Brian

P9-AQD-692

American Fiction

American Fiction

The Intellectual Background

by

D.E.S. MAXWELL

New York: Columbia University Press

© D. E. S. Maxwell 1963

First printing 1963
Fourth printing 1971

ISBN 0-231-02612-9
Printed in the United States of America

Contents

Acknowledgements

Permission to quote from the works listed below was kindly given by those named:

Little Gidding and *The Waste Land* by T. S. Eliot (Faber & Faber)

The Quest by W. H. Auden (Faber & Faber)

The Great Gatsby by F. Scott Fitzgerald (The Bodley Head)

The Just and the Unjust and *Guard of Honour* by James Gould Cozzens (Longmans, Green; Harcourt, Brace & World)

Castaway: copyright 1934 by James Gould Cozzens; copyright renewed 1961

The Custom of The Country by Edith Wharton (Charles Scribner's; Appleton-Century-Crofts)

The House of Mirth by Edith Wharton (Charles Scribner's)

The Age of Innocence by Edith Wharton (© 1923, 1951 William R. Tyler; John Lehmann)

Summer by Edith Wharton, (Appleton-Century-Crofts)

The Poetical Works of Edward Taylor ed. Thomas H. Johnson (Princeton University Press)

Chapter One

The Poetic Inception

THE Americanness of the American novel is as readily apparent as it is elusive of definition. It is the purpose of this study not to discover the reluctant formula, the comprehensive statement of national identity, but to examine the evidences of this identity in the work of some individual American writers. First, however, it is desirable to lay down some critical premises.

With the general tenor of Lionel Trilling's argument in his essay, 'The Meaning of a Literary Idea',[1] one gladly agrees. We must not, he says, deal with art 'as if it were a unitary thing, and by making reference only to its "purely" esthetic element, requiring that every work of art serve our contemplation by being wholly self-contained and without relation to action'. For Professor Trilling, the link between literature and what we may rather crudely call the life of action is its exposition of 'formulable ideas', a strongly intellectual grasp of ideas which have value and meaning in themselves, whose significance is not restricted to the part they may play in the structure of a literary work. By them we are led back to moral and philosophical considerations, back through aesthetics to the daily life in whose irresolutions a literary work originates. As will appear, any such contribution to liberalising literary criticism should be welcomed. It is in the development of this admirable doctrine, in its application to particular cases, that one begins to have misgivings. Going on to speak of

[1] Lionel Trilling: 'The Meaning of a Literary Idea' in *The Liberal Imagination*, pp. 281–303.

modern European fiction, Professor Trilling observes that, unlike its American counterpart, it 'refuses to be understood as a "symptom" of its society, although of course it may be that, among other things. It does not submit to being taped.' Modern American prose writing seems to him 'essentially passive . . . we incline to speak of (an American author) not merely incidentally but conclusively, in terms of his moment in history, of the conditions of the culture that "produced" him', and this 'leaves students with a too comfortable sense of complete comprehension'.

It is not, I think, misrepresenting the argument to suggest that Professor Trilling ascribes the superiority of the European writer to the unobtrusive felicity of the artistic rules and traditions which administer and sustain an easy intercourse between a complex civilisation and the primitive, unconscious urges of the human fancy. These traditions facilitate the transit of ideas, help to mediate between the intellectual and the primitive aspects of the creative tensions referred to in T. S. Eliot's comment that 'the artist is more *primitive*, as well as more civilised, than his contemporaries'. Of what is implied in his relating the respective cultures of the old and new worlds to the quality of their fiction there will be more to say later. More obviously at variance with Professor Trilling's anxiety to go beyond the '"purely" esthetic element' is the reserve with which he treats the prospect of relating fiction to its immediate social and historical environment, surely admissable once we concede that a work of art cannot ever be considered as wholly self-contained.

It is true that a great deal of critical energy has been expended on this kind of exposition, which he deplores, while apparently considering that it disposes well enough of modern American writing. The fault, one feels, is more in the critics than in the writers they pretend to explain, and it is very largely a fault of emphasis: the temptation, in dealing with an American writer, to insist on what is most clearly American in his experience—his environment and the historical situation in which he and his country find themselves. The method is attractive because it emphasises nationality by invading the already massively documented fields of indigenous sociology and politics, though it is likely in the end to submerge the lonely figure of the artist and his struggle to come to terms with ideas, feelings and the words to express them. However we may disagree with Professor Trilling's estimate of modern American literature, we must admit the truth of his strictures on the essentially peripheral quality of some of the criticism it has attracted. Still, the remedy is to handle the material more temperately, not to abandon it, for it is in his setting that we must see the writer if we are to understand him fully. It is something of a romantic simplification to speak of 'the lonely figure of the artist'. He may be lonely in the sense that the aims, ideals and manners of his society are not his and may even be repugnant to him; lonely in a feeling of detachment and because of his peculiar talents; but he is inescapably a part of his society and his times, which he at once stands aside from and embraces. He finds his audience in them and is nourished by them: their speech, habits and manners, their spiritual and political conflicts. It is a pointless exercise, for instance, to consider the novels of Fenimore Cooper without taking account of his deep involvement in the post-Revolutionary turmoil of political philosophies, though he was increasingly out of sympathy with the developing character of his country. The ideological dialectic of his period locates precisely the disturbed area of belief which Cooper's novels inhabit, though it offers us neither a simple abstract, so to speak, of his themes nor any commentary on the form in which he chose to dramatise the issues.

Professor Trilling does grant the relevance of such matters but he inclines to play down their importance, though it is in this domain that ideas are most likely to set up their reverberations in works of art. This inclination springs from a very definite and dominant critical attitude, which may be further considered here because it has greatly influenced modern assessments of American writing. Primarily, it is distinguished by a tendency to evolve schemes of abstraction, to arrive at a procedure by which works of literature could be examined as wholly self-subsistent creations, without reference to their social or psychological sources and by purely aesthetic criteria. M. D. Zabel, summarising the situation in American criticism in the middle of the twentieth century, draws attention to two fashions which illustrate this tendency. The first is 'a continuation of the aesthetic line initiated by Pound and carried on by Eliot, now bent more systematically than ever toward integrating the study of craftsmanship with metaphysical

3

or philosophical elements in literature: thus John Crowe Ransom with his demand for an "ontological" criticism. . . .'[1] By this, Ransom does not, of course, propose simply 'to isolate and discuss the "ideology" or theme or paraphrase of the poem'.[2] He argues that a poem consists essentially of its structure and texture and that the importance of the words which are its material lies not in the objects, feelings and ideas they represent but in the *architectural* relationship that exists between these within the poem. This relationship is the poetic analogue of the wholly abstract tonal patterns of music, or of the attempts of abstract painting to divorce art from representation. The aim is to disengage poetry from so-called 'extraneous' attachments, as in the second of Zabel's critical fashions, 'the discipline of formal and textual analysis' inaugurated by but, Zabel claims, 'now rejecting the empirical methods of I. A. Richards'.[3] Two other principal lines of activity are described, but the demarcation lines are again blurred. We have 'a continuing investigation of the social and cultural bases of literature . . . which now attempts to bring such realism to terms with aesthetic and moral claims: thus the work of men like Lionel Trilling and F. O. Matthiessen. . . .'[4] This investigation is in fact much closer to the 'ontological' criticism of Ransom than to the 'critical realism' which preceded it. In the essay already cited, Trilling in fact comes to lay less stress on ideas as 'principles of action' in human behaviour than on ideas as the formal components of a work of art, used to establish the 'dialectic' of the work, which is 'just another word for form'.[5] The fourth variety is 'a renewed effort to apply criticism to the practical business of education',[6] that is, instruction in the techniques of I. A. Richards's practical criticism'. Zabel goes on to describe a fifth variety which does have a genuine independence of approach, but the strong resemblance between the other four he mentions demonstrates a widespread uniformity of assumptions. There is a great deal of

[1] M. D. Zabel: Introduction to *Literary Opinion in America*, p. 39.

[2] John Crowe Ransom: 'Criticism as Pure Speculation', in Zabel, *op. cit.*, p. 643.

[3] Zabel: *op. cit.*, p. 39.

[4] Zabel: *op. cit.*, p. 39.

[5] Trilling: *op. cit.*, p. 283.

[6] Zabel: *op. cit.*, p. 39.

quarrelling among the critics but it does not conceal the marked family resemblance.

Common to all these modes is close attention to a carefully restricted topic or minute and detailed analysis of a particular text or part of a text, with the object of unfolding subtle undertones of meaning and illuminating refinements of structure. As with all techniques, a great deal depends on who is exercising them, and these are no more free from dangers than any other system. The search for subtlety of meaning can produce absurdities, the analysis of structure a dull shuffling of a few stereotyped counters—notably, as examples, 'irony' and 'ambiguity'. At its best, however—and it is at its best that it should be judged—the 'new criticism' has encouraged a valuable precision, eliminated vague sentimentalism and hazy subjectivity and insisted on what must always be the primary critical exhibit, the text itself. If it has fundamental poverties, these must be seen in its concern with explanation to the exclusion of judgment, in its vein of dogma, in its addiction to technical language and in an intense eclecticism which both arbitrarily restricts merit to a drastically narrow range of writers and also denies the value of any critical approach other than its own. An interesting speculation is the reasons for its present supremacy.

Malcolm Cowley sees in the current predominance of critical over creative writing and in the character of the criticism, an analogy to 'the Roman Empire during and after the age of the Antonines, which was also the great age of the rhetoricians'[1], and ascribes the rebirth of this mood to the feeling of the post-war generation 'that it has been asked to share in too many public emotions. After the fighting stops it leaves the fate of the world to professional politicians—most of whom are conservatives in such periods—and concerns itself with the questions it regards as personal and immediate or eternal . . . a movement away from socially oriented writing toward abstract or subjective literature, toward pure poetry, dream fiction or dogged scholarship.'[2] This may well have stimulated the growth of criticism and of this particular kind of criticism, but its ultimate cause is farther back, for it began long before the Second World War and its genesis may

[1] Malcolm Cowley: *The Literary Situation*, p. 4.

[2] Cowley: *op. cit.*, p. 5.

be seen even as far back as Spingarn's proclamation in 1910 that: 'We have done with technique as separate from art. . . . We have done with the history and criticism of poetic themes. . . . We have done with the race, the time, the environment of a poet's work as an element in criticism.'[1]

The new configurations of criticism may be plausibly attributed to the way in which the example of science, imperceptibly and perhaps hardly consciously sought, has, in the phrase of A. N. Whitehead, 'affected other regions of thought'.[2] Science is distinguished by its concern with means. Its aim is to amass and interpret accurate data, the scientific evaluation of which has no moral significance—though their eventual application may have. There is of course a point at which speculation must be led to break through the tightly-knit system of scientific materialism—as Whitehead's does—into a metaphysic concerned with ends as well as with means. The sudden illumination of a general, unifying principle, the lightning jump from particular instance to universal law, is, with the scientist as with the poet, the summit of the craft. But this is a faculty of the imagination by no means peculiar to science. The concept of science which has entered the grain of general ideas—and which would be accepted by a great many scientists—is that of a 'cosmology which presupposes the ultimate fact of an irreducible brute matter, or material, spread throughout space in a flux of configurations'.[3] Within this particular system it is assumed that, as A. D. Ritchie puts it, 'science is inherently capable of solving all problems . . . and outside the sphere of science there are no genuine problems'.[4]

The present century has been pre-eminently an age of technological advance, of increasing delicacy and exactitude in measuring both surface natural phenomena and the invisible structures of sub-atomic physics. The effect of this advance has been to close the gap between what may be theoretically hypothesised and what may be empirically demonstrated or tested. As Hermann Bondi explains, 'A scientific theory is one that it is in principle possible to disprove by empirical means. It is this supremacy of

[1] J. E. Spingarn: 'The New Criticism.' Quoted in Zabel, *op. cit.*, p. 22.

[2] A. N. Whitehead: *Science and the Modern World*, ch. I.

[3] Whitehead: *op. cit.*, ch. I.

[4] A. D. Ritchie: *Civilisation, Science and Religion* (Pelican Books), p. 164.

empirical disproof that distinguishes science from other human activities.'[1] Speaking of cosmology, he says that it is 'a subject, like any other scientific subject, in which there are means of disproving theoretical forecasts by experiment and observation. It is true that most of these are still rather difficult to make and require expensive equipment and great skill'.[2] Beside the metallic precision and certainty of the instruments, man himself is an untidy and enigmatic mess of unpredictable impulses and emotions, innately hostile, however he may accede to the superficial uniformities of his group, to any violation of the unique human personality —a personality which is in fact increasingly violable, and not only by ingenious agents of mass destruction. The personality can be broken down, reshaped to conform to politically desirable patterns, by a combination of modern drugs, techniques of promoting shock and psychiatric methods designed to eradicate neuroses but turned to inducing them. The human heart and intellect are, equally with the other aspects of nature, experimental fields, explored, controlled, by means which may be directed to malign or benevolent ends but which are in themselves concerned only with acquiring knowledge of the physical world.

Science in the popular mind is identified not only with what A. D. Ritchie calls 'newly invented gadgets that are by-products of science and often trivial appurtenances of the material side of civilisation',[3] but also with the intricate machines which are the agents of its profounder researches. The symbol is in many ways appropriate. It embodies the notions of infinite precision, of an advanced technology—both the product and the servant of science—of human inquiry divorced from moral and emotional distractions and of an intellectual system for which human beings themselves are, from one viewpoint, no more than material for study: man subservient to the machine. This does not, of course, mean that scientists are impervious to emotion and without moral sense, nor is it the whole truth about science, for whose ultimate survival are needed 'respect for truth and respect for persons as

---

[1] Hermann Bondi: *The Steady-State Theory of the Universe; The Listener,* 3 ix: '59.

[2] Bondi: *op. cit.*

[3] Ritchie: *op. cit.,* p. 170.

part of the general social tradition'.[1] Nevertheless, the symbol, if it is partial, does have its source in distinctive features of the scientific method.

A less pessimistic view of science exists and it is argued from time to time that literature has impoverished itself by its failure to achieve some kind of cross-fertilisation with the discipline of science and the sensibility of the scientist. Just what this ideal synthesis means and how it is to be achieved are obscure. Most recently it has been advocated by C. P. Snow, who describes the typical literary response to science and scientific advance as 'a scream of horror'.[2] This he exemplifies in the innumerable protests against industrialisation to be found in, for example, Morris, Emerson and D. H. Lawrence, protests which Snow considers invalid because they ignore the prospect of universal plenty offered by the applications of science. In point of fact, the uneasiness at its deepest level springs from an imaginative insight into perplexities and dilemmas of the human condition which are beyond the reach of the most ubiquitous prosperity and enter into a sphere beyond the mandate of science. Linked with this disquietude is a basic wariness, a feeling that science, circumscribed by the material and restricted to investigating means, may find no firm distinction between man and his environment as subjects for research. It is this feeling which creates the undertow of meaning in W. H. Auden's *The Quest*, the sinister innuendo of perversion in the working of scientific paraphernalia, a much more radical hostility than any to be found in the authors cited by C. P. Snow:

> *All had been ordered weeks before the start*
> *From the best firms at such work; instruments*
> *To take the measure of all queer events,*
> *And drugs to move the bowels or the heart.*
>
> *A watch, of course, to watch impatience fly,*
> *Lamps for the dark and shades against the sun...*
>
> *In theory they were sound on Expectation*
> *Had there been situations to be in.*
> *Unluckily they were their situation:*

[1] Ritchie: *op. cit.*, p. 70.

[2] C. P. Snow: 'The Two Cultures and the Scientific Revolution.'

> One should not give a poisoner medicine,
> A conjurer fine apparatus, nor
> A rifle to a melancholic bore.

Generally, the imaginative writer is more at home, and finds more sustenance, in this mood of rejection than in the occasional raptures which technological progress provokes. The naïve enthusiasm of Emerson's welcome to the transatlantic cable now strikes dully on our ears:

> Loud, exulting cries
> From boat to boat, and to the echoes round,
> Greet the glad miracle. Thought's new-found path
> Shall supplement henceforth all trodden ways,
> Match God's equator with a zone of art,
> And lift man's public action to a height
> Worthy the enormous cloud of witnesses,
> When linked hemispheres attest his deed.
>
> *(The Adirondacks.)*

The view of science held by C. P. Snow and the position of men like Auden, Lawrence or Yeats, who declared against 'this pragmatical, preposterous pig of a world'—these are fundamentally irreconcilable. They represent, it may be, complementary activities of the human mind and spirit and for this reason it is proper that the creative writer should remain, as he traditionally has been, the *advocatus diaboli* rather than the enthusiastic propagandist of science.

This inveterate partition has not, however, persisted in criticism. One would hesitate to equate scientific methodology with Auden's rifle, the new critic with his 'melancholic bore', but the analogy is not without point. The example of science has persuaded critics into attempting to import its certainties into the consideration of literature, to translate its essentially limited ends, its successful establishment of strict rules and categories, into aesthetic equivalents. Thus we have *Practical Criticism, Poetry as an Instrument of Research, Seven Types of Ambiguity*, and so on. It is as if, in the words of Malcolm Cowley, the critics 'regarded criticism as one of the learned disciplines, almost like biometrics or paleontology'.[1] R. S. Crane has pointed out that the object of

[1] Cowley: *op. cit.*, p. 10.

9

Richards's speculations is to secure a critical terminology fashioned 'as nearly as possible according to the pattern of natural science'.[1] Richards acknowledges this aim:

'(Science) can only tell us *how* so and so behaves. And it does not attempt to do more than this. Nor, indeed, can more than this be done. Those ancient, deeply troubling, formulations that begin with "What" and "Why" prove, when we examine them, to be not questions at all; but requests—for emotional satisfaction.'[2]

Some of the less desirable effects of this austere doctrine have been already suggested. Whitehead's comments on the limitations of scientific materialism can be applied to them with considerable justice:

'(Scientific materialism) is not wrong if properly construed. If we confine ourselves to certain types of facts, abstracted from the complete circumstances in which they occur, the materialistic assumption expresses these facts to perfection. But when we pass beyond the abstraction, either by more subtle employment of our senses, or by the request for meanings and for coherence of the thought'—'what' and 'why' rather than 'how'—'the scheme breaks down at once. The narrow efficiency of the scheme was the very cause of its supreme methodological success. For it directed attention to just those groups of facts which . . . required investigation.'[3]

In the same way, the new criticism was ideally suited to examining, in English poetry, the Metaphysicals. It so happened that the Metaphysical poets offered a happier example to modern poetry than nineteenth-century Romanticism. But the critical favour they found was not so much a judgment of their value as a rejection of a whole divergent tradition of poetry—the Romantic line, central to English literature—on whose compositions the new methods could not be efficiently deployed. With the novel, for the same reasons, the new criticism is equally partial. It dissects admirably novels whose structure is very consciously organised in

[1] R. S. Crane: 'I. A. Richards on the Art of Interpretation', in Zabel, *op. cit.*, p. 712.

[2] I. A. Richards: quoted by Crane, *op. cit.*

[3] Whitehead: *op. cit.*, pp. 18–19.

accordance with clearly defined postulates and which may therefore most usefully have their anatomy disembowelled, exhibited
and reassembled. Since the novels of Jane Austen, George Eliot,
Henry James and Joseph Conrad are the most consciously 'composed' and the most overtly 'intellectual', they are held to constitute the great tradition. Again, we see the murderous eclecticism,
the narrowed frontiers and the dogmatic cast induced by the capitulation of aesthetics to the alien assumptions of scientific methodology. Applying its principles to the American novel, the new
criticism has succeeded in establishing a number of equally categorical propositions.

The currently received version of the progress of American
fiction contains, however, two anomalous premisses. The first—
almost the essential hypothesis of 'ontological' criticism—is that
the critical data are embodied in the work itself. The questions to
be decided relate to themes, structure, ideas as ciphers in an
organisational scheme, linguistic texture, and the degree of efficiency with which these are inter-related. John Crowe Ransom's
dicta that 'a poem is a *logical structure* having a local *texture*', and
its corollary that 'The intent of a good critic becomes therefore to
examine and define the poem with respect to its structure and its
texture',[1] these have been extended to the other genres. R. P.
Blackmur, for example, commending 'the technical approach',
says that its advantage is that 'it treats of nothing in literature except in its capacity of reduction to literary fact . . . it is only the
facts about a poem, a play, a novel, that can be reduced to tractable form, talked about and examined. . . . The rest, whatever it
is, can only be known, not talked about'.[2] The second premiss is
that American fiction's commitment to allegory, as well as certain
congenital deficiencies of form and theme, are directly attribu-
table to the tenuity of American society. Conversely, the European novel is better than the American—which tends to mean that
it's better material for practical criticism—because European
society was so much richer and more complex than American.
Where so intimate a relationship subsists between the shape of
society and the very form of an art, we have something at the

[1] Ransom: *op. cit.*, p. 648.

[2] R. P. Blackmur: 'A Critic's Job of Work', in Zabel, *op. cit.*, p. 789.

least 'genuinely ulterior', not 'merely irrelevant'[1] and cannot ignore it in order to preserve the closed circuit which insulates criticism from the sources of literature.

The second premiss has acquired a certain sanctity through its enunciation by Henry James. Orthodoxy claims him as the crown of achievement in classic American fiction, partly because of his elegantly coherent theories of fictional structure and partly because of the efficient formal economics of his own novels of manners, in which Europe had hitherto been supreme. If a novel does not use the Jamesian artifices and devices, so the argument runs, if it is not, in addition, concerned with the individual in the setting of a complex social organism, then it is not a novel. Thus all pre-Jamesian American novelists are disqualified. Whatever their virtues, they were not writing novels. This rigid—and oddly apologetic—interpretation is advanced in Richard Chase's *The American Novel and its Tradition*. It applies strangely to a genre so fluid as to contain the disparate figures of Jane Austen and James Joyce. It also, of course, writes in a defining clause whose origin is exterior to both the 'logical structure' and the 'local texture', the self-contained 'facts', of any specific work, and this is the anomaly.

Being such a compendious form, the novel is not submissive to generalisations about its subject and structure. We may perhaps, however, be permitted the fairly malleable generalisation that the novel deals with the individual in the setting of a clearly visualised, concretely realised community, in some way mirroring the tensions, forms and *mores* of actual human society. The 'way' of course may range between a close fidelity to observed fact and outright myth and fantasy. The precise balance struck by individual novelists will be considered in later chapters. In the meantime, it will be sufficient to consider a little further the general thesis that American society was so thin that one side of the correspondence just didn't exist in any exploitable form, so that in order to write at all Henry James had to go to Europe.

The main objection to the theory is that, like most dogma, it is over-simplified and much more doctrinaire than in its original formulation. Adopted as an article of faith along with the rest of James's theories, it is in fact an extremely useful and illuminating suggestion, embodying considerable truth. But it is not, even for

[1] Blackmur: *op. cit.*, p. 776.

James, the whole truth. Quoted usually in association with similar remarks by Hawthorne and Cooper, the classic statement of the doctrine comes from James's study of Hawthorne:

'The negative side of the spectacle on which Hawthorne looked out, in his contemplative saunterings and reveries, might, indeed, with a little ingenuity, be made almost ludicrous; one might enumerate the items of high civilisation, as it exists in other countries, which are absent from the texture of American life, until it should become a wonder to know what was left. No State, in the European sense of the word, and indeed barely a specific national name. No sovereign, no court, no personal loyalty, no aristocracy, no church, no clergy, no army, no diplomatic service, no country gentlemen, no palaces, no castles, nor manors, nor old country-houses, nor parsonages, nor thatched cottages, nor ivied ruins; no cathedrals, nor abbeys, nor little Norman churches, nor great universities, nor public schools—no Oxford, nor Eton, nor Harrow; no literature, no novels, no museums, no pictures, no political society, no sporting class—nor Epsom nor Ascot! Some such list as that might be drawn up of the things absent in the American life—especially in the American life of forty years ago, the effect of which, upon an English or a French imagination, would probably, as a general thing, be appalling. The natural remark, in the almost lurid light of such an indictment, would be that if these things are left out, everything is left out. The American knows that a good deal remains; what it is that remains—that is his secret, his joke, as one may say.'[1]

That James is here as much playful as serious is indicated by the unmistakably ironical tone—'might, indeed, with a little ingenuity, be made almost ludicrous', 'it should become a wonder to know what was left', 'the almost lurid light', 'that is his secret, his joke, as one may say'. But even if we accept the statement at its face value as a somewhat pessimistic audit, we must consider it together with James's other, less melancholy views. In his letter to a Massachusetts summer school on 'The Novel', he said of 'the American world' as a subject for fiction that, 'The field is vast for freedom, for study, for observation, for satire, for truth'.[2]

[1] Henry James: *Nathaniel Hawthorne.*
[2] James: 'The Great Form', in Zabel, *op. cit.*, p. 56.

Elsewhere he had, more specifically, commended the exciting potential of the American language, whose essence, as in any language, is image and idiom, the slow deposit of man's transactions with his environment. James makes the point:

'Homogeneous I call the huge American public, with a due sense of the variety of races and idioms that are more and more under contribution to build it up, for it is precisely in the great mill of the language, our predominant and triumphant English, taking so much, suffering perhaps even so much, in the process, but giving so much more, on the whole, than it has to "put up" with, that the elements are ground into unity. . . . What forms, what colours, what sounds may the language take on or throw off in accommodating itself to such a growth of experience; what life may it—and most of all may the literature that shall so copiously testify for it—reflect and embody?'[1]

The effect of this long collaboration has been, in Edmund Wilson's words, to 'change the intonations of English, develop a new vocabulary, break the language into a new syntax'.[2] Still, of course, English, the American language is distinguished now by 'attachments and associations which, during the past two or three hundred years, have been acquired in North America instead of the British Isles'.[3] The environment, the developing society and culture in response to which it has evolved, rich enough to quicken a transplanted language with new life, we cannot dismiss as, by its very nature, hostile to fictional treatment. The new directions taken by the language themselves attest social and philosophical adjustments which the novelist may properly investigate. By relating a work to the society in which it was written we may uncover significances of imagery, of symbol, or relationships between ideas, of simple meaning, which the book itself does not fully disclose. Every writer has in mind an audience between whom and himself there is an implied common ground, the exploration of which is a necessary critical task. We may be counselled, then, to admit a close and positive relationship between the American novel and American society, which presented the

[1] James: 'The Question of the Opportunities', in Zabel, *op. cit.*, pp. 51-52.
[2] Edmund Wilson: *Classics and Commercials*, p. 631.
[3] Wilson: *op. cit.*, p. 424.

writer, certainly, with problems which, perhaps unprecedented, were yet not impossible of solution. We may presume a valuable line of inquiry in each novelist's attack on the problem of 'imitating' his society, without agreeing that the nature of the society must presuppose some inevitable artistic inferiority. We cannot dispense with what are loosely called extra-literary considerations. The words on the page are not separable from the objects they represent or the feelings that assembled them. By themselves—if such a condition is at all imaginable—they are no more a complete guide to the significance of a work than are biographical facts, social and historical correlations, psychoanalytical surmise or the pursuit of a mythic or symbolic content. Equally, none of these lines of inquiry is irrelevant: by the intricate and centrifugal associations of the words on the page we must be led into all kinds of dispersed responses, each in some way contributing to determine the total effect of the work. Macbeth's 'hangman's hands', for instance, will be meaningless to us if we do not know of the specific gruesome duties of the Elizabethan hangman.

The foregoing, considered as an attempt 'to lay down some critical premises' may seem somewhat negative. Its purpose is to dissociate the present work from the fashionable cult of critical chastity, to resist the imposition of a purely methodological approach, by which the critic 'is concerned with the work in front of him as something that should contain within itself the reason why it is so and not otherwise'.[1] There is more to literary merit than can be displayed by ingenious analysis of the 'oracular tongue and a nice derangement of epitaphs'; more to ideas than their abstraction into some organisational scheme. It is an illiberal view which holds that critical approaches other than its own are not merely wrong but do not, in the context of literary appreciation, really exist. We need not swing to the antithetical crudity of Marxist criticism to believe that literature is inseparable from life, from the bewilderingly complex web of attributes which identifies a nation. One would be hard put to it to extract a universally applicable formulation of that identity from the intricate confluence of—the list is not exhaustive—laws, politics, customs, history, geography and social patterns (forging new memory-clusters) which composes it. Hence it is necessary to select some

[1] F. R. Leavis: *The Common Pursuit*, p. 224.

one tributary whose effects are at once generalised in the national fabric and particularly the concern of the imaginative writer. One of the cardinal realities of the American experience has been the persistence of European memories and traditions and their traffic over the ocean through the centuries. The developing phases of European culture continued, after the first migrations, to be transferred to the New World and there accepted as a part of the American heritage. The main, though not the exclusive, theme of this book is the way in which American writing placed new constructions on the varied impulses of the European imagination.

II

The thesis of Frederick Jackson Turner's illuminating essay on the American frontier has an application beyond the social phenomena it was originally designed to explain. Turner accounts for the development of characteristically American institutions by the effect on the 'European germs' of the novel and harsh conditions of their American environment. 'The outcome,' he says, 'is not the old Europe, not simply the development of Germanic germs . . . here is a new product that is American.'[1] As the frontier moved westwards, the process of evolution from primitive conditions to a more complex society was repeated in each belt of settled land. Each time, the process owed less to the European nucleus, more to the American precedents that gradually accumulated and to the demands of the particular frontier belt involved. 'Thus,' Turner concludes, 'the advance of the frontier has meant a steady growth away from the influence of Europe, a steady growth of independence on American lines.'[2] It is a plausible and attractive theory, though Turner minimises the persistence of European influences. It could be wholly true only if America had been completely isolated from Europe, as in fact it never was. New waves of immigrants brought with them, even in revolt, their ingrained social aspirations, their cultural inheritance and their traditional cast of thought. European literature suffered no embargo and its predominance was, if often regretted,

[1] F. J. Turner: 'The Significance of the Frontier in American History.'
[2] Turner: *op. cit.*

usually acknowledged. Even the Revolutionary leaders, steeped in European culture, fought a great deal of their constitutional battle over European precedents. As Sir Herbert Read reminds us, for the American writer 'there will always be a centrality, an overtone, a tradition, towards which the fully conscious artist will aspire'. For Sir Herbert, the tradition is European. If he certainly exaggerates the dependence of the American writer in saying that his relation to Europe 'only differs in degree from that of a provincial novelist in England to the culture of the metropolis',[1] this is a corrective to Turner's minimising the tenacity of the European influences. Yet substantially Turner is right in contending that the European nuclei developed in ways dictated by their new environment and hence acquired a distinctive American character.

The divergence that Turner notices in social forms and institutions had its counterpart in the national literature. The American writer responded to the inflexions of European literature, but he habituated them to an alien experience and a divergent society. While, for example, the great upsurge of Romanticism in nineteenth-century Europe did carry over the Atlantic, the American apprehension of its styles and attitudes was not the same as the European, so that American Romanticism, though fundamentally akin, in practice assumed new contours. The consequent friction in the American sensibility is of the kind exemplified in Hester Prynne's turbulent thoughts which, as she leaves prison, oscillate between the poles of the American reality around her and the intrusive memories of Europe:

'Yet there were intervals when the whole scene, in which she was the most conspicuous object, seemed to vanish from her eyes, or, at least, glimmered indistinctly before them, like a mass of imperfectly shaped and spectral images. Her mind, and especially her memory, was preternaturally active, and kept bringing up other scenes than this roughly-hewn street of a little town, on the edge of the Western wilderness . . . she saw again her native village, in Old England, and her paternal home; a decayed house of grey stone. . . . The intricate and narrow thoroughfares, the tall, grey

[1] Sir Herbert Read: 'The International Situation in American Fiction', in *A Coat of Many Colours*, p. 280.

houses, the huge cathedrals, ancient in date and quaint in architecture, of a Continental city; where a new life had awaited her
. . . but feeding itself on time-worn materials, like a tuft of green
moss on a crumbling wall. Lastly in lieu of these shifting scenes,
came back the rude market-place of the Puritan settlement, with
all the townspeople assembled. . . . These were her realities.'

(*The Scarlet Letter*)

The episode invites an allegorical interpretation that Hawthorne
did not—consciously at any rate—intend it to imply. In Hester we
may see personified the antithesis which it is the American writer's
business to resolve, between the seemingly barren territory of a
simple community, its culture still unfurnished, and the culture of
Europe, 'ancient in date' but 'feeding iself on time-worn materials,
like a tuft of green moss on a crumbling wall'. Where European
precedents are adopted, they must acquire new life in their new
setting. The writer must see his material through them as Hester
sees her surroundings through her memories of Europe. Her
mood is nostalgic, regretful, but it is in her new surroundings that
finally she works out her drama of private guilt and public
punishment, of sin and atonement: 'struggles of fierce power', as
Hawthorne says elsewhere of America, 'love, hate, grief, frenzy—
in a word, all the worn-out heart of the old earth . . . revealed
under a new form.'[1] By contact with these 'new forms' of experience, which it is required to assimilate, the European aesthetic
will necessarily develop along unfamiliar lines.

The process is *engineered* only in the sense that any artist consciously applies his intelligence to the problems of his craft.
Where it becomes confused with nationalist fervour, it degenerates into a kind of programme for subsidising native industries or
ensuring a favourable balance of artistic trade. We shall see
Freneau side-tracked in this way by the less subtle coercions of
patriotism. Whitman's more ebullient outpourings are similarly
flawed:

I will report all heroism from an American point of view;
(*Starting from Paumanok*)

writing of the Muse,

[1] Hawthorne: 'The Prophetic Pictures', in *Twice-Told Tales*.

I say I see, my friend, if you do not, the illustrious émigré
    (having, it is true in her day, although the same, chang'd,
    journey'd considerable,)
By thud of machinery and shrill steam-whistle undismay'd,
Bluff'd not a bit by drain-pipe, gasometers, artificial fertilisers,
Smiling and pleased with palpable intent to stay,
She's here, install'd amid the kitchen ware!
                          (*Song of the Exposition*)

But these quotations must not obscure certain discrepant facts. First, Whitman's poetry on the whole effectively circumstantiates with the data of American experience his central faith that 'opposite equals advance': the unity whose parts are multitudinously varied in *Song of Myself*; the interplay of flux and stability in 'As I Ebb'd with the Ocean of Life'; the American pastoral myth and the novel beauties of urban life in *Starting from Paumanok*; death acknowledged in the midst of fruitfulness in 'When Lilacs last in the Dooryard Bloom'd'. Admitting an elegiac sense of tragedy into his poems, Whitman consolidated that 'American dream' which never quite convinces us in Emerson. Secondly, even the skirmishes into the narrow concerns of nationalist politics, which deranged Freneau's artistic vision, can be elevated above the immediate political issues involved. Just how this may come about can be illustrated from a literature even more contingent on the English than America's, that of the Anglo-Irish writers, who in may ways shared the American dilemma. Swift's poetry is a case in point. In his own peculiar outcropping from the general tradition of eighteenth-century English poetry, Swift struggled with the experiences of his years in Ireland and his reluctant consciousness of his Irish nationality. A study of the effects on both Swift and his poetry of this unsought predicament illuminates the likely consequences for the earlier American writers of their cultural disseverance, the distinctive features of which have been generally outlined above.

Swift is a poet as close to the Ahab-Philoctetes figure as we are likely to find—the exile, the maimed leader, the outsider who can yet do the state some service through his art. Though in his own country he was in a sense exiled. Of his life in Ireland he complains that he is 'obscurely here alone' and we have it on the authority of Dr. Johnson that Swift's return to Ireland meant 'the interception of his views, the extinction of his hopes, and his ejection from gay scenes'. His disabling wound was the insanity that eventually claimed him, clearly enough prefigured in the distempered imagery of his verse. Swift did not merely skirt the depths of filth and squalor. He dredged them with revealing persistence and often, it would appear, for no better reason than a perverted delight in dirt. His *Love Poem from a Physician* has no other purpose than to disgust. This kind of thing, and his recurrent outbursts against feminine hypocrisy, it would be simple, but wrong, to explain as solely the product of a morbid psychology. On occasion Swift could write graciously and charmingly of women, as in his poem, *On Mrs. Biddy Floyd: or The Receipt to form a Beauty*. He was, however, acutely sensitive to the dichotomy between appearance and reality: between overt prudery and hidden lusts; between assumed finery and all too human dirt. As a result, his verse is for the most part a ruthless stripping of social and literary artifices.

Augustan poetry delighted in graceful embellishment, ingenious fancy. There is a pressure towards idealisation, away from naturalism. Specifically, the woman and the man, with their untidy and often embarrassing needs and desires, are replaced by the odourless nymph and shepherd. The grosser elements are eliminated or achieve some tasteful apotheosis. Swift, however, was too keenly aware of sensuous impressions—unpleasant ones particularly—to accept this idealisation. Nor does his satire deal in the dignified generalisations of Dr. Johnson. Swift envisages abstract vice primarily in concrete particulars, not in an intellectual void.

The Progress of Love shows us the prudish Phyllis in a series of vignettes:

> *In church, secure behind her fan,*
> *She durst behold that monster man;*
> *There practis'd how to place her head,*
> *And bite her lips to make them red;*

Her ultimate fate is a social fate, a foolish marriage encumbered by infidelity and debt. Similarly, Corinna's nightmares in *A Beautiful Young Nymph Going to Bed* are social nightmares:

> *Or, if she chance to close her eyes,*
> *Of Bridewell and the Compter dreams,*
> *And feels the lash and faintly screams;*

The characters in his poems are unequivocally set in society, on which their immorality registers, with which it is integrated. *The Progress of Beauty*, in just the same way as *A Beautiful Young Nymph*, establishes the squalid contrast between the poise and beauty of the public woman and the filth and decay of the private, the real woman, hidden by cosmetic art. In each poem, the revolting details are intentionally corrective, the coarse, violent language designed to amend more euphemistic habits. We find coarseness in Pope also, of course, but not deliberately set against linguistic elegance. In *Strephon and Chloe* Swift directly juxtaposes the pallid conventionality of

> *To silver meads and shady bowers,*
> *Dressed up with amaranthine flowers*

and the uncompromising bluntness of,

> *In summer had she walk'd the town,*
> *Her armpits would not stain her gown.*

There is a certain pleasure in the spectacle of feminine hypocrisy exposed, but the brutality of Swift's attack suggests an unbalanced disgust. This is the appalling, one-sided vision which, once having recognised the sham, becomes obsessed. This is 'Swift's dark grove', of which Yeats wrote, the abnormal sensitivity to the foul and revolting, to the essential irreconcilability of human life with human ideals. And this was a temperament stimulated by the frictions of Swift's life in a country for which he felt only an inhibited sympathy, which was inevitably associated with his own thwarted ambitions. The Irish were an alien race on the fringe of civilisation. The wretched peasant life, so evidently lacking the pastoral veneer, gave a sensuous edge to his deflationary eclogues. In Ireland, the ingredients for his sustained antimasque were ubiquitous.

The verse of his Irish poems is urgently concrete. Swift's restless senses plague him with their impressions: 'A rotten cabin dripping rain' at Quilca; the weeds, the stones and the torn breeches of the *Pastoral Dialogue*; the cattle 'meagre and lank with fasting grown'; Stella's 'return to Ormond Quay' and to her lodgings:

> *She curst the narrow winding stairs;*
> *Began a thousand faults to spy;*
> *The ceiling scarcely six feet high;*
> *The smutty wainscot full of cracks;*
> *And half the chairs with broken backs.*

We are never allowed to lose sight of the material setting, recorded with lucid honesty. Swift's imagery and symbolism are similarly concrete. One of his fundamental perceptions, of the antagonism between counterfeit and genuine, finds a new social articulation in his treatment of the proposals to debase the Irish coinage. He threatens to

> ——*ring Wood's copper in our ears*
> *So loud till all the nation hears.*

It is the same duality we have seen in Corinna between illusion and reality, actualised in sensuous images. Swift brilliantly documents the Irish scene and the Irish people, from the Newry attorney of *The Answer* to the miserable Dermot and Sheelah of *Pastoral Dialogue*. A whole society comes to life in these poems, drab often and stark, but with tremendous colloquial energy— there is in fact an appreciable amount of actual dialogue. The laconic rhythms, as in these lines:

> *'Tis strange, what different thoughts inspire*
> *In men, Possession and Desire!*——;

the consistently unpoeticised language; the vivid observation; the unfamiliar settings: these give Swift's verse a tone unique in its age. As T. S. Eliot remarks, it was an age in which one of the virtues of poetry was that it had many of the characteristics of good prose. None of its poets, however, is so consistently in debt to the vulgar idiom as Swift. We find it in Pope, but more typical of his verse is the intricate scaffolding of the passage on Dryden and the critics in Book II of the *Essay on Criticism*. This has still the virtues of prose, but of a subtly ordered and strongly intellectualised prose. It is quite beyond the scope of Swift, whose verse commands limited resources. He is sustained more by the prose of narrative than of argument. His sentences are normally uncomplicated and their effects gained by simple accumulation of co-ordinate phrases and clauses. The colloquialism is that of a slanging street-corner brawl, not the delicate refinements of the salon.

So he found in his native country much that fed his predilections. His *Description of an Irish Feast* is a contemptuous burlesque of national pretensions to a noble antiquity, 'translated almost literally out of the original Irish'. The O'Rourkes, the O'Enagins, the Grinagins meet for a banquet which degenerates into a drunken free-for-all. Occasional stage-Irish nonsense though it is, it is more human than the cloudy princesses with whom Yeats was to infest the scene. Swift's harshness and ribaldry are in fact wholly in keeping with the traditions of Gaelic poetry. Yet with Swift's contempt for his surroundings there is also a kind of love, disappointed though he was and increasingly obsessed with his cruel vision of life as filthy and deformed. *Stella at Wood-Park* speaks, it is true, of 'Liffey's stinking tide at Dublin', but only in contrast to the Irish countryside; and the *Birthday Verses on Mr. Ford* insists,

> *The difference is not much between*
> *St. James's Park and Stephen's Green;*
> *And Dawson Street will serve as well*
> *To lead you thither as Pall Mall.*

Swift is more balanced than is sometimes allowed, but here as elsewhere he is at his best observing the bleak, the uncomfortable, the ramshackle.

Remarkably enough, Swift did have a lingering sensation of vanished greatness. In his paraphrase of *Horace* Book I Ode xiv, he allegorises Ireland as a ruined ship. The broken mast is the lost leader, 'the single pillar' who has led the people 'as a staff directs the blind'. Particularising, he equates himself with the 'aged patriot', betrayed by his 'fond' reliance on popular enthusiasm. Something of the legend remains, however, transcending the betrayal, as a defence against 'supple patriots of the modern sort'. His verses on the drying-up of St. Patrick's Well, with their oddly Miltonic passage on the corruption of the Irish church, is a blend of allusions to Christianity, classical myth and Celtic history. St. Patrick, Jason and Murrough King of Leinster are all laid under contribution to establish the notion of past Hibernian grandeur and heroic resistance to the 'ravenous isle'. But this, the poem concludes, is all gone and St. Patrick withdraws his patronage from the 'spurious and degenerate line'. It is Swift the aristocratic leader who speaks in this poem, contemptuous of the nation's servility and with an almost wistful consciousness of a heritage betrayed. Ostensibly, St. Patrick speaks, but the sentiments are Swift's. In the controversy over the proposal to debase the Irish coinage, Swift succeeded first in creating a hostile public opinion, then in establishing himself in the public mind as its effective advocate. But even here, though Swift was identified with public feeling as completely as a man can be, he is exhorting the people from across a gulf. Despite a number of ballad-type 'come all ye' poems, he never loses his patrician scorn.

Swift's poetry is not the 'product' of his environment and nationality. In them, however, lie the origin and maintenance of the deflationary style—bitter sarcasm, harsh abuse, brawling colloquialism; the anti-pastoral motif; the tumbledown properties; the brilliant evocation of a society beyond the purview of his English contemporaries; the disillusionment, the pervading sense of disinheritance; the formulation of a leader-principle with Swift himself as the aristocratic hero. From these Swift created a cantankerous but genuine poetry. What he does is to give poetic form, within the Augustan tradition—his central attachment—to this body of experience, themes and attitudes, whose nature is determined by the complex interconnexions of the individual perception and the native region.

III

Swift is a very special case, if only because of his innate morbidity. The issue of even so difficult a cultural relationship need not necessarily be as bitter in tone as Swift's poetry generally is. It is not Swift's spleen we may expect the American situation to duplicate, but the resourcefulness with which he extended literary forms to include a new range of imagery, themes and symbols. In the work of the earlier American poets we find the inception of the process. They grapple with problems of the kind that faced Swift and were, on a larger scale, to face the American novelists.

At first, the settlers looked on themselves primarily as English-men, but even at that stage their ideas and their way of looking at things were affected by their new surroundings. Attempts at literary assimilation were unco-ordinated. Outside European practice there was no coherent tradition, no common knowledge of a securely germinating line of descent on which the isolated experiments of individuals might depend, by which they might be directed. Nevertheless, a pattern of development was established and in the relatively uncomplicated circumstances of the early days we may perhaps discern it most clearly. It is of the kind we see in Swift and may be exemplified in the poetry of Edward Taylor, who wrote within the Metaphysical tradition very much as Swift wrote within the Augustan.

In the meagre context of New England poetry, Taylor's achievement seems breathtaking. A poetic imagination lights up the best Puritan sermons but rarely penetrates their poetry, most of which is on the abysmal level of the elegy on William Bradford's death:

> *The Ninth of May, about Nine of the Clock*
> *A precious one God out of Plimouth took:*
> *Governor Bradford then expired his breath,*
> *Was called away by force of cruel death.*[1]

The only genuine talent was Anne Bradstreet's and for her the historian's claims are grossly inflated. Her descriptions are derivative and conventional. She rarely encouraged her eyes and sensibility to operate on the actual surroundings in which she wrote. There is little sense of immediate observation, of a sensuous appreciation of real scenes. These are not the only qualities of poetry, but they are certainly part of the kind of poetry Mrs. Bradstreet set out to compose. In *Spring*, from *The Four Seasons of the Year*, there is the stock apparatus of nightingales, thrushes and frisking lambs, unenlivened by any individual vision. A gardener carries out unparticularised tasks:

> *——superfluous branches lops,*
> *And poles erects for his young clamb'ring hops.*
> *Now digs, then sows his herbs, his flowers and roots*
> *And carefully manures his trees of fruits.*

All this is a faded reminiscence of what was common in the lower

[1] Quoted in Nathaniel Morton's *New England's Memoriall* (1669).

reaches of contemporary English poetry. Her ideal is a lifeless correctness and as her detail is borrowed so is the diction. Contemplation is 'richly dight'; fish are 'wat'ry folk'. It is all very enervated. The first nine verses of *Contemplations* describe the various scenes that catch her eye as she walks through the autumn countryside. In this, A. H. Quinn recognises a definitely New England landscape, but only because he looks with the eye of faith.[2] There are too many rhetorical questions for any clear impression of the scene to emerge. The work of observation is hampered by the naïvely emblematic reading of nature: 'there is no object that we see . . . but we may make some spiritual advantage of . . . and he that makes such improvement is wise, as well as pious'.

(Anne Bradstreet: *Meditations*)

That is, all the phenomena of life have a moral lesson to expound; such exposition is too often forced upon her poetry. Here and there it develops more naturally. Thus she writes *Upon the Burning of our House:*

> And when I could no longer look,
> I blest his name that gave and took,
> That layd my goods now in the dust:
> Yes so it was, and so 'twas just.
> It was his own: it was not mine:
> Far be it that I should repine.

Yet repine of course, she does, despite the exercise of faith, and what remains with us from the poem is not the pious acceptance of disaster, feelingly expressed though it is here. We remember instead the pathos of her loss, the heartfelt imaginings of the homely scenes that the house might have witnessed had it been spared:

> No pleasant tale shall e'er be told,
> Nor things recounted done of old.
> No Candle e'er shall shine in Thee,
> Nor bridegroom's voice e'er heard shall be.

Part of our response comes, no doubt, from the contrast between the intensity of her emotion and the small scale of the material loss: a primitive cabin, a trunk, the simplest household goods, 'my pleasant things'. We realise that there is in fact no disparity

[1] A. H. Quinn: *History of American Literature.*

26

between the emotion and its cause, for in her life these bare necessities were everything. The diction is admirably pure and unaffected, the statements gain power from their refusal to elaborate, simple words to express basic emotions. This is very much a pioneer poem, dramatising the narrow margin that lay between survival and disaster.

Mrs. Bradstreet finds her best expression in what we may call domestic verse, the homely level of daily life. She is not unlike William Cowper, though without his technical skill, and she experienced, of course, none of the mental instability which informed his darker poems. But where they are comparable— Cowper was very good on both domestic trivialities and friendship—the comparison is worth undertaking—between, for instance, Mrs. Bradstreet's *To My Dear and Loving Husband* and Cowper's *To Mary Unwin*. The poems share the same modest simplicity, the same faith in the value of human love, the same unemphasised statement, translating hyperbole, so to speak, into common speech—'I prize my love more than whole mines of gold.' The difference between the two poets is, revealingly, Cowper's infinitely greater poise and assurance.

Mrs. Bradstreet's society never fully inhabited her verse and she did not participate emotionally in any tradition that might have schooled her in technical discrimination: hence the rattling polysyllables, the jarring rhymes, inappropriate imagery and platitudinous moralising. In her more ambitious flights, withdrawing from her adopted settings, she attempted simply to duplicate her models. Poetry buttresses the general with the particular, the remote with the familiar, the abstract with the concrete. Mrs. Bradstreet rarely took a clear and sustained look at what lay around her. She did not apprehend her own set of particulars— not just the physical surroundings but the imaginative logic of Puritan thought as well; nor did she grasp the tradition of abstract, speculative verse. Necessarily, she failed to bring about any conjunction of the two, whereby each might influence the other. Her often charming verse, then, never awakened to the profounder opportunities of her situation. Edward Taylor's poetry is infinitely more enterprising, as he was, intellectually, much the stronger of the two.

Edward Taylor did not come to New England until 1668,

when he was about twenty-three years of age. His poetry seems to have been written between 1680 and 1725, that is, after he had spent some years in his new country. The fact is significant. To discover just what, for Taylor, the significance was, it will be necessary to look briefly at the Puritan prospectus and the effect on it of its violent transplantation.

The American Puritans conceived their intentions very clearly. Their aim was to establish a theocracy in which the civil and religious structures would be identified, where the political machinery would be activated by theological principles. From William Bradford's *Of Plymouth Plantation* we gather something of the efforts that were made to secure a compact, tightly knit community where the social system dictated by Puritan theology could be established and more easily preserved than in any scattered, less cohesive grouping. Bradford was very uneasy over the dispersal of families, which removed them from the supervision of their superiors, and 'by which means', in his own words, 'they were scatered all over the bay, quickly, and the towne, in which they lived compactly till now, was left very thine and in a short time allmost desolate.' Ideally, society was to be hierarchical and Bradford's suspicions of this drift were, from his own standpoint, thoroughly justified, though what he opposed was historically inevitable. Gradually the stronghold did split up and we are presented, over the years, with the unique spectacle of a Puritan society slowly, undramatically, but remorselessly disintegrating. The unique feature is that it succumbed to the seeds of decay that it carried within itself. The other forms of Christianity, which opposed it in Europe, were in large measure excluded from the community, most of whose members acquiesced in the same theological principles. We need not trace in detail the progress of this deterioration but its main causes are of interest since they most clearly demonstrate the *interior* nature of the relapse. In a condensed account such as follows a good deal is bound to be left out. Thus there is no mention of the celebrated ideological dissenters Roger Williams and Mrs. Hutchinson, both of whom defected in the mid-1630s on the question of toleration. There is a venomous account of their activities in Morton's *New England's Memoriall*. They were, in any case, outside that central Puritan doctrine whose decay is the topic here.

Though the Puritans revered reason, learning and science, seeking to compose them, with religion, into an harmonious interpretation of spiritual and mundane life, by their opposition to episcopal government they strengthened the doctrine that men were saved by the infusion of Grace. Hence they diminished respect for priestly guidance and for learned interpretation of the Gospels. Their insistence that the motive for good deeds was more important than the action itself decayed into the belief that deeds are unimportant as compared with possession by the true spirit: hence the anti-intellectual, loudly evangelical 'fundamentalism', with its rabble-rousing appeal to the emotions, quite contrary to the original Puritan demand for scholarship and an educated laity. Then again, by their very enthusiasm for learning and the eagerness with which they welcomed the new science of Newton, seeing no conflict between it and their theology, they strengthened the habit of sceptical re-assessment of belief whose validity had always been assumed. From this sprang rationalism, free-thinking and agnosticism. As a corollary to the theological deviations, social theory became more liberal. Emphasis began to shift from the divine authority of the magistrates to the importance of popular election. This duality in the social covenant the Puritans had always recognised. The magistracy expressed the will of God, as His vice-regents, and embodied the will of the people, as being elected. But in the early days all the stress was on the former element. The liberty of the people, in the words of John Winthrop's *Speech to the General Court* (1645),

'. . . is the proper end and object of authority and cannot subsist without it; and it is a liberty to do that only which is good, just and honest . . . This liberty is maintained and exercised in a way of subjection to authority.'

Yet it was the reluctant admission of public concurrence that was to lay hold of political thought, in spite of all discouragement and with a human perverseness whose strength the Puritans would have been the first to recognise. 'Democracy,' said John Cotton, 'I do not conceyve that ever God did ordeyne as a fitt government eyther for church or commonwealth. If the people be governors, who shall be governed?' (1636.) Even Cotton, however, in his *Limitation of Government*, spoke of 'the people, *in whom fundamentally all power lies'*. This statement, once liberated from the restrictions he hedged round it, could be used as a foundation for philosophies that would have horrified its author. John Wise, John Barnard and Jonathan Mayhew mark distinct stages in the progress of social theory to the point where biblical guidance became not the primary source and justification of Governmental practice but merely a secondary confirmation of what reason established as right and practicable. By 1717, John Wise, in his *Vindication*, was arguing that 'Civill Government...must needs be acknowledged to be the Effect of Humane Free-Compacts and not of Divine Institution'. The movement towards democratic thought, a *trahison des clercs* more than a popular agitation, culminates in Jonathan Mayhew's *Discourse* (1750): '. . . nothing can well be imagined more directly contrary to common sense, than to suppose that millions of people should be subjected to the arbitrary, precarious pleasure of one single man (who has naturally no superiority over them in point of authority)'.

So the hard core of Puritan thought dissolved. The natural sequel was that it should be replaced, eventually, by a vague wishy-washy benevolence, sentimental and optimistic, believing in the perfectibility of man. In its later stages the process was accelerated by the impulses from eighteenth-century Europe of the French Revolutionary egalitarian philosophies. Before that, however, the history of seventeenth-century New England demonstrated how Puritan theories evolved through contact with the stresses of administering an actual Puritan society, voluntarily created. The circumstances of living in a Puritan society so cohesive and so isolated from dissident opinion is not duplicated elsewhere, and it is in the developments briefly outlined above that its unique character most clearly appears, the first distinctively American experience.

It was equally unparalleled, of course, in the heyday of Puritan authority. At that point, a great deal was made of the closeness in time between the Reformation and the settling of the new continent. The colony was a refuge from persecution in Europe and the colonists' vision was that in it should be established the Kingdom of God according to the Calvinist discipline. 'The Lord's promises,' said William Stoughton, 'and expectations of great things, have singled out New England, and all sorts and ranks of men amongst us, above any Nation or people in the World.' In *New England's Memoriall*, which appeared in 1669, two years before Taylor graduated from Harvard, Nathaniel Morton wrote of a new influx of colonists in 1630 that 'the Lord began in a manifest manner and way to make known the great thoughts which he had of Planting the Gospel in this remote and barbarous wilderness'. Cotton Mather's *Magnalia Christi Americana* set out to 'write the wonders of the Christian religion, flying from the deprivations of Europe to the American strand'. Nowhere else could the devout Puritan find such unanimity of aim, such boundless possibilities, such a zealous response to the heavy demands which the religion laid on its followers. In these years the community was still united, as far as any group of men may be, their faith tested but not broken by years of hardship, their beliefs still sturdy. All around Taylor, despite the backslidings and sinfulness inherent in the human condition, were the evidences, in laws, government, church and daily life, of an abstract theology assuming concrete social forms. It is difficult not to believe that it was Taylor's absorption into and communion with this reality which equipped his intellectual command of doctrine with the sensuous and emotional references that made it poetically valid. What emerges from the poetry is not a straight exposition of Calvinism but its incarnation in Taylor's transcription of everything he saw and thought and felt. He found aesthetic guidance too not in the tradition of Metaphysical poetry alone but in certain stylistic affiliations between it and the permitted rhetoric of the Puritan sermons, the religion's major weapon in the tutelage and admonition of its followers.

The Puritan ideal was, of course, the 'plain style'. According to Perry Miller the purpose of this was 'to keep attention from ever being beguiled by flourishes . . . all the resources of rhetoric, illustration, metaphor, simile, were skilfully employed—as long, that is, as the rhetoric never became an end in itself but was rigorously subordinated to conveying the meaning'. One must, however, to some extent disagree with Professor Miller's unconditionally contrasting their 'stylistic code' with 'the ornate "metaphysical" orations . . . . such as those of John Donne or Lancelot Andrewes'.[1] Differences there obviously are. The great Anglican sermons tend to be less rigidly intellectualised. There is a

[1] Perry Miller: *The American Puritans* (Anchor Books), p. 165.

much stronger pull on the emotions, a richer and more consistently embellished language. But in its most settled feature the Puritan style has a strongly 'metaphysical' character. This feature is its fondness for allegory, for the emblematic interpretation of personal experiences and natural phenomena. Thus we find Mrs. Bradstreet writing in her *Meditations* that, 'Iron till it be thoroughly heated is incapable to be wrought: so God sees good to cast some men into the furnace of affliction, and then beats them on His anvil into what frame He pleases'. It was a popular exercise and was practised commonly with extreme naïvety, or, in its later excesses, with a dusty and self-destructive ingenuity. In Professor Miller's words, 'a languid generation, no longer capable of creating its images, was becoming enslaved to the images given arbitrarily in experience'.[1] A notable example of the decadence is Cotton Mather's *Agricola, or the Religious Husbandman* (1727), its intention 'To Spiritualise the Common Actions of Life'. But the device is fundamentally an attempt to express abstractions in concrete analogues, to make the spiritual world visible, to forge links between actuality and the limitless mazes of such enigmas as the paradox of free will and predestination. In that it is 'metaphysical' and in the best of the Puritan sermons it does express these abstractions with great force and genuinely sensuous imagination.

The American Thomas Hooker (1586–1647) discourses on meditation—'the register and remembrancer that looks over the records of our daily corruptions, and keeps them upon file, and brings them into court and fresh consideration. . . . It's the traversing of a man's thought, the coasting of the mind and imagination into every crevis and corner. . . . Meditation lifts the latch and goes into each room . . . satisfies himself not to overlook carelessly on a sudden view, but unlocks every chest, romages every corner, takes a light to discover the darkest passages'. His sermon on *Wandering Thoughts* opens with a comparable little allegory of the mariner who, 'because the Channel is narrow, and the wind somewhat scant, he toucheth in many places, tacks about, and fetcheth many points, but still because it's to attain the Haven. . . . It's so in the carriage of the soul; the cause why a man fetcheth

[1] Miller: Introduction to Jonathan Edwards's *Images or Shadows of Divine Things* (Yale), p. 16.

such a compass, and tacks about in his own contrivements; now this, now that; one while one way, another while this or that presented and pursued busily; yet in the issue we land all our thoughts and look at the last to bring in content to such a lust: It's certain the vanity of that lust drew the vanity of my thoughts after it'. In John Cotton's *Wading in Grace*, 'faith saith not, Give me such a calling and turne me loose to it; but faith lookes up to heaven for skill and ability, though strong and able yet it looks at all its abilities but as a dead work, as like braided ware in a shop, as such will be lost and rust, unless God refresh and renue breath in them'. There are innumerable such examples of this allegorising faculty worthily employed to carry recondite abstractions into latitudes in themselves more familiar but having the shock of novelty in their application. We notice particularly the effect of sharply observed detail—rummaging in corners, taking a light along dark passages and so on. It is this power which brings the allegorical set pieces to life and it is apparent in all the best Puritan writing: in Bradford's report of a severe November that, 'it frose so hard as the sprea of the sea lighting on their coats they were as if they had been glased'; of a battle with the Indians—'a fearful sight was it to see them thus frying in the fyer, and the streams of blood quenching the same'; in Morton's description of a plague of caterpillars which 'did eat off the leaves of the trees, so they looked so bare as if it had been winter: and in some places did eat the leaves from off the Pease straw, and did not eat the Pease'. In the prolific example of Puritan homiletics Taylor found a domestic usage that countenanced the naturally Metaphysical bent of his style.

The preceding analysis may seem an unnecessarily devious approach to the poetry itself. Its justification is that it fills in the background from which the poetry acquired the features that set it perceptibly aside from English Metaphysical verse. Taylor's verse springs from a remarkably unified awareness of all the varied particulars which composed the experience of being a Puritan cleric in seventeenth-century New England.

Stylistically, Taylor has flashes of Donne's heated ingenuity and the same ability to link in rapidly unfolding sequence the most diverse ideas. The *Preface* to *God's Determinations* begins with a contrast between the void, the nothingness, that preceded Creation and the teeming variety of the world. The viewpoint is cosmic but not abstract. The vivacious imagery, delicately scaled to the proportions of miniature, gives a host of superbly imagined details:

> *Who laced and filleted the earth so fine*
> *With rivers like green ribbons smaragdine?*
> *Who made the seas its selvage, and its locks*
> *Like a quilt ball within a silver box?*
> *Who spread its canopy? Or curtains spun?*
> *Who in this bowling alley bowled the sun?*

The poem has progressed to this intimate description from the opening questions about Creation:

> *Upon what base was fixed the lath wherein*
> *He turned this globe and riggaled it so trim?*
> *Who blew the bellows of His furnace vast,*
> *Or held the mould wherein the world was cast?*
> *Who laid its corner-stone? Or whose command?*
> *Where stand the pillars upon which it stands?*

The images of the blacksmith and the mason, typically metaphysical, bring into engagement things apparently disconnected, the majestic and the prosaic. Next the poem goes on to the regularity of physical events: dawn and sunset, the motions of the stars, perpetually sustained by the direct intervention of God, trivial, despite their vast scale, as compared with their Creator,

> *Whose Might Almighty can by half a looks*
> *Root up the rocks and the hills by the roots——*

such an elaborate resonance of sounds as often occurs in Donne. All these wonders, Taylor concludes, are given to man who is 'nothing' and who has, by his first disobedience, rejected the gift: his soul—

> *. . . . his brightest Diamond is grown*
> *Darker by far than any Coalpit stone——*

blemished by inherited and insuperable depravity. The imagery, the coherent logic of the thought, advance by perfectly controlled steps from the creation of the world to the unworthiness of man, very much in the manner of Donne.

The theology, of course, is different. Taylor was not, as Donne was, perplexed by the conflict between the old, once universally accepted philosophy, and the new disruptive science of Copernicus: he lived, as the *Preface* makes clear, in the still orderly world of scholastic physics, which dismissed natural laws as an illusion. Taylor's poetry lacks Donne's confused and agonised hinterland of unsettled loyalties, with its considerable residue of Roman Catholic thought. In *Good Friday* Donne addresses the Virgin, in terms utterly foreign to the Puritan, as 'Half of that sacrifice which ransom'd us'. Even the titles of Donne's poems—*The Annuntiation and Passion, The Litanie*—suggest concepts alien to Puritanism. A recurring subject is repentance, which in his thinking implies an established church as intermediary between God and man, able in some degree to alleviate, by the power invested in it, the weight of man's sin. The closest we come to this in Taylor—and it is not very close—is in his poem, *The Joy of Church Fellowship*, where the emphasis is on the power of communal worship, not on a clerical power inherent in the church as an institution. These ideological differences are to be expected between a confident Puritan and a self-questioning Catholic poet caught in an age of shifting faiths. It is perhaps less apparent that, partly because of Donne's more hectic curiosity, Taylor's language and imagery are not so habitually bizarre, nor so frequently at the tightest intellectual and emotional stretch. Taylor has his incandescent moments, as when, 'Kenning through astronomy', he divines 'The world's bright battlement' of stars—a phrase that Donne himself might have struck. But 'a poem of any length', as Coleridge remarks, 'neither can be, nor ought to be, all poetry', and Taylor ascends to his heights from a 'natural style' more pervasive than and different from Donne's. At this level, he reverts to the plainest of Puritan rhetoric, finding it here and there, indeed, a trifle intractable:

> . . . . *perhaps some few you'll find*
> *That to notorious sins were ne'er inclin'd:*
> *Some shunning some, some most, some great, some small;*
> *Some this, that, or the other, some none at all.*
> *But all, or almost all, you'st easily find*
> *To all, or almost all, defects inclined.*
>
> > (*The Forwardness of the Elect.*)

Elsewhere he managed the transfer more adroitly:

> *Nature doth better work than Art, yet thine*
> *Out vie both works of nature and of Art.*
> *Natures Perfection and the perfect shine*
> *Of Grace attend thy deed in ev'ry part.*
> *A Thought, a Word, and Worke of thine, will kill*
> *Sin, Satan, and the Curse: and Law fulfill.*
>
> (*Meditation LVI.*)

In these we hear unmistakably the accent of the homelier pulpit manner, as in the following, from Increase Mather's sermon on predestination:

'Most certainly, altho' we cannot say, That if men improve their natural abilities as they ought to do, that Grace will infallibly follow, yet there will not one sinner in all the Reprobate world, stand forth at the day of Judgment and say, Lord, Thou knowest I did all that possibly I could do, for the obtaining Grace, and for all that, Thou didst withhold it from me.'

Taylor, though not bound to the extreme plain style—as the fact that his poetry does resemble Donne's sufficiently testifies—does admit its discipline into his verse and its effect is to keep it, in content, tone and spirit, closer to Herbert than to Donne.

The theme of Herbert's *Jordan* resembles closely that of Taylor's *Meditation LVI*. Herbert is saying that poetry is defiled by being thought proper only for 'fiction and false hair'—the fashionable subject of love and the stale diction that flourished with it. Poetry should be devoted to God and the affairs of the soul. Taylor too is writing about poetry:

> *Should I with silver tools delve through the Hill*
> *Of Cordilera for rich thoughts, that I*
> *My Lord, might weave with an angelick skill*
> *A Damask Web of Velvet Verse, thereby*
> *To deck thy Works up, all my Web would run*
> *To rags and jags——*

—the glory of God cannot be fittingly expressed through the medium of any natural or artificial wonder. He enumerates some of these (obviously, despite his argument, fascinated by them) in the sixth verse:

> *The Clock of Strasburgh, Dresdens Table-sight*
> *Regsamonts Fly of Steele about that flew,*
> *Turrians Wooden Sparrows in a flight,*
> *And th' Artificiall man Aquinas slew.*

His conclusion is that

> *Nature doth better work than Art, yet thine*
> *Out vie both works of nature and of Art.*

Basically, his thesis is the same as Herbert's, that the only really proper interest for human beings is God and that all other human business is vanity.

Herbert's advocacy of everyday parables, also, Taylor would certainly have approved:

'This is the skill, and doubtlesse the Holy Scripture intends thus much, when it condescends to the naming of a plough, a hatchet, a bushell, leaven, boyes piping and dancing; shewing that things of ordinary use are not only to serve in the way of drudgery, but to be washed, and cleansed, and serve for lights even of Heavenly Truths.'[1]

But though the principle is common to both poets their practice is not altogether identical. The physical characteristics of the church offered Herbert a source of imagery which was absent from a community where even churches were necessarily crude and makeshift enough. There was no counterpart in New England to the long tradition and solidity behind European church architecture. Indeed, the tendency would have been in any case to take pride in a break from traditional design as a visible symbol of the spiritual separation. Herbert's poems, *The Churchfloore* and *The Windows* are obviously inspired by the material characteristics of the church buildings—the marbled floors and the stained-glass windows which he uses to represent spiritual states. In Taylor's *Meditation XXVI*, on the other hand, the church floor 'paved with graces bright' has an entirely figurative origin, and so has the 'censer trim' (his heart) in *The Ebb and Flow*. Yet there is considerable common ground between the poets.

Herbert's dramatic little poem on the crucifixion, *Redemption*, presents Christ as a landlord from whom the poet seeks a favour.

[1] George Herbert: *The Country Parson*, ch. xxi.

He finds Christ not in fashionable places but among the 'ragged noise and mirth' of thieves and murderers where, just as He dies, He grants the poet's request. We don't find this narrative content in Taylor's poems but we do find him very often using a series of similar but more violently condensed allegories. His *Sacramental Meditations* are inspired by different biblical texts. Taylor's technique is to convert the teaching of the text into a series of closely-knit allegories. It is revealing that a number of the texts on which the poems are based are themselves expressed in metaphorical terms of this kind: VIII, 'I am the living bread'; X, 'For my flesh is meat indeed, and my bood is drink indeed'; XXXVIII, 'And if any man sin, we have an advocate with the Father'. In these poems, Taylor elaborates the implications of the image used in the text. Where the text states an idea in more abstract terms, Taylor translates the theme into his own imagery. The epigraph to *Meditation XL* is I John II : 21—'And He is the propitiation for our sins; and not for ours only, but also for the sins of the whole world.' The imagery with which the poem opens, castigating the poet's own sinful, despairing unworthiness, is vehement but static. His heart is

> *A Sty of Filth, a Trough of Washing-Swill,*
> *A Dunghill Pit, a Puddle of mere slime.*

Between the second and third verses it develops movement and conflict. His heart becomes the scene of a moral drama, a fortress· surrendered, Satan's

> *. . . Palace Garden where his courtiers walke;*
> *His Jewells cabbinet. Here his caball*
> *Do sham it and truss up their Privie talk*
> *In Fardells of Consults and bundles all.*
> *His shambles and his Butchers stalls herein.*
> *It is the Fuddling Schoole of every sin;*

it entertains riot and confusion:

> *. . . Pride, Passion fell,*
> *Ath'ism, Blasphemy pot, pipe it, dance,*
> *Play Barlybreaks, and at last couple in Hell:*
> *At Cudgells, Kit-Kat, Cards and Dice here prance:*

The concrete nouns, the verbs of violent motion, the bustling sequence of vignettes have the dramatic force of Herbert's familiar allegory and recall too Hooker's explicitly circumstanced portrayal of meditation. Where Hooker sustained and elaborated a single image, Taylor condenses each of a variety of scenes and rapidly transposes them, but essentially the method is the same. In the final three verses of his poem, Taylor turns to the second part of the text—Christ the propitiation for human sins. The imagery is of physical cleansing, using the commonest words and the names of the homeliest substances for washing, the successive labours of the housewife exactly paralleled:

> Lord, take thy sword: These Anakims destroy;
> Then soak my soule in Zions Bucking-tub
> With Holy Soap, and Nitre, and rich Lye.
> From all Defilement me cleanse, wash, and rub.
> Then wrince, and wring mee out till th' water fall
> As pure as in the Well: not foule at all.

The manner of simple pastoral expostulation is apparent here and, although Taylor never published his poems, that, however indirectly, is their tenor:

> A verse may find him who a sermon flies,
> Saith Herbert well.[1]

He deals often in downright antitheses—squalor and cleanliness, light and darkness—strikingly furnished from the odds and ends of domestic life in an unsophisticated society. *The Reflexion* uses a variation on the image of cleansing to express the idea of man's spiritual depravity, which obstructs the operation of divine grace:

> Had not my Soule's, thy Conduit, Pipes stopt bin
> With mud, what Ravishment would'st thou Convay?
> Let Graces Golden Spade dig till the Spring
> Of tears arise, and cleare this filth away.
> Lord, let thy Spirit praise my sighings till
> These pipes my soule do with thy sweetness fill.

---

[1] Preface contributed by 'a fellow Minister' to Michael Wrigglesworth's *The Day of Doom* (1662). Quoted in the *Oxford Anthology of American Literature*, p. 761.

Taylor's power to re-enliven is not confined to these more depressing regions of Calvinist theology. He feels sensuous delight and, at times, a kind of religious ecstasy as well as despair, an acknowledgment of the abundant potentialities of man's spiritual being as a willing instrument of God's purposes. Rather as Herbert cries,

> *O that I were an orange tree,*
> *That busy plant!*
> *Then should I ever laden be*
> *And never want*
> *Some fruit for him that dresseth me,*

Taylor pleads,

> *Make me, O Lord, thy Spinning Wheele compleat;*
> *Thy Holy Worde my Distaff make for mee.*
> *Make mine Affections thy Swift Flyers neate,*
> *And make my Soule thy holy Spoole to bee.*
> *My Conversation make to be thy Reele,*
> *And reele the yarn thereon spun of thy Wheele...*
>
> *Then mine apparell shall display before yee*
> *That I am Cloathd in Holy robes for glory.*

No Metaphysical poet is more consistently indebted to common speech and to metaphors adapted, with unstaled clarity of vision, from common speech and common experience. The skills from which he so often derives his imagery were those of a craft society, the accomplishments of every household. Through this medium he weaves into the fabric of his verse the intellectual creed which held the society together and dictated its form.[1] In these ways, Taylor is both genuinely in the tradition of the English religious Metaphysical poets and an adapter of their methods and approach to a different culture and a different theology. In Taylor's day, the amorphous figment, 'the American

---

[1] In this connexion we may recall the remark of Sir Herbert Read that 'no one who has given the least thought to the morphology of societies will be disposed to deny that they always depend for their cohesion and survival upon some unifying idea, which unifying idea has generally been of a mystical or religious kind'. (Read: *op. cit.*, p. 315). Of this principle there could be no more complete example than Puritan New England.

point of view' had, paradoxically, a more compact reality than it has now, because society then was homogeneous, dedicated to precise objectives and animated by a widely—one might say ubiquitously—accepted faith. It is this which Taylor manages to contain in his verse, reshaping, in the process, an inherited tradition. The substance and style of his poetry, his own temper and interests, the community in which he wrote, it need hardly be remarked, diverge widely from their counterparts in Swift. But these very differences in the constituents and their outgrowth emphasise the similarity of the process. The surroundings—in the most inclusive sense—of each poet stimulate him to creation, supply his material and enforce the extension we have observed of an established mode.

The verse of the last poet we shall consider, Philip Freneau, more explicitly resembles Swift's. Neither of them wrote, as Taylor did, out of a body of doctrine so definitively synthesised and so universally diffused that it intervened at every junction of imaginative and social life.[1] Both Swift and Freneau wrote on more narrowly political subjects and displayed a similar interest in the intrinsic importance of social manifestations, often writing poems on specific contemporary events. That this should be true of Freneau is an indication of the degree to which, with the passage of time, politics had replaced religion as the province of the intellectual. The Puritans had busied themselves with political theory and organisation, but only as an appendage of theology. With the death of the theocracy, politics was considered exclusively in the context of social affairs, of the rights (rather than the spiritual duties) of the individual, of efficient administration, of—particularly—the problem of combining republican and democratic ideals with the claims of stable government. In general terms, what this means is that the erstwhile 'American point of view'—which was wholly a Puritan point of view—had disappeared and a new ethos was in the making. In its evolution Freneau and his poetry were deeply involved.

[1] Professor Miller makes the point that 'The great difference between Calvin and the so-called Calvinists of the seventeenth century is symbolised by the vast importance they attached to one word, "method". Systematic organisation of the creed had indeed been of great concern to Calvin, but never the obsession it was to his followers.' Perry Miller: *The New England Mind—The Seventeenth Century*, p. 95.

A period so important in American history has of course been thoroughly chronicled and argued over. It will be necessary to present some view of it here, because its contentions are embedded in the work both of Freneau and of Cooper, whom we shall consider in a later chapter.

With a symmetry almost poetic, the essence of the debate was represented in the clash of ideas between Thomas Jefferson and Alexander Hamilton. Favouring state autonomy and firm checks on federal power, Jefferson had 'no fear', as he wrote in 1787, 'but that the result of our experiment will be that men may be trusted to govern themselves without a master'—men in whom he optimistically saw, as reformers do, his own tolerance, common sense and intellect. Jefferson venerated the commonalty not only through sympathy with the French *philosophes* but also, Claude G. Bowers points out, because during his youth in the American backwoods he found the levellers' theories in effective daily practice.[1] He envisaged an America expanding to the farthest frontiers while preserving its agrarian character, the mystique of husbandry, exalted by Crèvecoeur, whose words perfectly enshrine the Jeffersonian ideal:

'These are the people who, scattered on the edge of this great continent, have made it to flourish; and have without the dangerous assistance of mines, gathered, by the sweat of their honest brows and by the help of their ploughs, such a harvest of commercial emoluments for their country, uncontaminated either by spoils or rapine. These are the men who in future will replenish this huge continent even to its uttermost known limits and render this new found part of the world by far the happiest, the most potent as well as the most populous of any. Happy people! May the poor, the wretched of Europe, animated by our example, invited by our laws, avoid the fetters of their country, and come in shoals to

[1] Claude G. Bowers: *Hamilton and Jefferson*, p. 96. Bowers quotes Professor William E. Dodd's comment on Jefferson:

'It is not difficult . . . to see how the great principle of Jefferson's life—absolute faith in democracy—came to him. He was the product of the first West in American history; he grew up with men who ruled their country well, who fought the Indians valiantly . . . Jefferson loved his backwoods neighbours, and he, in turn, was loved by them.'

Still, this must not blind us to Jefferson's debt to the very much chillier metaphysic of universal equality.

partake of our toils as well as of our happiness . . . the laws, the indulgent laws, protect them as they arrive, stamping on them the sympathy of adoption.'[1]

Hamilton, governed by his conviction that 'the passions of men will not conform to the dictates of reason and justice, without constraint', argued the necessity of a central government with arbitrary control over the nation's economy and politics, secure from the pressure of popular discontents. There can be little doubt that in the confused and volatile post-revolutionary society, with its inheritance of what Cooper called 'justice . . . administered subject to the bias of personal interests and the passions of the strongest',[2] Hamilton's authoritarianism was, at the very least, expedient; equally, that Jefferson's egalitarianism was a salutary corrective. But Hamilton more clearly than Jefferson recognised the existence of the less tractable human motives, which, though they could not be eradicated, might be directed to beneficent ends:

'By multiplying the means of gratification, by promoting the introduction and circulation of the precious metals, those darling objects of human avarice and enterprise, it serves to vivify and invigorate the channels of industry, and to make them flow with greater activity and copiousness. The assiduous merchant, the laborious husbandman, the active mechanic, and the industrious manufacturer—all orders of men, look forward with growing alacrity to this pleasing reward of their toils. The often-agitated question between agriculture and commerce has, from indubitable experience, received a decision which has silenced the rivalship that once subsisted between them, and has proved to the satisfaction of their friends, that their interests are intimately blended and interwoven.'[3]

The inclusion here of these motives considerably modifies Crèvecoeur's utopian picture of what, in a letter to Adams, Jefferson called 'a good world on the whole . . . framed on a principle of benevolence'. Hamilton acknowledged the impure motives and his endeavour was to refine and emend them, not to

---

[1] H. St. J. de Crèvecoeur: *Letters from an American Farmer*.

[2] J. Fenimore Cooper: *The Spy* (Dodd, Mead ed.), p. 2.

[3] Alexander Hamilton: *The Federalist*. No. xii. (Everyman), p. 54.

rest passively in the faith that 'Those who labour the earth are chosen people of God, if ever he had a chosen people, whose breasts he has made his peculiar deposit for substantial and genuine virtue'.[1] The linguistic tone of the passage from Hamilton carefully balances the two poles of his thought. Proposing first the lures of 'gratification', 'the precious metals', 'darling objects of human avarice', he then elevates them to 'vivify and invigorate', to the dignity of 'the assiduous merchant', 'the laborious husbandman' and so on.

Marius Bewley, in his recent book on the American novel, *The Eccentric Design*, associates Jefferson's agrarianism with Adams's faith in the virtue of a landed rather than a moneyed aristocracy. Against this he pictures Hamilton as the champion of capitalist rapacity, concluding that 'There is nothing in Hamilton's character that suggests he could not easily have adjusted his tastes to the worst excesses of his financial doctrines as they developed later.' Such polemical projections are of dubious value. This particular one accords ill with the man who, in defeat, urged the election of Jefferson; of whom Bowers says that, 'Nowhere in the literature of invective is there anything more vitriolic than (Hamilton's) attack on a war speculator and profiteer.' One might as logically ascribe isolationism to Jefferson, the unlovelier features of frontier life (admitted by Crèvecoeur), or the present illiberal opposition of some state legislatures to federal reform. There is a measure of truth in Bewley's criticism of Hamilton's unrelieved distrust of the people, its consequent oligarchical philosophy and tendency to indulge acquisitive speculation—from which Hamilton himself profited not at all. But we must recognise also that Hamilton's vision of a commercial aristocracy shared the romantic idealism of Adams's conception of a propertied aristocracy or Jefferson's of a smallholding peasantry. A vast amount of nonsense is talked about the virtues of a landed as opposed to a moneyed aristocracy. Virtues they had, but no monopoly of them, and they were capable, of course, of conduct quite as ruthless and self-seeking as that of any *entrepreneur*. Wiser than opposing Jefferson and Hamilton in any pejorative sense is to see them as, simply, embodying the antitheses of their periods, each requisite to the unfolding pattern.

[1] Jefferson: *Notes on Virginia*.

Hamilton's sympathies were monarchist. We may discount the suggestion that, in proposing the constitution he did, he was merely following the gambit of over-pitching his demands. There is ample evidence that to his death he advocated the election for life of a President empowered to ignore or nullify laws as he saw fit. Working within the constitution the Philadelphia Convention finally adopted—'a frail, worthless fabric', he called it—he sought to fortify it against democratic infringement by creating, and allying with the government, a wealthy and aristocratic élite which could be induced to act for the common good. In the *Report on the National Bank* he wrote that 'Public utility is more truly the object of public banks than private profit, and it is the business of government to constitute them on such principles that, while the latter will result in a sufficient degree to afford competent motives to engage in them, the former be not made subservient to it'.[1] Hamilton was a partisan more of aristocratic values—responsibility as well as power—than of lawless financial trafficking. For all his political manipulations, for all the excesses implicit in his ideas, they did precipitate for the future an honourable myth of executive and commerical decorum, a concern for order, tradition and continuity, all of them vulnerable in the new America. Like Jefferson, though with an industrial not an agrarian bias, he envisaged an expanding economy and a nation, in the words of Jefferson's first Inaugural Address, 'advancing rapidly to destinies beyond the reach of mortal eye'.

[1] Quoted by W. R. Brock in 'Alexander Hamilton': *British Essays in American History*, ed. H. C. Allen and C. P. Hill, pp. 42-43. This idea of judicious regulation was a cardinal principle with Hamilton. We find it again in *The Federalist*, xxx. :

> Reflections of this kind may have trifling weight with men who hope to see realised in America the halcyon scenes of the poetic or fabulous age; but to those who believe we are likely to experience a common portion of the vicissitudes and calamities which have fallen to the lot of other nations, they must appear entitled to serious attention. Such men must behold the actual situation of their country with painful solicitude, and deprecate the evils which ambition or revenge might, with too much facility, inflict upon it.

There is an interesting parallel to Hamilton's reasoning in Burke's *Reflections on the Revolution in France*. Justifying the social value of settled wealth, Burke says that it 'tends the most to the perpetuation of society itself. It makes our weakness subservient to our virtue; it grafts benevolence even upon avarice.' *Works* (Nimmo 1899), p. 298.

These complementary political attitudes carried over into literature, and not only in the sense that writers espoused one party or the other. The political aspirations of Federalists and Anti-Federalists had their artistic cognates. As Hamilton felt the attraction of English constitutional security, so the Hamiltonian tradition in literature lamented American crudity, leaned towards English fashions and models and envied the poise and elegance of Johnson, Richardson and Sterne. 'A tradition essentially servile, imitative, timid', Bewley calls it, and the criticism is justified.[1] Even the opposition, however, anxious for a national literature, could find no way to cut itself off from English precedents and the embarrassment of the shared language, as Freneau discovered. He was violently pro-Jefferson in politics and his poetry, as one might expect, celebrates the presumptive union between French republican philosophies and the political institutions of the new democracy:

> *Genius of France! pursue the chace*
> *Till Reason's laws restore*
> *Man to be Man, in every clime.*
> (The Republican Genius of Europe.)

Its 'Republican Genius' aside, Europe is considered solely as a point of departure:

> *From Europe's proud, despotic shores*
> *Hither the stranger takes his way,*
> *And in our new found world explores*
> *A happier soil, a milder sway. . . . ,*
> *There Reason shall new laws devise,*
> *And order from confusion rise.*
> (On the Emigration to America.)

Elsewhere Freneau berates Federalist efforts to impede this Utopian progress:

> *In ten short years, of freedom weary grown,*
> *The State, Republic, sickens for a throne.*

Ideologically, the above quotations display Freneau comfortably at home among the expected declarations of approval and dissent. As a profession of Jeffersonian democracy, however, Freneau's

[1] See Appendix A.

poetry reveals dormant anomalies, discernible in the following verses:

> *What charming scenes attract the eye,*
> *On wild Ohio's savage stream!*
> *There Nature reigns, whose works outvie*
> *The boldest pattern art can frame;*
> *There ages past have rolled away,*
> *And forests bloomed but to decay.*
>
> *From these fair plains, these rural seats,*
> *So long concealed, so lately known,*
> *The unsocial Indian far retreats,*
> *To make some other clime his own,*
> *When other streams, less pleasing flow,*
> *And darker forests round him grow.*
>
> *Great Sire of floods! whose varied wave*
> *Through climes and countries takes its way,*
> *To whom creating Nature gave*
> *Ten thousand streams to swell thy sway!*
> *No longer shall they useless prove,*
> *Nor idly through the forests rove;*
>
> *Nor longer shall your princely flood*
> *From distant lakes be swelled in vain,*
> *Nor longer through a darksome wood*
> *Advance, unnoticed, to the main,*
> *Far other ends, the heavens decree—*
> *And commerce plans new freights for thee.*
>
> (On the Emigration to America.)

The peculiar excellence of this setting Freneau sees in its venerable innocence of the European contagion. The orthodox enough Romantic feeling gets a new purchase, beyond the eastern seaboard, in the western frontier, whose 'charming scenes ... outvie the boldest pattern art can form'. Yet the condition of unspoilt nature eulogised by Freneau is, it turns out, the prelude to a commercial development, a curiously inappropriate sequel. It is not so much that the charms of the wild and the claims of commerce are incompatible as that Freneau seems unconscious of any antagonism between them. A rather similar point, it will be noticed, is made by Hamilton with considerably more address in the passage quoted earlier from *The Federalist*. As a variant on the Wordsworthian view of nature, Freneau's development of the theme is most interesting. It is an American act of faith which permits him to visualise nature as simultaneously the auxiliary of commerce and the perennial repository of virtue, in a way impossible for his European contemporaries. Philosophically, his grasp of Romantic thought was as clear as so amorphous and emotionally constituted a body of concepts permits. As a Jeffersonian journalist he experienced no difficulty in carrying these values into the various political disputes of the era. As an American he was enchanted by the tremendous potentialities—moral and economic—of the growing nation. His problem was to compound these diverse attachments and responsibilities in poetic form. In the *Emigration to America* the two ideas fail to cohere, but Freneau returned frequently to such recensions of Romantic principle as his taste and circumstances suggested. He was inhibited in this not only by the difficulty of concerting his themes but also by the fact, as the *Emigration to America* suggests, that while his sentiments were predominantly Romantic, his diction had a strong Augustan turn. Freneau is usually represented as a straight forerunner of American Romanticism, in precisely the manner of Thomson in English poetry and exhibiting the same confusion between eighteenth-century ideas about correctness of diction and the Romantic version of nature spiritualised. In point of fact, as is argued above, his involvement in the European shift from Classicism to Romanticism is simply one factor in a fairly complex set of adjustments. The following poem attempts yet a different amalgamation between a received convention and what he had to say:

> *Ours not to sleep in shady bowers,*
> *When frosts are chilling all the plain,*
> *And nights are cold and long the hours*
> *To check the ardor of the swain,*
> *Who parting from his cheerful fire*
> *All comforts doth forego,*
> *And here and there*
> *And everywhere*
> *Pursues the prowling foe.*

48

> *But we must sleep in frost and snows,*
> *No season shuts up our campaign;*
> *Hard as the oaks, we dare oppose*
> *The Autumn's or the winter's reign.*
> *Alike to us the winds that blow*
> *In summer's season gay,*
> *Or those that rave*
> *On Hudson's wave*
> *And drift his ice away.*
>
> *For Liberty, celestial maid,*
> *With joy all hardships we endure.*
> *In her blest smiles we are repaid,*
> *In her protection are secure.*
>
> (*The Northern Soldier.*)

That Freneau was, in European terms, very much a classical poet is shown by the number of his poems that have, like this one, a public subject—formal odes and declamations, satires on contemporary events, wholly in the classical tradition. But the classical restrictions irked him. The unaffected simplicity of

> *When frosts are chilling all the plain,*
> *And nights are cold and long the hours*

clashes with the 'shady bowers', 'the ardor of the swain', the frigid eighteenth-century personification of 'Liberty, celestial maid', which is so patently an uncritical stereotype that its use eliminates any possibility of Freneau's having intended the other odds and ends of diction ironically, as Swift did. Yet his intention is evidently to modify the pastoral formula. The 'swain' in this poem, 'hard as the oaks', looks out on a comfortless vista of snow and wind, where 'The cold may freeze, the ball may kill', different from both pastoral gloss and Wordsworthian pantheism. Similarly in *To the Memory of the Brave Americans*, the 'shepherds', called away to die on a 'bloody plain', are not the pastoral Corydons of classical tradition, idling away their lives in decorative rural peace. Equally, the 'wasted rural reign', the 'shepherds sunk to rest' are objective, realistic pictures, rooted in the land: agrarian rather than pantheistic, concrete rather than mystical. Freneau holds more firmly than the English Romantics to the natural setting, sets off less frequently on ethereal philosophising. *Stanzas* pokes oblique fun at the whole business of romantic antiquity. The ruins of a country inn are playfully graced with an illustrious pedigree as 'A temple once to Bacchus', the 'Coy nymphs and sprightly lads' now vanished. Like his 'Indian student', 'No mystic wonders fired his mind.' Nature and its beauties had their own self-sufficient reality, the domain less of the seer than of the woodsman with

> sense enough to find
> The squirrel in the hollow tree.
> (*The Indian Student.*)

But in some of the lyrics we do find a genuine urge to elicit more remote and haunted qualities from the American scene. The student recognises 'Nature's God', 'dreadful secrets of the sky', 'The image of my God—the Sun'. In *The Indian Burying Ground* the spirits of the dead Indians still hunt by 'midnight moons'—

> The hunter still the deer pursues.
> The hunter and the deer—a shade!

Some of these effects are very nicely judged—the concrete, uncluttered vocabulary, the frugally condensed solidity of scene, the laconic rhythmical ease, the note of graceful, acquiescent melancholy. But the general impression is of somewhat random improvisation. The uncertainties come partly from the fracture in American political thought between faith in the rude virtues of bucolic simplicity and recognition of the demands and consequences of trans-continental expansion. This particular deadlock we have seen in the *Emigration to America*. In that poem, an earthy and material nature is idealised in the purely Jeffersonian sense that it encourages robust zeal and preserves morals corrupted by the cities. Of this agrarian pastoral, as we may call it, Freneau depicts the hardships—and the fortitude they inspire—in *The Northern Soldier* and *The Brave Americans*. Finally, we have the embryonic pantheism of the Indian poems. The confusion implicit in these unco-ordinated interpretations of the natural scene is deepened by stylistic indecision. It is not that Freneau imparts an artful rendering of confusion but that, caught up in the limited certainties of his own sector of the battle, he failed to realise that confusion existed, or chose to ignore it. Unlike Swift, he evolved no commanding *persona*, nor settled to any stylistic equilibrium. What is really remarkable, however, is that in circumstances so unpropitious, he succeeded at all in giving a bearing at once novel and persuasive to some of the established literary procedures on the basis of which, like Taylor and Swift, he worked. It is no wonder that, within an ambit of ideas so fluctuating, and able to turn, in Europe, only to traditions either deliquescing or rudimental, he should at times have felt not only that he had failed but that failure was inevitable:

> *On these bleak climes by Fortune thrown,*
> *Where rigid Reason reigns alone,*
> *Where lovely Fancy has no sway,*
> *Nor magic forms about us play,*
> *Nor nature takes her summer hue,*
> *Tell me, what has the muse to do?*
>
> *An age employed in edging steel*
> *Can no poetic raptures feel;*
> *No solitude's attracting power,*
> *No leisure of the noonday hour,*[1]
> *No shaded stream, no quiet grove*
> *Can this fantastic century move.*
>
> (*To An Author.*)

These well-made verses have something of the bare, restrained precision of the best American writing in any medium; the attachment to concrete particulars—hence the series of negative assertions; the casual tonal contour of the last line in the first verse, so very reminiscent of Robert Frost's vernacular pliancy. These qualities were always within Freneau's grasp, but he never consistently achieved them. Still, it is probably in this astringent simplicity of tone that Freneau did his best service to American verse, never more strongly sinewed than when undemonstrative, obliquely off-hand, its most intense effects contained, as Freneau's are, within the simplest clause sequences.

If the foregoing seems a churlish appreciation of Freneau, this should not obscure the real, if minor, pleasures of his verse. But we

---

[1] A savage gloss on this musically regretful line is Dickens's picture of the American lunch-time in *Martin Chuzzlewit*.

must recognise the imperfections. There is little point in inflating his merits beyond their due. It may be argued that what he set out to do was, at that time and for Freneau particularly, impossible, but the fact is that he failed. Failure, however, can be as informative as success and it is for this reason that Freneau's incursions into the European tradition interest us here. He confirms both the reliance on English example—still at this stage inescapably paramount—and the possibilities of augmenting and diversifying it by securing a confluence of precedent and experiment. Taylor's society was unique in its concentration and homogeneity. These conditions were never to be repeated, though American Puritanism has left a durable imprint on the national mind. The modern American nation, on the other hand, has developed in directions laid down by the great debate of the Revolutionary period, the echoes of which, however distantly, we catch in Freneau's poetry. Hence the ideas Freneau tried to contain happen to have a more direct relevance than Taylor's to the work of the earliest American novelists; but this is a quite fortuitous association. The basic interrelation is that all these writers refer to the old forms their search to release and methodise the tensions and engagements of the new society. As we have seen, the old forms, responding to new annexments, assume new capacities. The same process will be seen to operate in the novel.

Chapter Two

Poe and the Romantic Experiment

S T. Thomas Aquinas, in the *Summa Contra Gentiles*, traces the scale of being up from 'inanimate bodies' through the plants to 'the supreme and perfect grade of life ... found in the mind, which can reflect on itself and understand itself'. Beyond the intellect is the spirit, 'where the mind does not proceed by introspection from outside things to know itself, but knows itself by itself', the culmination of this being 'the highest perfection ... in God, where acting is not distinct from being, and where the concept is the divine essence'.[1] The Thomist system arrays society in a like confederate gradation, ideally with respect to intelligence—'men of outstanding intelligence naturally take command, while those who are less intelligent but of more robust physique seem intended by nature to act as servants'.[2] A society thus ordered in its perfect form has its apex in the monarch, as God is the apex of the scale of being, because 'unity enters into the nature of goodness' and: 'It is in fact evident that a number of individuals could not unite and bring others to harmony unless they were themselves in some way united. But what is a natural unity can be more easily a cause of unity than that which is artificially united. So a multitude can be better ruled by one than by several.'[3] Both the moral and the social lineages are different

[1] St. Thomas Aquinas: *Summa Contra Gentiles*, in *Aquinas: Philosophica Texts*, ed. Thomas Gilbey, pp. 182–3.

[2] Aquinas: *op. cit.*, in *Aquinas: Selected Political Writings*, ed. A. P. D'Entrèves, p. 101.

[3] Aquinas: *Summa Theologica*, Entrèves, *op. cit.*, p. 107.

asspects of a universal symmetry, presided over and given meaning by the infinite God. Their congruity lies in the inter-relationship of the consecutive stages and in the final dependence of the subordinate whole on its culminating rank, where all the properties are fused and transmuted. Paraphrasing Aristotle, St. Thomas distinguishes 'two systems . . . in the universe; by the first, the whole is ordered to something outside itself, as an army to its general; by the second the parts are ordered to one another, as the various formations of an army among themselves. The second co-ordination is on account of the first subordination.'[1]

Clearly apparent in this is the Christianised precipitate of the Platonic 'Form' or 'Idea'. Without going into the intricate associations between medieval Christianity and Platonism, it may be observed that their ideas impinge at many points, their concept of society being one. Though the hierarchical structures they commend resemble one another, for Plato the soul fulfilled itself in the correct performance of the duties demanded by one's status in society—only so crude a summary can elicit the necessary distinction from Plato's subtleties. The medieval schoolmen looked on earthly life as very much more a secondary attachment, the social virtues praiseworthy but in the last resort merely incidental to the progress of the soul. Platonism was interpreted so as to comply with the church's rejection of the evil and imperfect world, its glorification of Heaven as the ideal to which man must aspire, though to attain it within material corruption was beyond mortal power. Thomism was in fact an harmoniously concerted synthesis of Christian teaching and such pre-Christian philosophy, science and mythology as could be assimilated. The most intense and concentrated expression of its essence is the celebrated passage in the last canto of Dante's *Paradiso*,[2] but the medieval church disseminated it through society generally, variously apprehended at different levels, gradually more and more securely lodged in common accordance, so that it held together the whole culture and intellectual life of Europe. In many of its parts unscathed by the Reformation, the importance of this teaching here is its remarkable durability.

Any philosophy will sooner or later provoke opposition and

[1] Aquinas: *Summa Contra Gentiles*, Gilbey, *op. cit.*, p. 162.

[2] Dante: Paradiso, canto 33, ll. 80–85.

amendment. A system of parts linked in such mutual dependence as those of Thomism is liable particularly to revisions of emphasis. Its Platonic content, for example, provides an opportunity for one such transference. Platonism, which defines perfection in non-material terms, admits the complementary emphasis that, although Earth might be imperfect, it does, as a copy, verge on perfection. Spenser's *Hymne of Heavenly Love* dismisses 'all earthes glories' as 'durt and drosse', but the *Amoretti*—even granting formal hyperbole—allows a much nearer approach of earthly and ideal. Sonnet LXXXXIII specifically says that his lady's beauty illuminates the substance beyond the 'shadow' which is the 'World's glory'. In the following century, Milton has Raphael ask,

> *what if earth*
> *Be but a shadow of Heaven, and things therein*
> *Each to other like,* more than on earth is thought?
> *(Paradise Lost, V.)*

The Platonic duality could contain either emphasis: there remains the overriding agreement that the mundane aspires to immaterial standards and that at least a perception of these standards is latent in human life. Similarly, whatever modifications the other elements of Thomism underwent, it bequeathed intact its most general propositions, primarily that the apparent flux and irresolutions of human life were part of a larger order, some of whose conditions were manifest, some inferible and some the subject of mystical revelation. The history of the ideas St. Thomas propagated—which, collectively or individually, it is convenient to refer to as Thomism—is of their adaptation to extended knowledge and different methods of inquiry. The adaptation became a task more and more difficult of accomplishment, as philosophy increasingly turned from 'Types' and 'Universals' to the individual soul and psychology, while science replaced abstract reasoning by experiment. But for a long time the solid core of Thomism proved notably resilient, and it was round this centre that novel discoveries and hypotheses oscillated.

This is not the occasion to rehearse the obscurely instituted causes of the Renaissance and Reformation, but it needs only a brief glance at sixteenth-century literature to establish how much, despite the upheaval, came through from the middle ages.

Morality play personifications were an obvious reflection of the contemporary interest in generalising on experience rather than analysing idiosyncrasies, but the towering individuals—Faust, Tamburlaine, Hamlet, Lear—who dominate Elizabethan drama do not imply a total break with medieval dogma. The lesson of Faust is the disaster of the brilliant, nonconformist intellect which can master but not evaluate techniques and which aspires, with tragic consequences, beyond the nature ordained to it. The Elizabethan concept of 'Nature' is the key to the motivation of much of its tragedy: 'See wee not plainly,' asks Hooker in the *Ecclesiasticall Politie*, 'that obedience of Creatures unto the Law of Nature is the stay of the whole World?' Chaos visits society (as in Shakespeare's histories) and the individual (as in *Faustus*) when either offends against this law, which, as Hooker defined it, was 'that high everlasting law' of God Himself, whose provisions were hierarchical and which legislated for the 'manifold and yet harmonious dissimilitude' of the world. Jacobean writing is more conscious of the dissimilitude than of the harmony, because the social status-barriers had weakened and the spirit both of sceptical review and of the most militant Protestantism had become entrenched. But it was not long before the attempt was renewed to bring the disruptive philosophies within the traditional scheme.

The inspiration of these philosophies was the quickened pulse of direct observation and experiment, very tentatively encouraged and accepted though this for a long time was. Even Bacon urged that: 'The desire of Knowledge in Excesse, caused Man to fall.'[1] His general position was that certain areas of human thought were proper to religion, certain to scientific investigation. In the end, the conclusions reached by science were irrelevant to spiritual matters. Each of them dealt with different kinds of fact. Bacon, encouraging another variety of truth, for centuries neglected, did not reject the truths of religion. While he speaks of 'the dignity and excellency of knowledge and reason, in that whereunto man's nature doth most aspire',[2] he also limits its scope: 'Sacred theology must be drawn from the words and oracle of God, not

[1] Francis Bacon: 'Of Goodnesse, and Goodnesse of Nature.' *Essays, World's Classics*, p. 50.

[2] Bacon: *The Two Books of the Proficiencie and Advancement of Learning, Works* (ed. Ellis and Spedding), Vol. III, p. 318.

from the light of nature or the dictates of reason.'[1] Some forty years later, though with an accent perhaps more defensive, Sir Thomas Browne too argued the supremacy of faith. Invoking 'the liberty of an honest reason',[2] he makes very much the same qualification as Bacon when he says, 'I teach my haggard and un-reclaimed reason to stoop unto the lure of faith':[3] in matters where reason fails to bear out the necessary beliefs, it takes second place to faith—*certum est, quia impossible est*. Apparently without realising the full implications of the statement—which he does not enlarge into a case against the self-sufficiency of reason—he says, 'I could never divide myself from any man upon the difference of an opinion, or be angry with his judgment for not agreeing with me in that from which, perhaps, within a few days, I should dis-sent myself.'[4] Reason, that is, is fallible, and can lead different people, and even the same person in changed circumstances, to different conclusions. Yet another forty years on, Dryden's *Religio Laici* opens with an appraisement of reason in which Browne would have concurred:

> *Dim, as the borrowed beams of moon and stars*
> *To lonely, weary, wand'ring travellers,*
> *Is reason to the soul. . . .*
> *And as those nightly tapers disappear*
> *When day's bright lord ascends our hemisphere,*
> *So pale grows reason at religion's sight,*
> *So dies and so dissolves in supernatural light.*

The pre-eminence of reason was disputed even while it was accepted, though on certain fronts retreat was inevitable.

The fragility of much Thomist doctrine was readily enough exposed by reason and observation, imperfect as they might be. Its least tenable ground was its endorsement of Ptolemaic astron-omy which, with its concentric spheres and scale of ascending purity, cohered so admirably with the rest of the system. The conclusions of Copernicus and Galileo, so demonstrably factual,

[1] *Ibid.*, III, 478.

[2] Sir Thomas Browne: *Religio Medici*, Everyman, p. 10.

[3] Browne: *op. cit.*, p. 12.

[4] Browne: *op. cit.*, p. 7.

could not be denied for ever. The controversy was neatly sum-marised by Joseph Glanvill, a cleric and a Fellow of the newly formed Royal Society, in 1665:

'That the Galaxy is a Meteor, was the account of Aristotle: but the Telescope hath autoptically confuted it. That the Heavens are void of corruption, is Aristotle's supposal: but the Tube hath be-tray'd their impurity; and Neoterick Astronomy hath found spots in the sun . . .'[1]

Medieval astronomy was vulnerable to the exposure of such dis-crepancies, but medieval social thinking was much more tenacious because it was an attempt to rationalise conditions that actually did exist. Unlike the astronomical system, the social order did not collapse under mere scrutiny. The division of societies into a hierarchy of classes was a fact, and a further revolution of thought would be required before the prospect of engineering changes, of redistributing wealth and power, could receive an assent suffi-ciently general to be effective. One of Bacon's reasons for esteem-ing English society was that a due and sensible proportion was kept between the different classes. The empirical test was that the country's strength and stability made it militarily superior to France. The origin of this superiority he saw in 'the Splendour, and Magnificence, and great Retinues, and Hospitality of Noble-men, and Gentlemen, received into Custome', coupled with a commons 'maintained with such a proportion of land unto them, as may breed a Subject, to live in convenient Plenty, and no Ser-vile Condition'.[2] He is sanctioning not a dream of equality but such a settlement of the classes as will preserve the chain of de-scent. The inquiries of natural science did not themselves threaten this settlement but in so far as they threatened any part of the divine ordinance, they enfeebled all of it, particularly at a time when the change from a feudal to a haphazard capitalist economy was making nonsense of inherited loyalties and ideals. The pro-gress of experimental science in the seventeenth century was a very piecemeal and unsystematic affair. In place of what it dis-credited it could offer only fragmentary items of information.

[1] Joseph Glanvill: *Scepsis Scientifica: Or, Confest Ignorance, the Way to Science.*

[2] Bacon: 'Of the true Greatnesse of Kingdomes and Estates', *Essays*, p. 123.

But the integration of these *disjecta membra* was not long delayed and, ironically, it was Newtonian physics which gave new backing to the chain-of-being philosophy and carried it with its appendages through most of the eighteenth century. At the same time it evoked the irritating Panglossian optimism and the Deistic philosophy that the 'Supreme Architect', having set things in motion, had prepared the stage for man to carry on unaided. Now that he had mastered the workings of his environment, man could dispense with suprarational revelation. But despite the strength of this belief, the century's *Weltanschauung* is not to be dismissed at that inane level.

Science was indeed presumed to have arrived at a definitive exposition of the Heavenly laws which directed the universe, but was none the less counselled, in Pope's less celebrated lines on Newton in the *Essay on Man*, to proceed 'with Modesty thy guide'. The world was 'A mighty maze! but not without a plan', though to grasp the plan entire was still not considered to be within man's scope. Eighteenth-century 'optimism' at its best was in fact a finely regulated suspension of conflicting impulses, between the ordered perfection of the ideal—now shown to exist in physical nature—and the inescapable dissymmetry of human life. Not infrequently, writers failed to preserve the nice mental equipoise. The abrupt and comfortless conclusion of the third epistle in Pope's *Moral Essays* hardly supports the theory he earlier proclaims:

> *Extremes in Nature equal good produce,*
> *Extremes in Man concur to gen'ral use.*
> *Ask we what makes one keep, and one bestow?*
> *That Pow'r who bids the Ocean ebb and flow,*
> *Bids seed-time, harvest, equal course maintain,*
> *Through reconcil'd extremes of drought and rain,*
> *Builds life on death, on Change Duration founds,*
> *And gives th'eternal wheels to know their rounds.*

Johnson's *Vanity of Human Wishes* also presents a bleak review of human life and destiny, with at least a partial restoration of the balance at the end, more successful than Pope's because considerably less glib. By and large, the precarious balance was maintained, so that we have a philosophy which, while it no longer stipulated the rigid association of 'the world, the flesh and the devil', did admit the existence of imperfections. These could either be reformed without disturbing the fundamentally perfect scheme of things, or simply accepted in a spirit of fortitude as a disagreeable but necessary part of the design. The principle was applied to all human experience, private, corporate and cosmic, spiritual and material. Thus, defending the régime overthrown by the Revolution in France, Burke says that it 'possessed that variety of parts corresponding with the various descriptions of which your community was happily composed; you had all that combination and all that opposition of interests, you had that action and counteraction, which, in the natural and political world, from the reciprocal struggle of discordant powers draws out the harmony of the universe.'[1] Here again we find the political *status quo* being justified on the ground that it extends to human relationships the same divine principle of 'reconciled extremes' that Pope's lines describe.

The essential conservatism of this outlook is most cogently argued by Burke, for as his career testifies, he was neither indifferent to wrong nor solicitous of aristocratic privilege. His aim was, as he says elsewhere in the *Reflections*, 'at once to preserve and reform'. Against the irrational enthusiasms of the century's latter years he set his faith in the established order, evolved through the accumulated experience and wisdom of centuries, as a bastion against anarchy. To this employment the co-operation of all the classes was indispensable and its condition was a freedom commonly apportioned, so that no one section could secure unregulated sway over the others, a tyranny either of an *élite* or of the mass of people. The British Constitution he revered because, extending from precedent to precedent, it kept faith both with its past and with the changing circumstances it had to embrace. The monarch was subject to its provisions as well as to the pressure of the hereditary wealth and position of the nobility; through Parliament the Commons could moderate the strength of both these parties and give permanent expression to the feelings of the people in general. The constitutional checks and restraints thus guaranteed the British *modus vivendi* and the benefits it conferred on all the classes.

[1] Edmund Burke: *Reflections on the Revolution in France, Works* (Nimmo 1899), Vol. III, p. 277.

These perfectly rational justifications, of the kind Bacon used, come from the part of Burke's mind which gave him his profoundly sensible understanding of current politics and the methods of empirical inquiry. But beyond that a more mystical spirit presides over his thoughts and places him in the line of the great religious philosophers. He exalts these forms not only because they work in practice, but because the hierarchical arrangement, the mutually dependent disposition of classes, draws society more closely into the communion of the whole visible and invisible universe. Political systems might alter—indeed, as organic growths, must be capable of assimilating new substance. The business of the politician is to accommodate growth to the settled relations both of society itself and of the transcendental union of all nature, by whose values society should be modelled. For Burke, national constitutions were both utilitarian arrangements and metaphysical treaties:

'Each contract of each particular state is but a clause in the great primeval contract of eternal society, linking the lower with the higher natures, connecting the visible and invisible world, according to a fixed compact sanctioned by the inviolable oath which holds all physical and all moral natures each in their appointed place.'[1]

These tenets were most strikingly requisitioned in Burke's project for conciliating the American colonies. The novelty of the situation lay in the fact that the colonists were British, not an alien race subdued by conquest. Burke perceived here the opportunity of extending to an American legislature a subordinate autonomy which would place the colonies in the line of consenting powers descending from the monarchy. 'An empire,' he said, 'is the aggregate of many states under one common head' and 'the subordinate parts have many privileges and immunities',[2] which do not, however, dispute ultimate allegiance to the supreme authority. All Burke's speech *On Conciliation with America* is devoted to analysing this fine division of functions, delegating to the imperial relationship a place in the monarchy's domestic equilibrium of power. To establish it thus was not only expedient.

[1] Burke: *ibid.*, III., p. 359.
[2] Burke: *On Conciliation with the Colonies, Works,* II., p. 136.

As well as securing the commercial benefits, this plan met the more abstract requirement that states should align themselves 'in a just correspondence and symmetry with the order of the world, and with the mode of existence decreed to a permanent body composed of transitory parts.'[1] The form of association with England suggested by Burke seemed admirably designed to this end, and, as we shall see, met with favour among the colonists too.

This summary account of the erosion of Thomist thought and its reclamation in the eighteenth century, newly recruited from the apparently hostile cosmology of science, bears on the American equally with the European scene. For obvious reasons, much of the material which illustrates the descent and evolution of these ideas comes from European sources. America participated directly only from the seventeenth century, when we find that the Puritan rebellion, like most revolts, did not in fact take up ground entirely different from the philosophies it opposed. When the Puritans came to the New World they brought with them, as part of their intellectual equipment, many of the propositions which the long domination of Thomist thought had rooted in the European mind. As the products of a complex and intricately stratified civilisation they were strange arrivals to the inhospitable shores and rudimentary society of America, but the Puritans projected into their new surroundings their consciousness of all that they had left behind. Prominent among these ideas was the proposition which has been described as the most tenacious because closest to observed fact, that men are unequal and that the organisation of society must reflect the inequality. An early Puritan writer observes that 'every man is to serve his generation by moving in his own orb; and discharging those offices that belong to that order that the government of heaven has assigned him to'.[2]

In 1676, William Hubbard's sermon *The Happiness of a People* set forth a social doctrine essentially indistinguishable from the Platonist (and Thomist) prescription. It assumes the propriety of approximating in the state the ascending moral scale, so as to bring about 'such a disposition of things in themselves equal and unequal as gives to every one their due and proper place . . . per-

[1] Burke: *Reflections*, III., p. 275.

[2] Quoted by Perry Miller in *The Puritans*, p. 19.

sons of differing endowments and qualifications need differing station to be disposed into . . . whoever is for a Parity in any society will in the issue reduce things into a heap of confusion'.[1] Nor was this merely pulpit-bound oratory. Theory was translated into fact. The viewpoint of Devereux Jarratt—that '"from gentlemen as being of a superior order" he kept "a humble distance"'[2] was not confined to his own colony of Virginia. Speaking of the years that immediately preceded the Revolution, Charles and Mary Beard say that 'every colony had this class heritage developed into a well-articulated scheme of social subordination.'[3]

Society, then, tended to conform to a traditional shape. Though there was of course no aristocracy of the European kind, there was a very considerable body of conservative feeling and the class establishment that did exist was secured by the presence of the frontier and what at that time seemed its well-nigh limitless potentiality for absorbing expansion. It offered colonists dissatisfied with their status—they were not all Jarratts—a resort unknown in Europe and so channelled off much of the familiar antagonism between the propertied and the dependent, the rich and the poor. While the frontier encouraged many of the virtues we have seen lauded by Jefferson, it also supported chaotic and lawless communities, neither prosperous nor enterprising: Crèvecoeur gives the classic description of them. They exhibited exactly the kind of anarchic conditions Burke feared could be artificially induced in Europe by any attempt to legislate equality into society by the abstract social arithmetic of the French reformers. Thus American society kept up both the increasingly complex clerical-merchant hierarchy of the seaboard colonies and the amorphous settlements of the frontier, many of whose characteristics seemed menacing to the conservatives of the eastern towns in just the same way that the theories and practices of the French Revolution seemed menacing to Burke: that is, they not only endangered the sensible benefits of the existing order, but they offended against Nature itself. An additional cause of this latter debility, among the conservatives themselves, was the slow clerical apostasy which has been described in the previous chapter. Jonathan Edwards thought

[1] *Ibid.*, p. 247.

[2] Quoted in *A History of American Life*, Vol. IV, p. 80.

[3] Charles and Mary Beard: *The Rise of American Civilisation*, p. 126.

that the Puritanism of his day consisted 'little in respect to the divine Being, and almost wholly in benevolence to men'.[1]

In setting out to redeem its integrity, one of Edwards's aims was to adjust its theology to the discoveries of Newtonian physics, that is, to rationalise the old ideas on the new scientific basis. As Perry Miller has demonstrated,[2] the radical innovation is Edwards's argument that natural phenomena do not merely illustrate spiritual truths—the Puritan allegories—but actually *prove* them. The regularity and predictability of physical events, their laws generalised by Newton, suppose a corresponding spiritual order and it is this correspondence which gives meaning to the luxuriant Gospel imagery. So in No. 7 of *Images or Shadows of Divine Things*, Edwards says this:

'That the things of the world are ordered and designed to shadow forth spiritual things appears by the Apostle's arguing spiritual things from them, I Cor. 15: 36—Thou fool, that which thou sowest is not quickened except it die. If the sowing of the seed and its springing were not designedly ordered to have an agreeableness to the Resurrection, there could be no sort of argument in that which the Prophet alleges, either to argue the resurrection itself or the manner of it, either its certainty or probability.'

The burying and subsequent growth of the seed is not an illustration but a proof that man is subject to the same experience, for he too is part of the same ordered universe, in which 'one thing seems to be made in imitation of another, and especially the less perfect to be made in imitation of the more perfect, so beasts are made in imitation of man, plants are a kind of types of animals, minerals are in many things in imitation of plants'.[3] Edwards's application of these ideas to Biblical interpretation is not relevant here. The point is that he adopts the empirical postulate that the experience of the senses is the only valid source of ideas, and so the progress is from fact to idea, not from abstract theory to facts that may have to be distorted to fit in with it. 'The wise man,' says Edwards, 'argues from an image in the natural world.' By arguing from this premiss, Edwards instituted in America the philosophi-

[1] Jonathan Edwards: *Images or Shadows of Divine Things*, ed. Miller.
[2] *Ibid.*: Introduction.
[3] Edwards: *op. cit.*

cal revolution that was taking place in Europe, and to the same end, that of grounding the traditional system on the science which had at first seemed to invalidate it. Edwards had no particular interest in the political component of the doctrine: his concern was the salvation of the timeless and placeless soul. Nevertheless the political implications were there and Edwards's restatement of Puritan theology provides the same kind of detached, speculative background to politics as Thomism—as defined in this connexion—did in Europe. And as the inferences of this background filtered through society into controversy, its direct political application became vulgarised.

A good deal of American Toryism, unlike Burke's liberal conservatism, was simply stubborn resistance to any kind of reform. But the path from St. Thomas and the Anglican and Puritan divines to the over-simplifications of popular conservative apologetics is, though devious, discernible. We see it, for instance, in such a contribution to the pre-Revolutionary debate as this:

> *The greatest number's greatest good*
> *Should, doubtless, ever be pursued;*
> *But that consists, sans disputation,*
> *In order and subordination.*[1]

While the currency of the idea at this relatively ingenuous level— it was an argument to which the polemicists had frequent recourse —shows that it had, inevitably, renounced some of its subtleties, it shows also the extent to which Thomist political thought had penetrated one set of American convictions. Many even of the Deists—their extreme wing, again as in Europe, shading into radical materialism—continued to accept the great-chain-of-being philosophy. Franklin was one of them. In the *Autobiography* he tells us that to a deistic panphlet printed in London (1725) he affixed these lines from Dryden:

> *Whatever is, is right. Though purblind man*
> *Sees but a part o' the chain, the nearest link:*
> *His eyes not carrying to the equal beam,*
> *That poises all above;*

He later retracted—for not very elevated reasons—his opposition

[1] Quoted by Merle Curti: *The Growth of American Thought*, p. 193.

to organised religion: the value of religion and of regular public
worship was to encourage the smooth running of the social
machine and to improve the conduct of the individual. That function he considered an end in itself and the clearly implied corollary was that the rewards of moral virtue were likely to be
commercial prosperity. Franklin was no wild-eyed revolutionary.
Before the final break with England he shared Burke's desire to
league the colonies and the mother country in a partnership which
would recognise the mounting strength of America. In a letter to
Lord Keynes he wrote, 'I have long been of opinion that the
foundations of the future grandeur and stability of the British
Empire lie in America.' Even the youthful Freneau found colonial
status acceptable and praised the association with Britain, by
which American greatness would be augmented. This is the subject of the first version of his Princeton commencement poem,
The Rising Glory of America. The American Village (1772) says of
America that it will,

> *With rising pomp divine*
> *In its own splendor and Britannia's shine.*

There is little point in multiplying examples of these hardy
survivals of traditional thought. They were sufficiently prevalent
to warrant Merle Curti's comment that, 'Many of the older
patterns of thoughts continued to endure and to retard the
acceptance of the doctrine of progress which European philosophers were developing into one of the favorite concepts of the
Enlightenment.'[1] Their value in their new context was that they
ensured to America a share in the fundamental congress of minds
that unified the sundry disagreements of Europe. Whatever the
specific differences of opinion, there was a consensus on the terms
in which human problems were to be defined, on the substanti-
ality of the material world, social intercourse and institutions, and
on the standards by which man and his works were to be evalu-
ated. America might reasonably be said, from one viewpoint,
to lack an eighteenth century: we miss the variety, the plenitude
and the security of the European literature which these general
habits of thinking animated. American writing of the period was
for the most part didactic or propagandist at a fairly humdrum

[1] *Ibid.,* p. 116.

level and such literary merit as it had was that of expository composition. Yet in this restricted field the same philosophical unity appears. All the disputants would have agreed with Washington that 'a government for the whole is indispensable'.[1] Even those who favoured the most radical changes agreed on the reality of the issues they argued. When Freneau bitterly attacked Hamilton's proposals, and Hamilton as virulently replied, both accepted as their goal the most efficient organisation of human life into social forms. Each attempted rather to confute the other's logic than to deny it any meaning at all, so that there was no question of the extreme Romantic withdrawal from any involvement in a 'social contract', nourishing instead the distant, interior life of subjective dreams and visions. There is thus a deeper meaning than the entirely political one he intended in Jefferson's celebrated remarks in his First Inaugural Address:

'But every difference of opinion is not a difference of principle. We have called by different names brethren of the same principle. We are all Republicans—we are all Federalists.'

The eventual divergence from this social orientation of ideas is, of course, one of the later Romantic inclinations, with which we are familiar in Europe. It is much more central to Romanticism than many of the qualities popularly associated with it: belief in human perfectibility, description of antiquities and natural beauty, even the picturesque attractions of solitude. All these make an appearance in Augustan writing too. Romanticism takes them further and explores them more fully, the last particularly. The Romantic poet is led thereby from a tranquil assurance that society awaits one's return to a fascinated, often terrified absorption in the outcast regions of his own mind: of this passage more will be said later in the chapter.

II

There is a more complete reference to Cooper than to Poe in the eighteenth-century solidarity of outlook whose evolution has been described in the preceding pages. It is convenient, however, to take Poe first. He was a Romantic in some ways more advanced

[1] George Washington: *Farewell Address*, 1796.

than his European contemporaries. As such, he so little admitted into his writings the matter of current social and political thought that they isolate admirably the more purely aesthetic elements in their version of the literary coalescence we have seen in Taylor and Freneau. This was a process complicated for Poe by the fact that for much of what he tried to do there was little precedent. Further, he was close enough to the years of transition to feel still the counter-attraction of classical theory and the achievements of eighteenth-century English literature, in which he seems to have been widely read. Finally, Poe very largely settled the path of American fiction in the Romantic, not, as in England, the Augustan, tradition.

It is now a critical commonplace that 'Poe's love of working out cryptograms and crimes, had been primarily stimulated by the desire to prove himself logical when he felt he was going insane'.[1] There is undoubtedly a measure of truth in this. It is a nice point, though, whether that neurotic condition inclined him to the eighteenth-century appetite for scrupulous analysis and classification of forms and methods; or whether the rationalising vein was a perfectly normal reaction against the refusal of his fellow Americans to think at all seriously about the technical demands of writing, where the Augustans had been supreme. The titles of Poe's essays in this direction—*The Rationale of Verse*, *The Poetic Principle*, *The Philosophy of Composition*—suggest their intellectualising bias. Though imperfectly successful, they have brilliant passages and signify not fear of madness, but a sensible recognition that any art—particularly one as innovatory as Poe's —is the better for a clear formulation of method and intent. As he said in praise of 'Rhetorician's Rules' in the *Marginalia*, they teach the author,

'not only to name his tools, but to use his tools—the capacity of his tools—their extent—their limit; and from an examination of the nature of the tools—(an examination forced on him by their constant presence)—force him also into scrutiny and comprehension of the material on which the tools are employed, and thus, finally, suggest and give birth to new material for new tools.'

[1] Edmund Wilson gives this summary of J. W. Krutch's conclusions in 'Poe at Home and Abroad', *The Shores of Light*, pp. 180–181.

Only in Poe's last work, *Eureka*, is the strictly rational faculty wholly inapposite. And here, with the dissonance of insanity so patent, he lodges his distracted reasoning on the lucid Newtonian data.

His opening thesis is that the world originated from a still centre—God—whose essence is Unity, Simplicity. A self-generated energy expelled the simple mass in atomic fragments, to furnish, by a series of such impulses, the emptiness of space. A necessary part of the principle which inaugurated this process is that the diffused matter should ultimately revert to its starting-point, and that at all times it experiences a *tendency* to reunification—Poe speaks of 'the plainly inevitable annihilation of at least the material universe', by which he means its reversion to its original state. A force exists which, up to the crucial point in time, will prevent the actual coalition of the elements into which the original mass has disintegrated. This force, in its physical manifestation, is electricity, as the force causing the tendency to reunification is gravity as defined by Newton: in more general terms, these forces may, according to Poe, be described as 'attraction and repulsion. The former is the body; the latter the soul: the one is the material, the other the spiritual, principle of the Universe'. The Thought of God, that is the emanation from God of mental power, having initiated the process, is withdrawn and the process is continued through the operation of the laws, the physical principles, which are the result of the completion of God's primary direct action. The original act of will is determinate not continuous. By analogy, Poe supposes also the existence of a series of universes, of which we can have no knowledge 'at the very least until the return of our own particular universe into Unity'. When this happens, the sequence will be started all over again, with fresh results, so that an infinity of creations lies in the future, radiating and concentrating 'at every throb of the Heart Divine'. Finally he claims that the God who originated the action exists only in the diffused matter—so that man himself is part of the Divine Being and will attain his true stature only when united again with the countless other constituent elements.

Two quotations, chosen pretty much at random, illustrate the dichotomous tone of the style:

'What does the Newtonian law declare? That all bodies attract each other with forces proportional to the squares of their distances. . . . Let us now adopt a more philosophical phraseology: *Every atom, of every body, attracts every other atom, with a force which varies inversely as the squares of the distances between the attracting and attracted atom.* . . . In the famous Maskelyne, Cavendish, and Baily experiments for this purpose, the attraction of the mass of a mountain was seen, felt, measured, and found to be mathematically consistent with the immortal theory of the British astronomer;'[1]

and in contrast to this scientific restraint:

'The equilibrium between the centripetal and centrifugal forces of each system, being necessarily destroyed upon attainment of a certain proximity to the nucleus of the cluster to which it belongs, there must occur, at once, a chaotic, or seemingly chaotic precipitation, of the moons upon the planets, of the planets upon the suns, and of the suns upon the nuclei; and the general result of this precipitation must be the gathering of the myriad now-existing stars of the firmament into an almost infinitely less number of almost infinitely superior spheres. In being immeasurably fewer, the worlds of that day will be immeasurably greater than our own. Then, indeed, amid unfathomable abysses, will be glaring unimaginable suns. . . . While undergoing consolidation, the clusters themselves, with a speed prodigiously accumulative, have been rushing towards their own general centre—and now, with a thousandfold electric velocity, commensurate only with their material grandeur and with the spiritual passion of their appetite for oneness, the majestic remnants of the tribe of Stars flash at length into a common embrace.'[2]

What most strikes us here is Poe's quite unconscious conversion of terms from simple physical measurements—'proportional to the square of their distances', 'mathematically consistent'—to oracular and entirely subjective suppositions—'commensurate . . . with the spiritual passion of their appetite for oneness', 'unfathom-

[1] Edgar Allen Poe: *Eureka* in *The Centenary Poe*, ed. Montague Slater, pp. 356 –357.

[2] *Ibid.*, p. 403.

able abysses'. For Poe, the truth could be reached only by the utter annihilation of the rational consciousness and, ultimately, of the Universe itself: a cosmic pattern of destruction of which he could easily see himself as part. In the closing words of *Eureka* he had travelled to the last fringes of reason:

'These creatures are all, too, more or less conscious Intelligences; conscious, first, of a proper identity; conscious, secondly, and by faint indeterminate glimpses, of an identity with the Divine Being of whom we speak—of an identity with God. Of the two classes of consciousness, fancy that the former will grow weaker, the latter stronger, during the long succession of ages which must elapse before these myriad of Intelligences individual become blended—when the bright stars become blended—into One. Think that the sense of individual identity will be gradually merged in the general consciousness—that Man, for example, ceasing imperceptibly to feel himself Man, will at length attain that awfully triumphant epoch when he shall recognise his existence as that of Jehovah. In the meantime bear in mind that all is Life—Life—Life within Life—the less within the greater, and all within the *Spirit Divine*.'[1]

There is an undeniable hysteria, a fevered desperation, in these frenetic periods, but this final isolation serves to confirm his symbolic, almost his mythical, stature. He is the broken, humiliated outcast whose sibylline words command respect, inspire a mystical awe. Even if more sinning than sinned against, Poe, in *Eureka*, was offering a perfectly valid, though oblique, commentary on the commercialised society that could find no place for him, calling attention and, in the most dramatic manner imaginable, bearing witness, to standards and ideals too little regarded. Again, it is a Romantic attitude carried, as Poe so often carried things, to its most extreme conclusion. He is standing counter to the social currents observed by Dickens in *Martin Chuzzlewit*, offering no solutions, but sensible of the murderous depths beneath the surface ugliness and with a spiritual discernment and a sense of form that were inert in his society. *Eureka* depends both on the trance-like Romantic vision and on the receptive, analysing intelligence. Nowhere is the pertinacity of Poe's belief in the importance of

[1] Poe: *Eureka* in Slater, p. 407.

reason and objective calculation more curiously indicated than in this last megalomaniac attempt to prove their unreality. In his writings, the belief takes the form of balancing Romantic extravagance with classical circumspection, least successfully in his poetry, which is full of extraordinary lapses of taste. His prose is a very different matter. It is there, in his longest fictional work, *The Narrative of Arthur Gordon Pym*, that we find him most openly and with the most fertile results drawing on the previous century for the government his irregular fancies needed.

III

In his essay on Fenimore Cooper's *Wyandotté*, Poe included *Robinson Crusoe* among 'the finest narratives in the world'. He praised it again in *The Philosophy of Composition* and in his *Marginalia* noted its 'potent magic of verisimilitude'.

Frequently, Poe's own conscious aim was the creation of just this 'potent magic', his apparent purpose to duplicate Defoe's orderly realism. His debt to Defoe's methods is most obviously to be seen in the diligent accumulation of 'factual' data that characterises, for example, both *MS Found in a Bottle* and, more particularly, *The Narrative of Arthur Gordon Pym*, with their cargo lists and their detailed geographical and meteorological observations: the air of authenticity depends on our feeling that here are matters which research might corroborate, which only experience could have amassed and the labour of recording which in so meticulous detail only personal interest could have justified. When *The Record* accepted *The Strange Case of M. Valdemar* as genuine, Poe did, indeed, sneer at 'all this rigmarole (of) testing a thing by internal evidence',[1] but in fact the sarcasm reflected rather his jubilant sense of intellectual superiority than any dissatisfaction with the effectiveness of the technique. Certainly, the opening of *Pym* is quite clearly modelled on the opening of *Robinson Crusoe*. Defoe begins:

'I was born in the year 1632, in the city of York, of a good family, tho not of that country, my father being a foreigner of Bremen, who settled first at Hull. He got a good estate by mer-

[1] Poe: *Marginalia* in Slater, p. 552.

chandise, and leaving off his trade lived afterwards at York, from whence he had married my mother....'

and Poe:

'My name is Arthur Gordon Pym. My father was a respectable trader in sea-stores at Nantucket, where I was born. My maternal grandfather was an attorney in good practice. He was fortunate in everything, and had speculated very successfully in stocks of the Edgarton New Bank, as it was formerly called....'[1]

Both books originated in the same way as imaginative extrapolations from factual narratives, the basis of Defoe's being the various accounts of Alexander Selkirk's adventures, and of Poe's the journals of a number of Antarctic expeditions, a lengthy résumé of which he incorporated in the novel. The claims to authenticity begin with a nice bit of deadpan sophistry in the preface. Referring to the supposed dual authorship—Poe and the eponymous narrator—of the story, it remarks that 'in spite of the air of fable which had been so ingeniously thrown about' it, and which was credited to Poe, 'the public were still not disposed to receive it as fable': as though the purpose had been to trick up fact as fiction, not to give fiction the appearance of fact. Poe, then, would seem to be engaged in substantially the same kind of enterprise as Defoe, and not just at the beginning of *Pym*, as a convenient mode of entry to different purposes, but through all the book's extravagant developments. In point of fact, the aim of both novelists may be stated in identical terms, though in a formula that conceals more than it makes explicit: to domesticate the unfamiliar, to make extraordinary events credible, to procure, in the words of Coleridge, a 'willing suspension of disbelief'. Defoe, however, documented exotic, not fantastic, adventures. His characters—Crusoe, Singleton—were social beings thrown from a developed to a primitive context and left to make the best of it. Defoe's interest was in showing how individuals strove to sustain normality in such difficult circumstances, to come as close as possible to a renewal of social existence, to overcome physical difficulties by applying the skills and training of their civilised life.

[1] Quotations from *The Narrative of Arthur Gordon Pym* are taken from the text in R. B. Johnson (ed.), *Poems and Miscellanies of E. A. Poe* (Oxford), pp. 251–429.

Their voyages were resolutely directed back towards normality, their world was solid, and secondary among Defoe's interests was the soul of his characters—or, it might perhaps be more accurate to say, their spiritual state was entirely contingent on their showing in the world of practical affairs.[1] Poe's voyages, on the other hand, are more akin to the *Flying Dutchman's*—obsessed, driven, compulsive, voyages compelled by guilt, or fear, or, more usually, his favourite quirk, perverseness; and set in surroundings whose tendency is to dissolve and crumble from reality to nightmare, as in the tumbling universes of his *Colloquies*, or of his poem, *Dreamland*:

> *Mountains toppling evermore*
> *Into seas without a shore;*
> *Seas that restlessly aspire,*
> *Surging, unto skies of fire.*

Inevitably, Poe read his own predilections into Defoe. *Robinson Crusoe* he considered a study 'of man in a state of perfect isolation'[2]—an innocent enough comment, until we recall Poe's notion of 'isolation', much more bizarre and much more destructive than Defoe's of the whole idea of communal existence, of the hypotheses of organised society. The solitaries of Poe's tales are isolated by psychic barriers, not remoteness in space, though

---

[1] Ian Watt in *The Rise of the Novel* offers a complete analysis of what Defoe's 'individualism' meant. Cut off from society though Crusoe was, he retained his very precise ideas of the purpose and proper direction of man's life in whatever environment he might find himself. There is none of Pym's submission to the mysterious invasions of the subconscious mind. 'Defoe's attitude,' says Watt (pp. 73–74),

> 'here exhibits a confusion of religious and material values to which the Puritan gospel of the dignity of labour was peculiarly liable: once the highest spiritual values had been attached to the performance of the daily task, the next step was for the autonomous individual to regard his achievement as a quasi-divine mastering of the environment.'

There is no prospect of such mastery in Poe. Crusoe's—and Defoe's—attitude is in fact (p. 78) a 'narrowly ethical' one and it is deemed good for the castaway (to that extent he is not 'autonomous') as it is for the individual in society. When Poe removed his characters from the defences of normal life, it was to isolate the totally irrational and subjective—ultimately 'autonomous'—urges which society inhibits, though they operate there as well.

[2] Poe: *Marginalia* in Slater, p. 542.

often the spiritual disjunction is actualised in a physical analogue. Pym 'entombed' in the ship's hold, in the coffin-like box, is the Pym whom the sea attracts, as he tells us in Chapter 2, by visions of a life 'upon some gray and desolate rock, in an ocean unapproachable and unknown . . . prophetic glimpses of a destiny which I felt in a measure bound to fulfil'; the Pym all of whose half-acknowledged yearnings are away from normal intercourse and who, in a sense, submits to the perpetuation of his captivity in the hold of the *Grampus* by deliberately wasting his last supplies of liquid. Of the same kind are Prince Prospero and his companions in *The Masque of the Red Death*. Poe's solitary is not merely someone accidentally cut off from society: the isolation is at least partly voluntary; it is frequently accompanied by the destruction of a unified group—a family (*The Fall of the House of Usher*), a ruling *élite* (*Hop Frog*), a nation (*The Masque of the Red Death*), even the world itself (*The Conversation of Eiros and Charmion*). Generally, the companion of isolation is death. Catalepsy, burial alive, chance or engineered entombment are the recurrent *motifs*, always viewed with reluctant fascination, always figuring mental states in the material situations.

In these ways, Poe's concept of isolation is as different from Defoe's as it could be. Yet in interpreting *Robinson Crusoe* as, bearing in mind this concept of isolation, we must consider him to have done, Poe's critical sense had not entirely misled him, though it had produced a revealing re-accentuation. Pym and Crusoe do share a number of experiences. Pym is, in effect, buried alive as a stowaway on the *Grampus*; Crusoe very narrowly escapes a similar fate:

'. . . two of the posts I had set up in the cave crack'd in a frightful manner; I was heartily scared, but thought nothing of what was really the cause, only thinking that the top of my cave was falling in, as some of it had done before; and for fear I should be buried in it, I ran forward to my ladder. . . .'

The last clause alone points the distinction between Defoe's hero and Poe's. Crusoe's response is an instinctive assertion of his urge to survive, with none of Pym's ambiguous compromises between safety and self-immolation. In these comparable circumstances, the divergence of attitude is unmistakable. Then again, both of the castaways have frightening dreams, Pym's 'of the most ter-rific description', imaging the claustrophobic terrors of his in-carceration, Crusoe's stimulated by and giving expression to the awakening of remorse over 'eight years of seafaring wickedness'. Crusoe's dream is a simple pictorialised allegory of his earlier speculations—a man 'all over as bright as flame' who utters a per-fectly coherent threat: '"Seeing all these things have not brought thee to repentance, now thou shalt die."' The images of Pym's dream are more remote—dislocated symbols of suffocation, sterility and despair—serpents, limitless deserts, dreary wastes—associated at a much deeper level of consciousness. Crusoe's re-ligious fears and self-questionings, tormented though Defoe in-tended them to be, are thoroughly conventional and most of his time he spends in planning, contriving, devising expedients to deal with wholly concrete difficulties. It is in handling these prob-lems that Defoe is most at home and it is then, not when he con-templates his spiritual state, that Crusoe most fully exists. Still, the other elements are there, though dissociated. Crusoe's collapsing cave is simply a cave, his spiritual despairs unexceptional and the two experiences quite distinct. But they are both consequences of his isolation and we might expect them to be seen in con-junction in the sensibility of a man like Poe, for whom external events were primarily emblematic.

Most interesting in the relationship between the two writers, then, are their contrasting attitudes to external reality. With apparently very much the same acceptance of the observed fact as having a self-sufficing reality, Poe applied Defoe's technique of establishing authenticity, assembling and manipulating his imagined facts and figures. Defoe's aim was fulfilled as the fic-tional world took shape and solidified, as it mirrored actuality with increasing substance and fidelity. For Poe that was merely a beginning. Almost, he persuades us to acquiesce in the truth of his creation in order, finally, to expose its illusoriness. The solidity is a sham and, in being sham, it reflects the unsubstantiality of the material world itself. Ultimately, Poe's work is a wholehearted rejection of the kind of reality Defoe believed in. The substance he fabricates with such care is designed to shadow the terrors and inadequacies of its inhabitants and to dissolve with their dissolu-tion. The narrator of MS Found in a Bottle rushes, with the crew of the ghost-ship, 'onwards to some exciting knowledge, some never-to-be-imparted secret whose attainment is destruction ... there is upon their countenances more of the eagerness of hope than of the apathy of despair'. Destruction and dissolution are the welcome ending, for only through them can we reach beyond the delusive substance to the ideal truth.

Unquestionably, much of Poe's defection from the sober world of fact is a rationalisation of his personal history. Profoundly at odds with society, his vast ambitions shattered against both the indifference of others and his own deep-seated revulsion from sustained enterprise, the attempts repeatedly abandoned to preserve the dream of a success commensurate with his ambitions. We notice about Poe's ventures into magazine writing, *The Literary Record* and *Graham's*, the inevitability with which, their prosperity assured, he parts company with them, through a drunken lapse, a quarrel, the inducement of a more glittering scheme to be embellished by his busy fancy. It is impossible to ignore the psychiatric testimony which has been admitted, so to speak, in Poe's case, since the publication of Joseph Wood Krutch's *Edgar Allan Poe: A Study in Genius*. The chief shortcoming of the psychiatric approach is its exasperating assumption of total understanding: uncover the neuroses and you explain the talent. About Poe, however, it does have much of value to disclose, though sometimes at the cost of distracting attention from other explanations at least equally plausible. Briefly, it depicts Poe as a man who fled reality down the traditional retreats of alcoholism and drug addiction. With Virginia Clemm he achieved the appearance of marriage without the demands of a fully adult partnership. In point of age, he could almost have been her father and emotionally the orphaned Poe must have responded to this aspect of the relationship. By his marriage he regained also the status of son and to Maria Clemm, most willing of mother substitutes, was encouraged to abdicate much of what capacity he had for responsible decision. While this arrangement may be taken to have satisfied many of his buried longings, it could not completely eradicate his intermittent awareness that it was an escape into a trap, though its perverse appeal was durable enough to cause the failure of his later attempts to break away from Mrs. Clemm. The underlying horrors and the immediate miseries of life, both of which he saw with such terrible lucidity, confirmed him in the role of victim and the condition of passivity. In life his only resource was to carry out his pitiful retreats; in his writings he could remould and reconstruct, objectify his neuroses by asserting the unreality of the phenomenal world. As the narrator of *The Assignation* says, 'There are surely other worlds than this—other thoughts than the thoughts of the multitude.' Poe's premiss as a writer was that the 'other worlds', the true reality, were to be attained by the annihilation of at least the rational part of the self, which was a type of the ultimate destruction of matter itself—a nihilistic revision of Platonism.

That this is substantially a correct statement of the relationship between Poe's unhappy life and the tortured philosophy behind his writings there can be little doubt. It does, however, neglect a certain duality in Poe's thought less easily reconcilable with this interpretation. It seems likely, for instance, that at another level of personality, Poe wanted desperately to accept the visible world at its face value. The fascination Defoe had for him, his own lust for 'the potent magic of verisimilitude', argue a longing that the real world should be as solid and reliable as its fictional image can be made to seem. This is the Poe who in one of his letters wrote of 'the . . . beauty which I adore—the beauty of the natural blue sky and the sunshiny earth—there can be no tie more strong than that of brother for brother . . .' In the *Colloquy of Monos and Una* we have a simply Romantic evocation of an idyllic time when 'blue rivers ran undammed, between hills unhewn, into far forest solitudes, primaeval, odorous and unexplored'. Against his melancholic recoil from society and his speculative disestablishment of the material universe, we must set, on the one hand, his exhilarated, though fitful, delight in natural beauty and, on the other, his wishful clinging to things as they are—the solidly recorded background of the English school in *William Wilson*, the precise delineation of scene in *A Descent into the Maelstrom*, the massive Gothic décor of *The Oval Portrait*. His anguished practice was to pull down the structures he had laboured to erect, but the pressure to build was there as well. Such duality was common in Poe. It may at times, as has been already suggested of his analytic bent, have a literary provenance—though whether that is indeed a source or merely another symptom may be interminably and unprofitably argued. In the end, of course, as will appear from the closing sequences of *Pym*, where Poe brought the dilemma of rational and supra-rational to an issue, logic and reason surrender to subliminal impulses. There is no point in trying to endenizen Poe finally among the Augustans; but it is fair to say that relics of the classical tastes do both moderate Romantic improvisations and to some degree regiment the psychological discords.

Even his personal abnormalities have a strangely 'literary' cast. Many of them may be traced to a purely histrionic identification of himself with commonplaces in the Romantic myth, an obvious enough gesture of defiance in a society so inimical to his concept of the artist. Thus his 'Bohemianism'; thus, perhaps, he saw his marriage as giving life to the Petrarchan ideal of a fatal, ethereal love beyond earthly consummation. This process of identification, however, got beyond Poe's control, was complicated and set on its depressive course by psychological accidents at whose nature and origin we can now only guess. In the upshot they crippled and drove underground the flickers of positive idealism we have seen. As circumstances more and more persistently drove him to the easy solution of withdrawal and each withdrawal weakened what resilience he had, his ambitions settled into fantasy-projects and the morbidity of his writings came to seem a complete and faithful allegory of the life and doom of the artist.

At one time or another, it may be concluded from this survey, Poe comprehended all the facets of Romanticism. If we find in his work—and in his life—Romantic attitudinising, we find also the abiding Romantic attitudes: the myth of the primitive beauty of nature, opposed to the stigmata of man's interference; the concurrent sense of man's identity with nature and with God; the further paradox of the melancholy awareness of human isolation from society and from other humans individually; the consequent psychological retreat to introspection. The list is by no means exhaustive but it covers most of the principal attributes. To it we must add the rider that Poe's Romanticism is not synonymous with European Romanticism. Its grouping of the attributes gives them an altogether novel direction and they find expression most effectively not in poetry—the central Romantic medium in Europe—but in prose. Furthermore, Poe's tastes were eclectic. He had not the same sense as, say, Wordsworth, of conducting a personal crusade against classical authority—partly, perhaps, because there was no native American analogy to the bulky English tradition. Such opposition as there was to tradition was directed as much against European domination generally as against classicism particularly. Whatever the reasons, Poe didn't neglect the classical lessons, and what he learned there significantly helped his experiments in fiction. Briefly, Poe's problem was that in the normal outlet for his intensely egocentric Romanticism, the personal lyric, there was no place for his supplementary role as the detached analytic recorder of the external reality of manners, customs and backgrounds. But in prose fiction, the classical instruction, the emphasis on representational exactness—'the eye on the object'— could add the dimensions of physical actuality to the range of the late Romantic lyric's inward-looking eye. Thus Poe was brought to the exercise of amalgamating realistic presentation with his transcendental, ultimately anti-realistic judgment of values. If this had its difficulties, it offered also the chance of pursuing with greater particularity than was possible in the lyric the transit to ultra-sensuous realities from the everyday life of things seen and accepted as seen.

IV

In his essay 'Poe at Home and Abroad', Edmund Wilson concludes that it was 'Poe who sent out the bridge from the romanticism of the early nineteenth century to the symbolism of the later'.[1] As a writer, then, Poe raises the problem of deciding to what extent he succeeded in marrying his subject matter to symbolic method, and in working out a method. To this inquiry, as to understanding Poe the man, while psychological surmise is relevant, it is more important to examine his literary affiliations, to see in what ways he has absorbed and transmuted them and how, as a pioneer, he has adumbrated procedures developed by later writers.

As has been indicated, Poe's interest in Defoe did not result in his taking over holus-bolus Defoe's trick of verisimilitude. From the systematically rendered physical data, Poe derives a symbolism whose very origin is some safeguard against the dangers of abstractness and at least partly answers for Poe the problem that

[1] Wilson: *op. cit.*, p. 190.

exercised Hawthorne of finding 'a neutral territory, somewhere between the real world and fairyland, where the Actual and the Imaginary may meet'[1]—though for Hawthorne the task was made more difficult by his attempting to carry it out in the unfamiliarised terms of the American scene, which Poe almost entirely ignores. Poe's awareness of the unsubstantiality of the material world never wholly liberated him from its toils nor enfeebled his ability to image it faithfully, whether his subject was an actual place, like the Benares of *A Tale of the Ragged Mountains*, or a scene with no specific counterpart, like the nightmare landscape of *The Fall of the House of Usher*. The settings come alive as places before they tremble into symbol, and in thus directing Poe the influence of Defoe was particularly beneficial, for it is in the ominous and illusively familiar settings that Poe gives tangible form to the terrors and perversions of the abnormal mind which were his subject-matter. The backgrounds—not only landscapes, buildings, rooms, furnishings, but the whole apparatus of social communication: speech, books, journals, shared assumptions—are effective as symbols because they are at once alien and familiar, palpable and dissolving. They mirror the secret kinship we must acknowledge between the abnormal mind and the most normal, and they link Poe's internal horror-world to the common ground of observed fact. Poe's artistic aims may have been, as Lionel Trilling argues, 'tangential to society', but he never loses sight of the point of contact between the tangent, which is exceptional sensation, and the circle, which is normal life. The hysterical energy of the opening sentences of *The Tell-Tale Heart* is authentically colloquial, modulating to the speaking tones of insanity, which impinges on the outer world in the experience—commonplace enough—of 'a shriek . . . heard by a neighbour during the night' and the police officers who 'chatted of familiar things'. In another mode, the balanced formality of style in the first paragraphs of *The Fall of the House of Usher* introduces us remorselessly to the exterior melancholy of the setting, which symbolises, we gradually realise, a more profound, less easily defined spiritual malady. The degree of fantasy varies. The excursion into the sensations of dying in *The Colloquy of Monos and Una* explores rare and intense but none the less actual areas of human experience,

[1] *Scarlet Letter* (Everyman), p. 47.

where the senses merge and vision is transposed into '*sound—sound sweet or discordant as the matters presenting themselves at my side were light or dark in shade—curved or angular in outline*': a visionary exaltation of rare states of being.

The Narrative of Arthur Gordon Pym is commonly enough interpreted as a 'good salt-sea yarn' miscarried. In the first few chapters especially, the fantasy and morbidity of much of Poe's work are subdued, so that it sets out as a novel where the normal association between fiction and reality seems to have replaced the soaring and toppling dream-worlds or the psychic horrors for which Poe is celebrated. In point of fact, *Pym* is the most sustained effort Poe made to adapt the methods of Defoe to his own very different purposes. It is not a realistic novel gone wrong but a symbolic novel that doesn't quite come off, partly because Poe's aims were confused (there was a commercial motive in the suggestion that a full-length book might find a readier market than collections of short stories) and partly because Poe's talent was happier in the necessary compression of the tale than in the wider ramifications of the novel. His whole aesthetic theory exalted the short over the long composition: we should decide 'upon a work of Art . . . by the effect it produces' and 'the brevity must be in direct ratio to the intensity of the intended effect'. [1] There is undeniably a great deal of pure hackwork in *Pym*: the twenty or so pages giving a lengthy account of Antarctic exploration are little more than padding. On the other hand they do have the purpose, which we find also in Defoe, of *wearying* the reader into credulity. More efficient is the passage in Chapter Six which describes in detail, with all Defoe's expertise and abundant particularity, the system of stowing ship's cargo. This is another of the deceptively reassuring paths along which Poe leads us to the abyss. The hold that so nearly becomes Pym's tomb is at once a measurable set of technical problems ('A hold filled with grain . . . will be found not more than three-fourths full upon reaching its destination') and a gloomy prison of 'innumerable narrow windings', 'dismal and disgusting labyrinths', 'windings innumerable'.

Just as Poe's symbolic method absorbed Defoe's circumstantiality, so it assimilated the common narrative theme of the voyage,

[1] Poe: *The Poetic Principle* and *The Philosophy of Composition* in Johnson, *op. cit.*, pp. 169 and 194.

with many of the accreted meanings of its Romantic acceptation. Of Pym's voyage there are of course many analogues in nineteenth-century Romantic poetry, and in more general terms, the Romantic poet's attitude to his material was closely akin to Poe's. Coleridge's, for all that it is fragmentary and haphazard, is the most suggestive commentary, from the Romantic viewpoint, on the nature of the poetic faculty, whose central drive he sees in the power of the creative imagination to achieve 'the balance and reconcilement of discordant qualities: of sameness with difference; of the general with the concrete; the idea with the image; the individual with the representative'.[1] All the emphasis here is on the principle of unification, on the imagination as an analysing force the end of whose analysis is resynthesis. Yet the distinctive feature of the Romantic sensibility is its response to the existence of conflicts not easily reconciled, its acknowledgment of

> *One thought, one grace, one wonder, at the least,*
> *Which into words no virtue can digest;*

and it is nourished by its own duality—the aspiration towards vast, cloudy ideals, the ecstasy in the beauties of the world, and the disgust with and revulsion from the imperfections of life as it is. 'Reconcilement' is the aim, but the turbulent Romantic aesthetic operates also in mysterious regions (ranging beyond social and metaphysical paradoxes) where we are made acutely conscious of unresolved flux, of incompleteness, of conflicts which it is the artist's job to mirror, not to unify, because discord is a necessary condition of their being. Consequently, the Romantic solutions: a world liberated from its torments and antinomies by a convulsive moral and political regeneration; or a life irreparably flawed but superseded by the perfection of death and its mystical sequel.

Either way, the Romantic rejects the present condition and from this stems the fondness for myths of dispossession and rebirth; the recurrence of images of decay and impermanence; the symbols of flight and the journey. The symbolic significance of the voyage is most concisely stated in the last stanza of Shelley's *Adonais*:

[1] S. T. Coleridge: *Biographia Literaria* (Everyman), p. 151.

83

> *my spirit's bark is driven*
> *Far from the shore, far from the trembling throng*
> *Whose sails were never to the tempest given;*
> *The massy earth and sphered skies are riven!*
> *I am borne darkly, fearfully, afar;*
> *Whilst, burning through the inmost veil of Heaven,*
> *The soul of Adonais, like a star,*
> *Beacons from the abode where the eternal are.*

Here we have the ideas of isolation from the unenlightened crowd, of the dedicated spirit embracing the perils of discovery and inspired by the visionary prospect of a haven beyond life. These *motifs* are given fuller expression in *Alastor* (the spirit of solitude, Poe's familiar). The poem is very close to *Pym* in theme and design. *The Ancient Mariner* does also suggest a number of helpful comparisons, mainly of narrative detail, but the mariner, renewed, comes back to the world. Both Pym and the protagonist of *Alastor* finally renege, passive but consenting instruments,

> *in mystic sympathy*
> *With nature's ebb and flow.*

'Nature's ebb and flow', as we shall see, provides the structural principle of *Alastor*. Its hero sets out in youth 'to seek strange truths', travelling to exotic scenes, barren and fruitful both. Though associated with the cities of antiquity, Athens, Tyre, Babylon, they are predominantly regions of dream. Among the ruined temples of 'Dark Aethiopia' he sees 'the thrilling secrets of the birth of time'. The 'veiled maid' who appears to him in sleep—'knowledge and truth and virtue were her theme'— vanishes as he is about to clasp her to him. The quest to find her again leads him, by mountains, tombs and 'deep precipitous dells', to 'a little shallop' on which he embarks. He is carried to a river which, passing through a cavern, winds its way to a ravine whose gloomy cliffs are relieved by a 'green recess' in which he takes refuge and, as the moon sets, dies.

Unlike Coleridge's and Poe's mariners, the hero of *Alastor* travels East, not South, but his quest resembles Pym's and leads him among very similar landscapes, possessed throughout by a half-reluctant desire for death. For him, 'silent death . . . exposed its own strange charms' and he asks if

> *'every shade which the foul grave exhales . . .*
> *Conducts, O Sleep, to thy delightful realms.'*

So Pym, descending the cliff, finds that 'my whole soul was pervaded with *a longing to fall*'; so, seeing the death-ship and its terrifying crew, 'in the last and most loathsome state of putrefaction', he and his companions beg that they should 'receive us among their goodly company'. These thematic resemblances are more or less to be expected. The remarkable—though loose— conformity between the two works is indicated even more clearly by the likeness of the surroundings in which the dramas are played out. In *Alastor*, the poet, having left 'his cold fireside and alienated home', wanders where

> *The red volcano over-canopies*
> *Its fields of snow and pinnacles of ice:*

the Antarctic scenes in Pym, which have the same paradoxical qualities, spring immediately to mind. 'Black bare pointed islets', 'secret caves', the boat swept on to a 'labyrinthine dell', 'the grey precipice' and in it 'one silent nook' of 'fissured stones': these recur in Pym, also with symbolic implications. The islands Pym visits (Desolation, Inaccessible) are described as sterile and precipitous. On Tsalal, the islanders massacre the party from the *Iane Guy* by collapsing the cliffside on top of them, in a ravine of which Pym says that it reminds him of 'those dreary regions marking the site of degraded Babylon'. From this catastrophe he and Peters escape by hiding in 'a fissure in the soft rock', later exploring the dark cavities that honeycomb this 'island of the chasms'. 'The Ethiopian characters so mysteriously written in their windings' and the letters formed by the shape of the caves themselves offer cryptic and tantalisingly incomplete explanations of the islanders' behaviour and beliefs, as Peters suspects. But Pym dismisses the idea as 'idle opinion' and comments only that 'these singular caverns afforded us no means of escape from our prison'. The 'thrilling secrets' remain hidden. Pym's wholly rational deductions mislead him and revelation is postponed to the novel's apocalyptic climax: 'And now we rushed into the embraces of the cataract, where a chasm threw itself open to receive us. But there arose in our pathway a shrouded human figure, very far larger in its proportions than any dweller among men. And the hue of the skin of the figure was of the perfect whiteness of the snow.' As with Verlaine's Saturniens,

> *L'Imagination, inquiète et débile,*
> *Vient rendre nul en (lui) l'effort de la Raison.*

The pattern of *Alastor* is determined by the imagery and is antithetical. The imagery proposes a series of conflicts: fire and ice, valley and mountain, fecundity and sterility, accomplishment and loss, understanding and incomprehension. In the Romantic mode, the external images symbolise the intricacies of the mind, as for Keats the world of his imagination was visualised as 'some untrodden region of my mind'; as, later in the tradition, the white jacket became for Melville at once an *alter ego* and a symbol of the tortuous byways of his personality: 'There were, also, several unseen recesses behind the arras; insomuch that my jacket, like an old castle, was full of winding stairs, and mysterious closets, crypts, and cabinets; and like a confidential writing desk, abounded in snug little out-of-the-way lairs and hiding-places, for the storage of valuables.' In *Alastor*, this kind of symbolism is found at its most overt in a phrase like 'the wide pathless deserts of dim sleep', or in the way Shelley uses the river-journey at the end to recapitulate what we have already seen of the poet's life. The stream, he says, 'images my life:

> *Thy darksome stillness*
> *Thy dazzling waves, thy loud and hollow gulfs,*
> *Thy searchless fountain, and invisible course*
> *Have each their type in me.'*

But in more general terms, the caves, valleys and windings of the landscape are the caves, valleys and windings of the mind, so that Shelley was presenting the dynamic antagonisms of 'nature's ebb and flow' as archetypes of the perplexing enigmas of the mind and thus developing a fruitful variation on the Romantic theme of the kinship between man and nature. Structurally, then, the imagery formulates the pattern of natural flux and relates it to the poet's tragic interior confusions. Within either frame of reference, the incompatibles may be reconciled, the ultimate satisfaction realised, only through death.

As a narrative, *Alastor* is patently defective. Poe's task in *Pym* was to superimpose its symbolic design on the structure of the realist novel without obstructing the narrative flow. The imagery and landscapes of *Pym*, as already suggested, strongly resemble those of *Alastor*. So too, within the narrative, we discern the *Alastor* pattern of radical antitheses. As in *Alastor*, tumultuous storm and placid calm alternate. Pym's voyages all end with the violent and violently described destruction of Pym's vessel: 'some fragments of our boat'; 'the longboat and starboard bulwarks torn off, and even the windlass shattered into fragments', 'a wild chaos of wood, and metal, and human limbs'. There is a succession of subterranean descents, generally marked by a dilemma of subjective and objective terrors. While Pym suffers his private terrors in the hold, above him the ship's ordered life disintegrates in the mutiny. In the ravine on Tsalal, he once again finds himself 'entombed alive . . . with the ghastly considerations that we are beyond the remotest confines of hope, and that such is the allotted portion of the dead': outside, the islanders massacre the rest of *Jane Guy's* crew. Other descents are through the water to the storeroom on the dismembered *Grampus* and into the caves on Tsalal. The descent is always an escape from a world that has got out of hand, often substituting its own terrors for those of reality. Hints of the equivocal boundaries between appearance, fantasy and reality permeate the novel. Pym brings about the overthrow of the mutineers by the pseudo-resurrection of the dead Rogers. Speculating on the success of this ruse, he remarks that usually 'the appalling horror . . . is to be attributed . . . more to a kind of anticipative horror, lest the apparition *might possibly be* real, than to an unwavering belief in its reality'. Here, the crew's 'unwavering belief' has been secured by a contrived resemblance. In his later hallucinations, Pym's actual surroundings take on the shapes suggested by his sick fancies, so that he 'for some time remained firmly convinced that I was still in the hold of the brig, near the box, and that the body of Parker was that of Tiger' (his dog). Safe in the *Jane Guy* and remembering his experiences on the *Grampus*, he records that the past reality now seems 'a frightful dream'. The external world of fact responds to the directions of the observing mind, and its objective existence is called into doubt. On Tsalal, the apparently solid cliffs crumble into ruin and destroy the ship's party, as though 'the whole foundation of the solid globe were suddenly rent asunder, and . . . the day of universal dissolution was at hand'. For Pym, of course, it is quite close at hand. In the closing sequence the world of reality dissolves with intensifying speed up to the climax. The novel is not unfinished, for no conclusion could more fitly summarise its intimations of destruction than the final union with the looming figure in the chasm.

This symbolism does not involve the precise correspondences of allegory. The ulterior meanings, as Poe said of Hawthorne's tales, are 'judiciously subdued, seen only as shadow or by suggestive glimpses . . . a not obtrusive and therefore not unpleasant *appositeness*'. The preceding outline of the novel suggests some of the symbolic implications. Pym is the voluntary 'outcast from his tribe' (a phrase used by Poe of Cooper's Wyandotté). In the course of his wanderings he reaches out not only to remote places (Desolation, Inaccessible, the fabulous Auroras, the Antarctic) but also to alien experiences and the disorders and traumas of the mind, which parallel and are reflected in events on the physical plane. The 'societies' Pym enters (on the *Grampus* and on Tsalal) are treacherous and violent, but the individual, thrown back on his own resources, turned in on his own mind, finds no safer refuge than in the deceitful and fluctuating reality he has fled. The novel traces a sequence of withdrawal and return. The oblivion to which the sequence leads is achieved by a coincidence of Pym's own longings—'I was still more earnestly bent on prosecuting the voyage to the southward'—and the natural forces driving the ship—'the constant tendency to the southward, both in wind and current'. Around these ideas is centred the theme of the novel: that the world of reality and the forms of society are unstable figments; that in them, destructive, supra-rational impulses lead to a mystical but undefined consummation (more fully set forth in *Eureka*).

The Narrative of Arthur Gordon Pym is a novel whose premiss is a rejection of society and its values and even of the individual consciousness. The point of no return we may place at the horror of cannibalism, after the destruction of the *Grampus*, the irrevocable denial of communal existence and at the same time, it may be, an image of the predatory society of Poe's time—there is an interesting echo of this in Twain's ghoulish joke, *Cannibalism in the Cars*.

In this respect, Poe is neither unrealistic nor out of touch with what lay around him; nor any the less a novelist because, like Melville, he is outside the usual social precincts of the form. Poe dealt in society reduced to its elements, in the basic conflict between what Locke called 'the fancies and intricate contrivances of (individual) men'[1] and the liabilities contracted by communal submission to a 'politic society'. Poe's, of course, was a much more sweeping recantation than such a straightforward refusal of civil obedience as Thoreau's but the principle is the same. His subject is the isolated individual or group of individuals—'*Isolatoes* ... not acknowledging the common continent of men ... now federated along one keel'.[2] Society proper is either more or less eliminated or mirrored in other ways than directly, as in *Moby Dick* Ahab's vial 'filled with Nantucket soundings' brings 'two remote associations together'. Thus Pym's temporary affiliations to the various groups he joins dramatise what Poe saw as the essential relationship between society and the individual. Society proper hardly enters directly into the novel—there are a few New Bedford scenes in the first two chapters—but we are nevertheless made aware of Poe's warped and limited but precise vision of the diabolic elements in it and in the human ethos. What is most important in *Pym* is his rendering of this vision: the steps by which he marked out the development from a Romantic viewpoint to a more purely symbolic technique.

The work of Coleridge, Keats and Shelley particularly among the Romantics has a strong and highly subjective symbolic content. Though the symbols are necessarily taken from the objective world, or have their simulacra in it, the effect of the poet's treatment is to abstract them from that world, first because their significance is decided by entirely personal associations and ideas, secondly because, very often, the poet lays all the stress on elaborating these multiple associations, not on establishing the symbol's physical existence. It is a symbolism erected on a substratum of some intense and evanescent emotional experience, moments of exalted joy or penetrating despair. The flashpoint provides the symbol—the nightingale, the skylark—but the poet has little perception of the object he uses to embody his feelings as a creature

[1] John Locke: *Of Civil Government*, II (Everyman), p. 123.
[2] H. Melville: *Moby Dick* (Collins Classics), p. 113.

of flesh and blood. Elsewhere, as in *Alastor*, the symbols exist in a fluid and agitated background, rich in sensuous properties it may be, but by its inconsequence immediately dissociated from rational actuality; a background, in short, 'to which . . . the attributes of time and space are inapplicable and alien, but which can yet not be conveyed save in symbols of time and space.' [1] It is at this point that we find the essential divergence between Poe's and the Romantic system. Poe imposes the irrational, chimerical dream-world on rigidly solid, concrete, even deliberately banal 'attributes of time and space' and commutes at will between the two, the Defoe-world perpetually at the mercy of the nightmare sub-world, much as the twisted phantoms of *Morella* grow unseen beneath the bright domestic veneer of Poe's life in New York with Virginia. What Poe did in *Pym* was to reclothe the symbol of the voyage in its common garb of observed fact— and to load it, in addition, with his own aberrant fancies. In thus attempting to order and substantiate his symbolism, Poe initiated the line which was to be continued by Hawthorne and Melville.

Hawthorne, like Poe, was concerned with a symbolism issuing from a fictional world 'so like the real world that, in a certain remoteness, one cannot tell the difference, but with an atmosphere of strange enchantment, beheld through which the inhabitants have a propriety of their own'. [2] Hawthorne's short story *Dr. Heidegger's Experiment* illustrates very clearly what his methods were and how fine was the adjustment that had to be made between reality and fantasy in order that the actual might be successfully transmuted into symbol. It offers an instructive contrast to Poe's novel. The story is about an elixir with the power to transmute youth—temporarily, as it turns out—and its effect on four aged friends of Dr. Heidegger. From their experience of the brief gift it is apparent that they have learned nothing from the follies of their lives and would, if given the chance, reproduce precisely all their former sins. Ignoring the dissuasion of Dr. Heidegger, they decide to journey to the source of the elixir to rejuvenate themselves again. That is the substance of the story. Its opening paragraph is sedately factual; the third paragraph begins to imply other sources than the narrator for what we are told—'if all stories

[1] Coleridge: *op. cit.*, p. 233.

[2] Preface to *The Blithedale Romance*.

90

were true . . .', 'it was fabled that . . .' There is much detailed cir-
cumstantial description. Shortly afterwards, Hawthorne says that
he himself has made up the stories about Heidegger and that he is
a 'fiction-monger'. This admission enfeebles the careful scaffolding
of authenticity and discredits in advance the later attempts to
insinuate the existence of other witnesses to the strange events 'the
tall mirror *is said* to have reflected . . .' The four participants in the
experiment are symbols, types of lust, vanity, gluttony, avarice.
The faded rose on which Dr. Heidegger first demonstrates the
elixir's power is the relic of a romantically cherished, irrecoverable love; the butterfly, whose declining vigour briefly returns
when it touches the liquid, signifies the ephemeral return of
youth, almost at once recalled 'far down the chill and darksome
veil of years'. The slight narrative sinks under this weightily
manipulated symbolism. Hawthorne vacillates indecisively between treating his material on the one hand as outright allegorical
fantasy, and on the other as actuality whose firm outlines gradually erode into symbol. The elusive passage from outer life to the
irradiating depths of symbol is never secured. Poe's own success
in *Pym*, it must be allowed, was partial. The structure of the novel
is, to say the least, ramshackle and rather distended than maintained by the pot-boiler stuffing. The tension relaxes and the
setting, losing its substance, loses also its shadows. Poe doesn't
consistently succeed in keeping the two levels simultaneously
alive, but they are never, as in *Dr. Heidegger's Experiment*, plainly
incompatible.

The induction to *Pym* is an interesting document. Written—
improbably—in the person of Pym, it refers, as has been pointed
out, to the supposed double responsibility for the narrative:
'Even to those readers who have not seen the Messenger, it will
be unnecessary to point out where (Mr. Poe's) portion ends and
my own commences; the difference in point of style will be
readily perceived.' This almost schizophrenic declaration may
well have been inspired by Poe's dissatisfaction with the novel,
which he was later to describe as 'a silly book'. He was a conscious
enough artist to have recognised its faults and this oblique disclaimer is characteristically evasive. It suggests, however, another
consideration. 'A difference in point of style will,' indeed, 'be
readily perceived.' It is of the same kind as the variation in

Eureka, but under better control, and it follows Poe's doubling between the contrarieties of objective reality and immaterialising fantasy. The first is mirrored in the business-like realism of present-ation, the second in the impressionistic 'dissolves' to states of mind and feeling. During the descent of the cliff on Tsalal the descrip-tion moves from its focus on the cliff—composition, height, method of descent—to the turmoil of Pym's fears. The language exchanges precise, quiescent terminology for words of vertigi-nous, hallucinatory motion; the exterior, 'the flat surface of the cliff before me', blurs and vanishes:

'At length arrived that crisis of fancy, so fearful in all similar cases, the crisis in which we begin to anticipate the feelings with which we *shall* fall—to picture to ourselves the sickness, and dizziness, and the last struggle, and the half swoon and the final bitterness of the rushing and headlong descent. And now I found these fancies creating their own realities, and all imagined horrors crowding upon me in fact. . . . And now I was consumed with the irrepress-ible desire of looking below. I could not, I would not, confine my glances to the cliff; and with a wild, indefinable emotion, half of terror, half of a relieved oppression, I threw my vision far down into the abyss. For one moment my fingers clutched con-vulsively upon their hold, while, with the movement, the faintest possible idea of ultimate escape wandered, like a shadow, through my mind—in the next my whole soul was pervaded with *a longing to fall*; a desire, a yearning, a passion utterly uncon-trollable. I let go at once my grasp upon the peg, and, turning half round from the precipice, remained tottering for an instant against its naked face. But now there came a spinning of the brain; a shrill-sounding and phantom voice screamed within my ears, a dusky, fiendish, and filmy figure stood immediately beneath me; and, sighing, I sunk down with a bursting heart, and plunged within its arms.'

These collocations of reality and reality assaulted, swallowed up in the disintegration of the perceiving consciousness, convey Poe's 'meaning', his final assessment of the events he portrays, his 'criticism of life', in Arnold's phrase.

Poe's scale of values and his method of evaluation are altogether different from those of the conventional novel. The eighteenth-century novelists had discovered the fascination of presenting clearly individualised characters whose personalities were simultaneously revealed through and affected by a causal sequence of action set in recognisable daily life. The presentment of *manners* played a considerable part in the building up of character and the author passed judgment on both characters and action by reference to generally accepted criteria—either directly stated or by various means implied—of good and evil; as the moral life of the characters was directed within the story by conceptions of guilt and innocence, probity and infidelity, bravery and cowardice and so on, similarly arrived at. Novelists, that is to say, created an artistically ordered microcosm based on the prevailing ideals of their society. Even when the novel was satirical and the ideals in actual life were paid only lip service, they still provided viable standards of conduct. For all that Poe had little regard. From that point of view he offers us only characterising gestures. Thus we are told that during the mutiny, the behaviour of Augustus, Pym's companion, seemed to indicate a 'falling-off in friendship and faith', that Peters 'treated Augustus all this day with great kindness'; or that Pym had an 'enthusiastic temperament'.

But comment and illustration of this kind are infrequent and hastily dismissed; character does not gradually synthesise and take shape as the events unfold. Instead, the narrative records the discrete, minute by minute responses of the type we find in Pym's rapid transitions of feeling in the hold of the *Grampus*. His periods of consciousness alternate with cataleptic sleep and hysteric coma. In his wakeful moments, at first contented with his surroundings ('at which I was excessively amused'), he moves to 'great disquietude' and 'a multitude of gloomy fealings'. When he thinks that he has effected an escape he feels 'exceeding joy', followed at once by 'extreme horror and dismay'. 'Some portion of presence of mind' is succeeded by apathetic 'despondency' and, finally, the 'perverseness' which makes him waste his last gill of liquid and disables him, when Augustus does appear, from uttering the 'one little syllable' that would save him. Sequences of this nature are the groundwork of the novel. If we are to adopt E. M. Forster's categories of 'flat' and 'round' characters we must say that Poe explores the 'roundness' to the virtual exclusion of the 'flatness'. The human being becomes, so to speak, a medium which receives stimuli and transmits its awareness of them, more often than not aberrant. The novel, then, advances the characters—in particular, Pym—through a series of situations the point of which is to emphasise their discontinuity, or, more accurately, that the only consistency in human behaviour is its compulsive liability to evil and to the irrational; and in the personality that it is fissile. Pym expresses horror and disgust at some of the actions in the novel. The appropriate conventional judgments on cruelty and wrongdoing are thus given a place. But the real interest is not that these actions are reprehensible but that they happen and that their occurrence is unpredictable: it is the 'sympathetic' characters, not the villainous mutineers, who eat human flesh. Poe's attitude is rather that of Pym when he comments on the dreadful results of his urging the captain of the *Jane Guy* to pursue their southward course:

'While, therefore, I cannot but lament the most unfortunate and bloody events which immediately arose from my advice, I must still be allowed to feel some degree of gratification at having been instrumental, however remotely, in opening to the eye of science one of the most intensely exciting secrets which has ever engrossed its attention.'

Such is the manner of Poe's 'criticism'. He is less moralist—in any restricted ethical sense—than, simply, investigator, displaying, not censuring, the eccentric longings he unearths.

The sundered world of Pym transcribes the most inward conformations of its author's mind as closely and unmistakably as that of any Romantic lyric. But where the Romantic poet does allow his settings an existence in physical fact, it is much less mundanely particularised, and much less a matter of communal experience than in the novel. In the lyric, we are looking back at concrete reality, not moving deliberately through it to the transcendent plane where proportions shift and new patterns of meaning are revealed. In *Pym*, the foundation is a world of seemingly tangible fact whose outlines fade and reform, suggest interior correspondences and an inner reality which controls the outward shapes. Poe's representation of reality has an aesthetic, not—in any practical sense—a sociological purpose. It brings within the circumference of his criticism that resolutely materialistic life which the lyric was not equipped to contain. We have seen the means by which Taylor and Freneau cultivated a felicitous poetic mode for the statement of, the one, a coherent body of sacred doctrine and, the other, a political debate. The material of their art, personal though their statement of it was, had a life of its own extraneous to their feelings about it. Poe's is almost entirely subjective in origin, the psychological discords for which he sought artistic expression. But the process at work is the same. They invaded, all of them, the sectors of the European tradition that seemed most useful to their needs and, in using them, produced new artistic forms for new forms of experience. Poe's work is not so positively an outgrowth from the central preoccupations of its society as the others', but it does, in the directions we have seen, touch on its society and certainly owes part of its character to Poe's revulsion from American life, or, at any rate, his image of it. It is not coincidental that there was nothing in Europe quite like Poe's writing.

To engage the diverse components of his art, Poe turned not only to the new Romanticism but to the repudiated precepts of Classicism as well. Without the latter he could hardly have given shape to his esoteric insights. As it happened, he had success enough to offer Melville a secure starting-point for his explorations of symbolism and reality. No writer, however, has ever lived on the strength of an arid abstraction like 'a contribution to the novel'. Poe has had the misfortune to acquire a popular curiosity value as the creator of the 'detective story'[1] and an academic reputation as

---

[1] It is worth pointing out that the writers of what is called the 'classic' detective story do themselves an unmerited honour in claiming Poe as an ancestor. Their stories are for the most part ill-presented, wholly artificial puzzles set in improbable country houses, employing unnaturally ingenious homicidal schemes and with an implausibly convenient accumulation of suspects. In *The Mystery of Marie Rogêt*, one of his most celebrated stories in this *genre*, Poe reasons out a common and sordid city murder, a girl strangled and mutilated. The enduring interest of the story is not that in it Poe edged his way towards the solution of an actual crime, remarkable though that is. What gives the story its substance is the nature of the crime and Poe's presentation of it. It becomes a parable of the violent elisions in the fragile security of social life, of outlawry breaking abruptly to the surface, of isolation enforced. The murderer has 'none of that confidence which the presence of numbers inevitably inspires. He is alone with the *dead*. He trembles and is bewildered . . . his fears

the earliest precursor of Kafka. Neither of these labels does justice to what we have seen of the considerable intrinsic merits of his work, his lucid intellect, his dedication to the craft of writing, the suffocating power with which he communicates his dreadful truths. The foregoing commentary deals with the origins and methods of Poe's art and with his place in the development from the European of an American tradition. A necessary footnote is that if Poe is not a 'major figure', then he has sufficiently the attributes of one to warrant attention of this kind. The origins and methods of a writer's art are a satisfying and legitimate study. They are not, however, an end in themselves. The final sanction for a work of art is the pleasure and the extension of wisdom it offers Johnson's 'common sense of readers uncorrupted with literary prejudices, after all the refinements of subtilty and the dogmatism of learning'—conditions amply satisfied by Poe in this novel.

---

redouble within him . . . The sounds of life encompass his path. A dozen times he hears or fancies he hears the step of an observer. Even the very lights from the city bewilder him.' (*The Mystery of Marie Rogêt* in Slater, pp. 303–4). The story, in fact, is another of Poe's glimpses into those lawless human passions which compose the obverse of social man.

Chapter Three

Politics and Pastoral in Cooper

P OE'S clairvoyant intuitions are those of the mystic
faculty Coleridge ascribed to the poet in *Kubla Khan*, but
with a diabolic rather than an Elysian inspiration:

> And all should cry, Beware! Beware!
> His flashing eyes, his floating hair!
> Weave a circle round him thrice,
> And close your eyes with holy dread,
> For he on honey-dew hath fed
> And drunk the milk of Paradise.

In Poe, the typical medium of disclosure is a narrator in a state
of intense or exalted emotion: near (or beyond) death, contem-
plating murder or undergoing a compulsion to confess it, possessed by what, in *The Premature Burial*, Poe called 'the grim legion
of sepulchral terrors'. The private trespasses which exclude these
spokesmen from the affairs of their fellow-men are at once the
source of their more intense perceptions and a retribution for
them. Their attributes, in fact, were of the kind with which Poe
himself was cursed. In this, like their creator, they are representative of the recurrent and well-defined concept of the artist we find
in the later Romantic and the French symbolist traditions. Its most
remarkable anticipation is in the story of Trophonius, in many
ways suggestive of both the psychic condition and the artistic role
of writers like Poe, Beddoes,[1] Baudelaire and Rimbaud.

[1] See John Heath-Stubbs, 'The Defeat of Romanticism', in *Penguin New
Writing*, No. 23. Heath-Stubbs comments on Beddoes that he passes, '. . .

After he had killed his brother, according to Pausanias, 'The earth yawned and received Trophonius,' who thereafter became a celebrated oracle, receiving petitioners, who could approach him only after elaborate rites and with considerable difficulty, in a deep cave at Lebadea. Plutarch tells us of Timarchus, who visited the cave, that, 'His experiences began with a feeling that his head had split with a loud crack and that his soul had passed out through the sutures.' After the visit, men returned worn and gloomy, rendered, by whatever the revelation was, a prey to melancholia and spleen. Again our witness is Pausanias:

'. . . . When a man has come up from Trophonius the priests take him in hand again; and set him upon what is called the chair of Memory, which stands not far from the shrine; and, being seated there, he is questioned by them as to all he saw and heard. On being informed, they hand him over to his friends, who carry him, still overpowered with fear, and quite unconscious of himself and his surroundings, to the building where he lodged before. . . .'[1]

Though much is obscure in the history of Trophonius, the shape of his experience is clear. Acquiring his divinity through a sinful deed, he construes the occult meanings of the individual destiny, though himself secluded underground from the life of common humanity. Marvellous sights and sounds accompany the secrets imparted in the cave. Though he dispenses wisdom at the cost of inspiring terror, his pronouncements continue to be solicited.

[1] Pausanias: *Description of Greece*, Fraser's translation, V, 204, and I, 494-5.

beyond the "easeful death" which could be called "soft names in many a mused rhyme", of Keats;—that ceasing "upon the midnight with no pain"—the Death which "is life's high mead"—to a fuller realisation of that state of merging, in dissolution, with the beauty of the natural universe which Shelley envisaged in *Adonais*. . . . In one form or other, the death-wish pervades the poetry of Beddoes; now a shadow, moving grotesquely, as a skeleton, or in the misformed and dwarfish shapes of his clowns; now striding forth in images of strange and terrible power. Sometimes Death is seen as a state of mystical and transcendental union with the Universe . . .', p. 152. Like George Darley and Thomas Hood, Beddoes, who committed suicide in 1849, explored 'fields of thought and experience beyond the waking consciousness . . . through the medium of the poetic imagination' (p. 145); and like them was 'born too late into an uncongenial world' (p. 142). The essay suggests many revealing similarities between Poe and this group of writers.

Worship of the blemished oracle elicits knowledge, beauty, fear and admiration. As with Trophonius, so with Poe and his kin. Cast out from society, their very isolation is the origin of their powers. The secrets they expound, in forms aesthetically pleasing, are those of the nether life common to both outcast and, fearfully admitted, conformist. With these powers, as exercised by Poe, the previous chapter has been concerned. Cooper returns us from the cave of Trophonius to that eighteenth-century world of social debate which for Poe had only a subordinate reality.

A good deal has already been said of the persistence in American life of the conservative European advocacy of a social hierarchy. It was between that and the promises of Jacksonian democracy that Cooper's sympathies veered and around the ideas contingent on these philosophies that he wrote his novels. On the conflict as it affected Cooper personally there is general agreement, at least among the older critics. By intellectual conviction a liberal and, more narrowly, a Democrat, he was emotionally an aristocrat. 'In spite of his deliberate acceptance of the democratic spirit,' says Parrington, '. . . he remained at heart as sturdily eighteenth century as any fox-hunting master of English acres.' Parrington adds that no other American 'was so unsettled by contact with European civilisation . . . Europe appealed to his native aristocratic prejudices, but repelled his democratic; Jacksonian America appealed to his democratic prejudices, but rode roughshod over his aristocratic'.[1] Van Wyck Brooks makes a very similar analysis.[2] James Grossman notes that Cooper's 'exposition . . . of the superiority of American democracy to European aristocracy' is regularly balanced by an appeal for the 'honest observance of class distinctions and the honest description of social classes'.[3] Less convincing than the fact of Cooper's divided sympathies is Grossman's argument that they involve no real disagreement. In appealing for the restraint of mob power and press irresponsibility, Grossman says, in contending for the positive value of an aristocracy, Cooper was applying the democratic principle of supporting

[1] V. L. Parrington: *Main Currents in American Thought*, II, 224 and 226.

[2] Van Wyck Brooks: *The World of Washington Irving*. See particularly pp. 168, 325–7, 331–3.

[3] James Grossmann: *James Fenimore Cooper*, pp. 5 and 260.

minority rights and keeping before him the essential democratic social ideals which the reality of American life was distorting and vulgarising.[1] A simpler explanation is that Cooper realised that if democracy could not support some kind of class system, the necessary curb of an aristocracy and of aristocratic ideals, the harmonious contention of different social levels, then it must inevitably vulgarise. Cooper believed in both democracy and aristocracy. His was a fairly disputatious nature. A certain thrawnness in his character more than any unified philosophy dictated his attitudes, so that in Europe he praised democratic rights, in America aristocratic privileges. If he had any consistent principle, it was that 'pure' democracy was impossible. His ideal was the eighteenth-century one of an enlightened and responsible aristocracy and a flexible class system.

Cooper described his European historical novels (*The Bravo, The Heidenmauer* and *The Headsman*) as 'a series of tales in which American opinion should be brought to bear on European facts.' In addition, they have been regularly interpreted as an oblique commentary on the American scene and hence as material to Cooper's ideas on domestic politics. The subject of *The Heidenmauer* is the revolt of the villagers of Durckheim, in the sixteenth century, against monastic power and wealth. *The Bravo* deals with the capitalist tyranny of the Venetian Republic. Van Wyck Brooks represents these novels as defending 'the rule of the people against irresponsible oligarchies who questioned the capacity of men to govern themselves'.[2] The implication that the progress of American affairs also demonstrated the beneficence of democratic principles is developed by Robert E. Spiller, who says of *The Heidenmauer*:

'In thus showing the effect of Lutheranism in liberating the mind of man from superstition, and the social order from corruption and hypocrisy, Cooper draws an obvious parallel to his own time in the effect of the American ideal in liberating the modern mind

[1] Marius Bewley advances the same argument in *The Eccentric Design* (pp. 67–68), where he contends that Cooper was hostile to the Whigs because he considered them to have failed to carry 'the civilising function of a cultivated upper class' into the new democratic society.

[2] Brooks: *op. cit.*, p. 264.

from the corruption of the world controlled by the *ancien régime*.'[1]

James Grossman disagrees with this simple equivalence of medieval Europe and evil, independent America and virtue. In describing the machinations of the Venetian capitalists in *The Bravo*, he says, Cooper had in mind that the 'American facts . . . were startlingly like the European. The reference to a bank is particularly significant since political radicals back home had already begun their attack on the Bank of the United States.'[2] In other words, Cooper is using a segment of European history to illuminate the disquieting growth of a parallel materialism in American life, not setting European corruption against a superior American morality. Marius Bewley adopts Grossman's view of *The Bravo* and reads *The Heidenmauer* similarly:

'The economic base of the Protestant Reformation was no new discovery in the nineteenth century, but it was soft-pedalled for at least half a century after *The Heidenmauer*. . . . (*The Heidenmauer's*) interest is centred in the shifting grounds from the world of the imagination to the world of profit which characterises the sixteenth century. Read in this way, *The Heidenmauer* may still not be an exciting or a successful novel, but it may claim its importance as a brilliant intellectual analysis far in advance of its time . . . Cooper had his eye on the American scene and on the Whig aristocrats with their drive towards a financial oligarchy. He was aware . . . that there were significant parallels between the economic situation in Germany in the sixteenth century, and modern America.'[3]
To describe as 'a brilliant intellectual analysis' of the Reformation a view which Professor Trevor-Roper has called the 'old clichés, the effronteries of Cobbett and Chesterton', is a trifle extravagant. A kinder view of the mercantile classes is nearer the truth. In England, to quote Trevor-Roper again, post-Reformation charity was efficiently and liberally dispensed by 'above all,

[1] Robert E. Spiller: *Fenimore Cooper; Critic of His Times*, quoted in Bewley, *op. cit.*, p. 49.

[2] Grossman; *op. cit.*, p. 77.

[3] Bewley: *op. cit.*, pp. 51 and 56–57.

merchants and professional men, using urban, especially London, wealth (the gentry were far behind them) . . . "We may say with full confidence that we deal here with one of the most amazing records of fiduciary responsibility that the western world has ever known."[1] The inadequacy of Cooper's analysis, which this exposes, is a relevant point. The preceding review of critical opinion indicates at least one thing clearly among the disagreements, that Cooper was a man of very decided but extremely unsystematic views. In the European novels he was both using the 'American ideal' as a moral criterion and drawing attention to its shortcomings in practice; he was trying to relate the American problem to much less straightforward European episodes which, in the upshot, he drastically over-simplified; he was charging a commercial aristocracy in Europe with ills which, in America, were the doing of a democratic majority. For this welter of ideas, Cooper inevitably failed to work out an adequate fictional form. The novels are, as Bewly acknowledges, laboriously written and make very heavy going. This commentary on them has been deliberately conducted somewhat at second hand because, although they provide a useful entrance to Cooper's themes, they are hardly worth direct and detailed study. Cooper as an expositor of the European situations he chose to investigate we cannot, in truth, take very seriously, and the popular judgment which has neglected these novels is a sound one.

In theory, we may conclude, Cooper admired The People, but he seems to have thoroughly detested, if we can judge by his law suits and his conservative position in the Anti-Rent disturbances, his personal encounters with them. He despised the policies of the Federalists, their successors, the Whigs, and the commercial *élite* with which they were associated. Much of his dislike was entirely rational. But insofar as it was simple prejudice against commerce, it prevented him from seeing that it was the Jacksonian policy of limiting governmental activity that made possible the wild and undirected scramble for wealth—in which The People enthusiastically participated—and the eventual consolidation of vast personal fortunes into the often unscrupulous capitalism of the

---

[1] H. Trevor-Roper: 'A New Classic of Social History', *Sunday Times*, May 24, 1959. A review of *Philanthropy in England*, 1480–1660, by W. K. Jordan, from which Trevor-Roper takes the closing quotation.

nineteenth and early twentieth centuries. According to Grossman, the argument of Cooper's European travel books is that 'a government that wants men to be truly free will regulate conduct that needs regulation'.[1] This is precisely the remedy proposed by Hamilton, whose policy of governmental regulation might well, rightly undertaken, have controlled both the avaricious commercialism and the trashy vulgarity which so distressed Cooper. Hamilton was alive to the fundamental difficulty of compromising between tyranny, order and anarchy:

'Government is frequently and aptly classed under two descriptions —a government of Force and a Government of Laws; the first is a definition of despotism—the last of liberty. But how can a government of laws exist when the laws are disrespected and disobeyed? Government supposes control. It is that power by which individuals in society are kept from doing injury to each other, and are brought to co-operate in a common end. The instruments by which it must act are either the Authority of the laws or Force. If the first be destroyed, the last must be substituted; and where this becomes the ordinary instrument of government, there is an end to liberty.'[2]

Cooper's American novels, where he most satisfactorily marshalled his ideas, come down, in the end and with perhaps a lingering regret, on the side of fortifying a government of laws.

The virtues which Jefferson, and Cooper after him, saw in the proprietors and smallholders of an agrarian community were not self-supporting. They—and the possibility of transferring them to both pioneer societies and urban industrialism—depended on the preservation of law and order, on the sodality of governors and governed, on the continuance of the social system which the whole drift of Jackson's *laissez-faire* democracy was to abandon, while offering no stable replacement. Without Cooper's ever admitting it, or even consciously realising it, the Hamiltonian ideals described in Chapter One would have satisfied many of his requirements. The dilemma referred to in the quotation from Hamilton given above Cooper dramatised in the Leatherstocking novels.

[1] Grossman: *op. cit.*, p. 102.

[2] Hamilton: quoted by W. R. Brock, *op. cit.*, p. 56.

In the process he displayed the same concern that respect for law should be inculcated, over easier and even, at times, seemingly more merciful and humane alternatives, as the most potent safeguard against both anarchy and tyranny. The organs of this necessary restraint—central government (however undeveloped), organised religion, the courts—were just the establishments stigmatised by the radicals as, in Hamilton's ironic words, impositions 'upon the freedom of man; as causes of the corruption of his nature, intrinsically good; as sources of an artificial and false morality which tyrannically robs him of the enjoyments for which his passions fit him, and as clogs upon his progress to the perfection for which he was destined'.[1]

Not unnaturally, it was when Cooper posed these questions in an American setting that he most fully grasped their implications. Setting them in a simple society of a time not long past, he reduced them to their fundamentals, kept their contemporary relevance and detached them from the passions of his own era. Cooper was incapable of the imaginative jump which could transpose the conclusions he reached from a rudimentary and comparatively settled, to a complex and expanding society. His half-acquired taste for democracy inhibited him from seeing the justice of ceding to the state powers and responsibilities which in a simpler period had been the prerogative of a paternalistic aristocracy, totally unfitted to compensate, on its own, for the rough justice of an economic free-for-all. Hamilton's achievement was to state the principles which should direct the transposition and they are principles at many points in accord with Cooper's. Their aim was to secure to the commercial dispensation that staple of aristocratic decorum which had preserved the agrarian community on a system of social degrees. Only by some such means as Hamilton proposed could the old virtues have been carried over into the new order. Jackson's doctrine of negative action (as by vetoing renewal of the Bank of America's charter) in the free play of industrial development let them go by default. As it happened, Hamilton, and Cooper so far as he favoured encouraging society to stratify, were, at least temporarily, on the losing side. The class divisions which—inevitably —did develop lacked most of the graces they admired, though it might with some reason be urged that the vulgarity of the Jack-

[1] Hamilton: quoted by Brock, *op. cit.*, p. 56.

sonian era—and of its successor, the Gilded Age[1]—was also its strength and that only this gross single-mindedness could so rapidly and efficiently have exploited the continent. However, to examine the vanished possibilities of history has, in this particular case, at least the academic value that it shows how Hamilton and Cooper, formally opposed in politics, shared the ideal of

[1] From Jackson's honest but misguided efforts to impose some kind of control, to the unscrupulous monopolising of the Gilded Age, the descent is clear. In *The Age of Jackson* (p. 316), Arthur M. Schlesinger puts forward the following analysis of what was at issue:

> The basic economic conception, which Adam Smith shared with Jefferson, was of a 'natural order of things', that, once cleared of monopolistic clogs, would function to the greatest good of the greatest number. This conception, for all its apparent clarity, soon turned out to be packed with ambiguities. Free enterprise might mean . . . a fighting belief in the virtue of competition, or it might mean, as with present-day conservatives, a fighting belief in the evil of government intervention.

Thus Jackson's intervention to veto the Bank Bill was intended to place the new competitors on a more nearly equal footing with the older-established. Having done this, the government retired, for Jackson, like the industrialists, was chary of anything more positive in the way of government action. Neither side saw at the time that this policy in fact benefited the more rapacious speculators. Nowhere in Jackson's programme do we come across anything like Hamilton's idea that it was up to the government to ensure that private economic power should be made to work for the national well-being. Thus, as Schlesinger points out (p. 337), 'The fate of Jacksonian economic legislation was that common historical irony: it on the whole promoted the very ends it was intended to defeat.' By a final paradox, the rampant capitalistic enterprise of the Gilded Age was justified as a democratic movement. In *The Growth of American Thought* (p. 300), Merle Curti says of the later economic predators that to justify their operations it 'was only necessary to argue that the system of free competition for natural resources was in accord with the doctrines of liberty and equality.' Later on, this was to be supplemented by reference to the heartening theories of Darwin on natural selection. One manifestation of this is Andrew Carnegie's essay on *Wealth*. It is interesting to note how very much less frank than Hamilton Carnegie is. Where Hamilton spoke, as has been noted, of 'avarice' and 'the precious metals' as 'darling objects', Carnegie is at pains to conceal these motives. The emphasis is all on the 'special ability' of the successful merchant, his 'talent for organisation'. Money, we are asked to feel, is not sought but mysteriously finds its way to the diligent trader—'it is inevitable,' we are told, '. . . that they must accumulate wealth'. For all its specious rationalising, however, the Gilded Age, as we shall see in Edith Wharton, was in its turn to represent a vanished age of standards no longer sufficiently regarded. But these are very much later developments. The foundations were laid, however unwittingly, during Jackson's presidency.

conserving the traditional class structure and maintaining government as an active mediator between private profit and public utility. This common ground between the two men is an inheritance from the eighteenth-century ideas of order, discussed in the previous chapter, which came down to Poe mainly in their aesthetic application, but which possessed Cooper's political being. To this, perhaps, he owed his ability to envisage a reconciliation of the best parts of the aristocratic and democratic philosophies. There is no final accounting for the differing reactions of different men. Where Poe withdrew to his oracular cave, Cooper, almost equally at odds with American society, remained to survey and analyse it in terms of its political ecology. In the Leatherstocking novels, the tough, stubborn and irascible Cooper, a man whose individuality and troubled sense of purpose we can only admire, did arrive at some kind of peace, some resolution of his intellectual dilemmas.

II

The argument between Hamilton and his opponents over specific matters of policy was, in the last analysis, the conflict between two different views of human nature debated in terms of civil administration. On the one hand we have the idea that human morality, naturally good, declines in proportion to the complexity and artificiality of society; and on the other that only restraint, the hope of reward or the fear of punishment, can neutralise the evil passions which predominate in human nature. Beyond the political lies the ethical or philosophical disagreement. The Puritan belief in human depravity we have already seen. Coupled with it was the temperate optimism engendered by removal to their new and uncontaminated settlements. Ever since then, the disparity between promise and achievement has been commonly recognised as almost obsessively present in the American mind, whether in the moral, political or material spheres. The purity of man in his natural state and the corruption of political societies, the spiritual grandeur of unspoiled rural scenes and the mischievous exploitation which degrades them: it is mainly around these basic antitheses that Cooper constructs the Leatherstocking novels. They are thus 'political' novels at, so to speak, one remove. Their immediate concern is not Whig-Democrat disputes but the more profound antagonisms of which political acts are an expression. Perpetually recurring in Cooper's version of these antagonisms is that obstinate sense of America as an Arcadia consecrated to some exalted destiny. For the Puritans it might be more appropriately designated an Eden, but the faith is differently manifested.

Captain John Smith, in his account of the settlement of Jamestown, begun in 1607, was the first to give a secular statement, as we might call it, to the vision of America as the land of infinite promise. He was not, he tells us, 'so simple to think that ever any other motive than wealth will ever erect there a Commonweale'. Nevertheless the new country did wring from the prosaic Captain Smith a lyrical description which, though its motive was partly, no doubt, the utilitarian one of inducing new immigrants to come to Virginia, had even for him a clear emotional truth:

'Heaven and earth never agreed better to frame a place for man's habitation, were it fully manured and inhabited by industrious people; here are mountains, hills, valleys, rivers, and brooks, all running most pleasantly into a fair bay, encompassed (but for its mouth) with fruitful and delightsome land . . . full of flowers of divers kinds and colours . . . and vines in abundance . . . fruits, as strawberries, four times bigger and better than ours in England. . . great plenty of fish of all kinds . . . many great and fair meadows . . .'[1]

It is not over-fanciful to see in this an early step towards domiciling in America the Arcadian myth of European tradition. Smith's history, in fact, contains the genesis of many attitudes we now think of as characteristically American and which reached a more or less definitive form in Cooper.

The landscape the Puritans first saw was considerably bleaker than the one Smith describes, but the later experiences of the Virginia colonists were no happier than those of the Massachusetts settlers. As Smith's account progresses, it becomes more and more a record of Indian troubles, of a rigorous pioneer life, of opposition and plotting both from home and within the colony. Constantly he stresses the need for hard work and, as President,

[1] Captain John Smith: *A Description of New England* in *Works* ed. Arber, 1884.

issues his 'proclamation against drones', in which he laid down that 'he that gathereth not every day as much as I do, the next day shall be sent beyond the river, and be banished from the Fort as a drone, till he amend his conditions, or starve'. These are the earliest of those pioneer hardships by which, ultimately, the nation was to be created. Although there may be no such thing as a National Character, every country has an ideal figure or set of ideal figures, to which it aspires and with which it is commonly identified. In Smith's history is the prototype of the resolute pioneer, practical, measuring success largely by material standards, inured to struggle against a hostile environment. Finally, Smith's descriptions of the American scene and background, of exploratory journeys, of skirmishes with the Indians and of Indian customs: these are the first stages in the task of codifying a whole new accumulation of physical data, of subduing a new area of observation which was to become a new area of imaginative writing.

The importance of all this to literature is that it set the tone of American pastoral, which, while remaining conscious of its European origins, acquired a distinctive factual bias. Of this we have already seen hints in some of Freneau's poetry. In connexion with Cooper's fiction, however, the differences must be more fully discriminated.

'Pastoral' is a term with strong but often imprecise connotations. One's instinctive response to the word is to think of an idyllic Arcadia of eternal youth and perpetual sunshine, the world of Milton's *L'Allegro*:

> . . . *many a youth and many a maid,*
> *Dancing in the chequered shade;*
> *And young and old come forth to play*
> *On a sunshine holiday . . .;*

of Goldsmith's 'sweet Auburn', with its 'dear, lovely bowers of innocence and ease'. Of this conception of pastoral, in which there is of course considerable truth, one of the purest English examples is Drayton's *Muses Elizium*. In it, the setting is uniformly graceful and placid: the sun will always 'glaze the gliding streams', 'the west wind stroaks the velvit leaves', 'the slyding hours so slyly stole away'. The nymphs are concerned only with building altars to Apollo, celebrating marriages, vieing with each other in complimentary exchanges or competing in writing poetry. Pastoral of this kind represents the countryside as an unflurried backwater in which contemplation, the release and moulding of serene emotions, were more easily achieved. It was made possible by the convention's gradual detachment from the real life of shepherds and country folk. Yet the very fact that this visionary rural scene was so different from daily life, and was attractive because of that difference, was bound eventually to inspire a satiric purpose, to encourage the poet to set against the beautiful scene the austere reality from which it was an escape: in the woods of pastoral lived satyrs as well as fauns. This might be called a perversion of the tradition, but in fact even in the *Bucolics* Vergil introduced controversial ideas. Milton wrote his diatribe against ecclesiastical turpitude in the pastoral *Lycidas*; Goldsmith converts Auburn, in his attack on economic evils, to a place of 'tangling walks, and ruined grounds'. Sidney's *Arcadia* is similarly designed. Its pastoral setting does not exclude evil and treachery, dishonesty, avarice and lust. Sidney presents discussions of political theory, propounds methods of dealing with rebellion against the state— Pyrocles and Musidorus in fact subdue a revolt; constructs a legal system in which a father must sustain the judgment of death he has brought against his unrecognised son, even when the son's identity is revealed. But though discussion of the moral and political questions so dear to Elizabethans occupies more of the *Arcadia* than the idyllic pastoral element, verisimilitude of setting is never the point. The land is 'clothed with a continual spring because no beauty here should ever fade'. Necessarily, the pastoral *locale* is not tied to time and place and the serious issues are debated against an idealised, not a realistic, setting.

In his *Virgin Land*, Henry Smith describes the flood of sub-pastoral writing that poured from American observers during the late eighteenth and nineteenth centuries—'a rapturous picture of luxuriant nature . . . coloured by literary convention and a stilted rhetoric.'[1] It was without exception blind to what was actually to be seen, as remote from the real world as Sidney's and without Sidney's awareness of what he was doing. Nevertheless it represented a genuine sentiment and it was to the strength of feeling this American rural utopianism represented that Cooper owed his

[1] Henry Smith: Virgin Land, pp. 129-30.

own more delicate appreciation of the pastoral features embodied in American life. Cooper's too is a setting of natural beauty and grandeur which has many claims to be called pastoral. Like the scene described by Captain Smith it has a wonderful charm and fecundity. But it is a pastoral to which the authentic shepherds have returned. As Sidney, so does Cooper examine against this setting the variable forms of human conduct as it bears on his society. Cooper's setting, however, is distilled from what actually lay around him, not drawn from legend. The manners he describes are manners of fact, not the rhetorically stylised models of Sidney. The difference is between two artistic conventions, that of a sixteenth-century writer interested in generalising, typifying, abstracting, in decorative formalities, and that of a novelist in the modern sense with his strong attachment to manners and appearances. In the Leatherstocking series the two worlds, of 'Golden Age' Elysian pastoral and of discongruent natural and human strife, are less anomalously associated than in Sidney's *Arcadia*, because both are grounded in observed fact. However idealised Cooper's descriptions at times may be, they retain their links with real places, where the seasons follow their appointed rounds and men carry out the laborious duties of husbandry. It is all in the pastoral tradition, but in going faithfully to the forests, lakes, prairies and settlers of America, Cooper restored the tradition to its origins in life and gave a new solidity to the well-established practice of using it as a medium of social criticism—'under the vaile of homely persons and in rude speeches', as Puttenham's *Arte of English Poesie* recommends, 'to insinuate and glance at greater matters'. Once again we find American writing best served by intelligent adaptation of European precedent, worst by the decorous withdrawal of fuzzily descriptive placards—'soft zephyrs', 'sweet songsters of the forest', 'genial clime'[1]—from the moribund European tradition. Cooper's own prose is far from innocent of blemishes like this, but there is enough honestly sensuous description to focus the scenes clearly. With Cooper, when it did happen, it was a stylistic deficiency only, not a fundamental incapacity of vision. Working in the more expansive

---

[1] These quotations are taken from Gilbert Imlay, *Topographical Description of the Western Territory of North America*, pp. 39-40. Quoted by Smith, *op. cit.*, p. 130.

world of the novel, and with ideas better suited to the novel than to the kind of poetry Freneau essayed, Cooper managed a reconciliation of the idealised and the realistic, of pastoral and agrarian, of the epic hunter and the yeoman, which Freneau was unable to support for any length of time.

III

According to the computations of F. L. Mott, all the Leatherstocking novels were best sellers over the three decades during which they were published. In Europe as in America, Mott tells us, readers liked them because they were written in the 'very spirit of high, clean, adventurous romance . . . romance of the forest, the Indian, and the pioneer . . .'[1] In point of fact, Cooper's narrative powers, his ability to convey the pace and movement of rapid, lively action, were modest enough. As we shall see, the most genuinely exciting and fully realised episodes in Cooper's novels are more often than not periods of arrested motion, the chilling pause in, or sequel to, violence, static or slow-moving tableaux rather than passages of urgent and complex incident. Certainly, whatever it was that sold *The Pioneers* (1823), the first of the Leatherstocking series, it was not, by any exacting standard, the quality of sustained and eventful action.

The lesion in *The Pioneers* between the main romantic plot and the real theme has been frequently noted. The plot is a highly conventional affair involving concealed identity, love whose course is hindered by accidental circumstances, an intolerably refined and lifeless heroine, Elizabeth Temple, and an equally unexciting hero, Oliver Edwards, who, some cryptic remarks suggest, is partly of Indian descent. It turns out that his name is really Oliver Effingham, that he is the son of a former business associate of Judge Temple, Elizabeth's father, and that he has wrongly believed himself cheated of his inheritance by the judge. Inevitably, all the misunderstandings are cleared up in the end. Judge Temple had not been dishonest and Oliver was merely an honorary member of the Delaware tribe. Thus freed from the suspicion that he was of mixed blood, he becomes an acceptable suitor and marries Elizabeth. It is at this point only that the stock intrigue

[1] F. L. Mott: *Golden Multitudes*, p. 75.

touches on the central core of the novel, which is the collision between a maturing society (Judge Temple, Templeton and the Government of Laws) and the free individualism of the wilderness (Natty Bumppo and Chingachgook, the Inner Light and the Noble Savage).

The latter part of this antithesis is a complicated one. Towards the end of the novel, when he refuses to leave the burning forests and, in effect, wills himself to death, Chingachgook acquires once again the stoic virtues of the Noble Savage he had been in youth. But during the course of the novel he has appeared as the decadent, drink-corrupted remnant of a vanished race:

'His hand seemed to make a fruitless effort to release his tomahawk, which was confined by its handle to his belt, while his eyes gradually became vacant. Richard at this instant thrusting a mug before him, his features changed to the grin of idiocy, and seizing the vessel with both hands, he sank backward on the bench and drank until satiated, when he made an effort to lay aside the mug with the helplessness of total inebriety.

'"Shed not blood !" exclaimed (Natty), as he watched the countenance of the Indian in its moment of ferocity; "but he is drunk, and can do no harm. This is the way with all savages; give them liquor, and they will make dogs of themselves."'

Even the noblest of savages is not proof against the temptation of the flesh and, as we gather from the other novels, not all savages are noble. On this issue Cooper is less indecisive than he is sometimes represented as being. Grossman says of *The Last of the Mohicans* that the 'possible problems that might be raised by Uncas' love for Cora and by Cora's love for the man in love with Alice are conveniently avoided by the deaths at the end of the tale of both Cora and Uncas.'[1] But in fact, as far as Cooper was concerned, there was no problem. He has never the slightest intention of permitting any inter-racial marriage and clearly disapproves of the idea. Cora, whose mother was of West Indian negro descent, is of mixed race and so is sufficiently non-white to give some sanction to Uncas' love—as distinct from the lust of the bad Indian, Magua; but they are not of the same race, so they may not marry. Nor, for the same reason, may Cora marry a European. When

[1] Grossman: *op. cit.*, pp. 43–44.

Cora's father tells Heyward of her ancestry, he feels, despite his denial, the instinctive recoil of which the father accuses him:

'"And you cast it on my child as a reproach! You scorn to mingle the blood of the Heywards with one so degraded—lovely and virtuous though she be?" fiercely demanded the jealous parent.

'"Heaven protect me from a prejudice so unworthy of my reason!" returned Duncan, at the same time conscious of such a feeling, and that as deeply rooted as if it had been engrafted in his nature.'

Thus in Cooper's eyes it would be unthinkable for Elizabeth Temple to marry Oliver Effingham while thinking him to be of Indian descent.

Cooper's views on this matter are undoubtedly displeasing to the liberal mind but that is not a reason for denying their existence. They are of particular interest here because, as has been remarked, it is at this point only that the romantic plot of *The Pioneers* has even the slightest bearing on the main theme. To Indian life and the Indian ethic Cooper concedes its virtues. It is a part of the 'wilderness code', which is opposed to the rule of law, but it is an inferior part. Cooper knew that European treatment of the Indians had been frequently unjust, but however far short of their ideal the Europeans might fall it was, being Christian, a superior ethic to that of the Indians. In *The Deerslayer* Natty makes the distinction, a kind of moral *apartheid*:

'God made us all, white, black, and red; and, no doubt, has his own wise intentions in colouring us differently. Still, he made us, in the main, much the same in feelin's; though, I'll not deny that he gave each race its gifts. A white man's gifts are christianised, while a red-skin's are more for the wilderness. Thus, it would be a great offence for a white man to scalp the dead; whereas, it's a signal vartue in an Indian. Then ag'in a white man cannot amboosh women and children in war, while a red-skin may. 'Tis a cruel work, I'll allow; but for them it's *lawful* work; while for *us*, it would be grievous work.'

The real conflict in *The Pioneers*, then, is not between the European and the Indian ways of life but between different European codes, one of which, Natty's, has a greater coincidence of habits with the Indian. Elsewhere, Cooper uses the Indians to provide an ironic contrast to the shortcomings of Europeans who, despising them, in practice descend to the same pagan level, the more shamefully because they are instructed by their higher ethic. But in *The Pioneers* the Indians have only this peripheral role, that Natty has, with some of their skills, acquired a sympathy with some of their *mores*. The clash of opposites here is worked out between Natty's responsible individualism and Templeton's centralised authority, with its system of legislated rewards and sanctions.

Cooper said of *The Bravo* that 'the government of Venice, strictly speaking, became the hero of the tale'. In the same way, Templeton becomes a protagonist in *The Pioneers* and it is the painstaking care Cooper devotes to establishing the place solidly in our minds that retards the action. By Chapter 16, almost one-third of the novel, we have covered only a few hours and not much has happened. This part of the book, in fact, gives quite strongly the impression of a series of factual essays on different aspects of pioneer life. The origin of Templeton is explained and its appearance, wrapped in the snow and ice of a hard Christmas, described in passages of considerable beauty:

'There was a glittering in the atmosphere, as if it were filled with innumerable shining particles . . . Immediately beneath them lay a seeming plain, glittering without inequality, and buried in mountains. The latter were precipitous, especially on the side of the plain, and chiefly in forest. Here and there the hills fell away in long, low points, and broke the sameness of the outline, or setting to the long and wide field of snow, which, without house, tree, fence, or any other fixture, resembled so much spotless cloud settled to the earth. A few dark and moving spots were, however, visible on the even surface, which the eye of Elizabeth knew to be so many sleighs going their several ways, to or from the village. . . . A dark spot of a few acres in extent at the southern extremity of this beautiful flat, and immediately under the feet of our travellers, alone showed by its rippling surface, and the vapors which exhaled from it, that what at first sight might seem a plain, was one of the mountain lakes, locked in the frosts of winter. A narrow current rushed impetuously from its bosom at the spot we have mentioned, and was to be traced for miles, as it wound its way towards the south through the real valley, by its borders of hemlock and pine, and by the vapor which arose from its warmer surface into the chill atmosphere of the hills . . . the frozen lake lay without a shadow on its bosom; the dwellings were becoming already gloomy and indistinct; and the wood-cutters were shouldering their axes, and preparing to enjoy, throughout the long evening before them, the comforts of those exhilarating fires that their labor had been supplying with fuel. . . . The paper curtains dropped behind our travellers in every window, shutting from the air even the fire-light of the cheerful apartments; and when the horses of her father turned, with a rapid whirl, into the open gate of the Mansion-house, and nothing stood before her but the cold, dreary stone walls of the building, as she approached them through an avenue of young and leafless poplars, Elizabeth felt as if all the loveliness of the mountain-view had vanished like the fancies of a dream.'

At one level, and it is not the least of the book's charms, this is a novel of the nostalgic homecomings of childhood. Into the experience of Elizabeth Temple's going home after four years away at school Cooper successfully projected his own imaginative re-creation of his father's early days in Cooperstown.

All the characters are introduced by way of a straightforward character sketch and most of them are represented as playing a typical role in pioneer society. At the beginning of Chapter 8 Cooper specifically claims this as part of his purpose. The place of the church (Chapter 8) and of the inn (Chapter 13) in the social life of the settlement is discussed; the village architecture is facetiously described and the effect on pleasures and occupations of the passing seasons—the coming of spring, for example, in Chapter 20. Leisurely this presentation may be, but Cooper succeeds wonderfully in building up his world and the pattern of life that obtains in it, the inconveniences, the crystallising traditions and customs, the rudimentary social divisions, the physical setting. Templeton, in fact, represents the growth of society in the fringe areas of populated America. It represents the laborious attempt to settle on standards, to retain valuable and discourage bad traditions, to import a sense of law.

The theme of law and order and of Templeton as their guardian is introduced early in the novel, when Natty complains, in argument with Judge Temple over which of them had shot a deer, 'I don't love to give up my lawful dues in a free country. Though, for the matter of that, might often makes right here, as well as in the old country, for what I can see.' His right to shoot deer, he says later, 'is of older date than Marmaduke Temple's right to forbid him.' The old dispensation of the wilderness, from which Natty derives his claim, comes to life in the frequent lengthy monologues in which he recalls his past. Then, he tells the judge, 'if one wanted a ham or so, he had only to watch a-nights, and he could shoot one by moonlight, through the cracks of the logs'. It is through Natty's sporadic bursts of reminiscent garrulity that the old life of pastoral freedom, heroic endeavour and violence finds a place in the novel beside the more humdrum Templeton of the 1790's. His conversation with Oliver Edwards in Chapter 26 brings into present focus most of these features of the vanished past:

'I had the place to myself once, and a cheerful time I had of it. The game was plenty as heart could wish; and there was none to meddle with the ground, unless there might have been a hunting party of the Delawares crossing the hills, or, maybe, a rifling scout of them thieves, the Iroquois . . . it was a comfortable hunting ground then, lad, and would have been so to this day, but for the money of Marmaduke Temple, and the twisty ways of the law . . . Yes, yes; when the trees began to be covered with leaves, and the ice was out of the lake, it was a second paradise. . . . I have met but one place that was more to my liking . . . up on the Cattskills. . . . You know the Cattskills, lad; for you must have seen them on your left, as you followed the river up from York, looking as blue as a piece of clear sky, and holding the clouds on their tops, as the smoke curls over the head of an Indian chief at the council fire. . . . Creation . . . all creation, lad. I was on that hill when Vaughan burned 'Sopus in the last war; and I saw the vessels come out of the highlands as plain as I can see that lime-scow rowing into the Susquhenna, though one was twenty times further from me than the other. The river was in sight for seventy miles, looking like a curled shaving under my feet, though it was eight long miles to its banks. I saw the hills in the Hampshire grants, the Highlands of the river, and all that God had done, or man could do, far as the eye could reach—you know that the Indians named me for my sight, lad; and from the flat on the top of that mountain, I have often found the place where Albany stands. And as for 'Sopus, the day the royal troops burnt the town, the smoke seemed so nigh, that I thought I could hear the screeches of the women.'

The imagery of these monologues is carefully restricted within Natty's imaginative scope—the river 'as blue as a piece of clear sky', the clouds lying on the mountain top 'as the smoke curls over the head of an Indian chief at the council fire', the distant river 'looking like a curled shaving'—and they are interspersed with such convincing visualisations as that of the marksman's chinks in the cabin logs. We are persuaded to accept as real both the character and the life that he so vividly recalls. Natty enlists a good deal of sympathy for himself and for the emancipated existence whose freedom he never abused.

It would thus be easy to identify Cooper's views with Natty's irascible condemnations of 'clearings and betterments', particularly as many of the agents of Templeton cut so much less agreeable a figure. The Judge's cousin, Richard Jones, who is made a sheriff, is a fool; the magistrate, Hiram Dolittle, is cowardly, avaricious and contriving. Yet Cooper's conviction is clearly that, while the arguments in favour of law can survive even such disastrous exponents as Hiram and Richard, the anarchic life of the wilderness could be practised in community only if everyone had Natty's self-command—and, as Judge Temple remarks, 'Thou art an exception, Leather-Stocking . . . for thou hast a temperance unusual in thy class . . .' It is this temperance to which the law tries to give form and countenance and it is significant that Natty and the Judge agree in condemning the mass destruction of the pigeon shoot as wasteful and immoral. The Judge deplores also the heedless wood-cutting of the foresters. Both he and Natty are men of goodwill, but the Judge, more realistic, sees that, although the Inner Light may be sufficient for the few, the many, brought together in social union, must accept a degree of compulsion. In these ways, and repeatedly in talk and situation,

Cooper keeps before us, throughout the novel, the conflict of opinion which is consummated by Natty's imprisonment after he has shot a deer out of season and resisted arrest. Although Natty had earlier saved Elizabeth Temple from death, Judge Temple must uphold the authority of the law—a situation strangely like that of the trial in the *Arcadia*. 'Society,' he says, in response to his daughter's appeal, 'cannot exist without wholesome restraints. Those restraints cannot be inflicted, without security and respect to the persons of those who administer them; and it would sound ill indeed to report, that a judge had extended favor to a convicted criminal, because he had saved the life of his child.' The crux, in fact, is that the law is valuable only when it is respected and to this necessity Natty must be sacrificed. His own case proves that, despite his earlier irony in the bar-room of Chapter 14, the law can be enforced. Wisely and firmly applied—for there is no magic power inherent in the law itself—it is a protection as much for Natty's individualism as for the fruitful development of community life: when he is first asked to furnish a search-warrant for Natty's cabin, Judge Temple says that 'the habitation of a citizen is not to be idly invaded on light suspicion'. What Natty represents—and his faith finds an echo in Judge Temple—is adamant, uncompromising but responsible individualism. In Judge Temple's view, and in Cooper's, the law is the collective voice of such individuals united in the necessary compromise against a less scrupulous egotism.

In connexion with the complex intercourse of principles which the novel canvasses it is relevant to note that the village of Templeton is evoked as tenderly as Natty's wilderness. It is by no means simply a graceless usurper. There is a shadowy third party to the comparisons between the two, and that is the great urban civilisation of which places like Templeton were the embryo. More often than not, when Cooper pokes playful fun at the village and its pretensions, it is by reference to the completeness and assurance of European civilisation, not to the romantic byways of the forest and prairie. A Templar, we are told, 'would smile at the qualifications of Marmaduke (Temple) to fill the judicial seat he occupied.' A graduate 'of Leyden or Edinburgh would be extremely amused with this true narration of the service of Elnathan in the temple of Aesculapius'. The village church is called New St. Paul's, 'though the imitation was somewhat lame'. Richard Jones's heated vision of hypothetical streets and avenues is ludicrous but it is also prophetic: Cooper draws attention to the speed with which the village is leaving behind its original air of makeshift: 'The village was alive with business; the artisans increasing in wealth with the prosperity of the country, and each day witnessing some nearer approach to the manners and usages of an old settled town.' Templeton has its laughable aspects, but the way it has chosen is the only possible one for a nation bent on emulating its European ancestors.

In the society he reviews here, Cooper found complexity enough to keep up a robust and satisfying dialectic. His counters are the romantic dangers of the wilds and the rude charm of pioneer settlements, the idyllic yet actual pastoral atmosphere which invests both these, the sanguine promise of society and its contingent claims, the transition from individual to corporate responsibility, the failures and achievements of each. It is not an unimpressive list. Though Cooper—largely because of his commitment to plot conventions—failed to impose on it that firmly unified structure which severe criticism might demand, he amplified the straight adventure story by making the action the intermediary of his subtly discriminated ideas. Templeton, its champions and antagonists are not mere blunderers through a chronological sequence of depthless events. They are meaningful because their actions yield a moral increment.

At the end of the novel, freedom and reputation restored, Natty, 'weary of living in clearings . . . where the hammer is sounding my ears from sunrise to sundown', sets off for the Big Lakes and 'the best hunting, and a great range, without a white man on it'. We leave him as 'the foremost in that band of pioneers who are opening the way for the march of the nation across the continent'—a race of men doomed to extinction with the subduing of the last frontier, but leaving behind a residue of strenuously independent spirit which, as in Templeton, informs even the increasing body of laws that accompanies more settled life. The world of the romantic hunter was one that flowered briefly and in Natty, Cooper idealised its best qualities, assessed its contribution to the growing nation and, with perhaps a lingering regret, acknowledged it inferior to the exciting potential of civilised life. Cooper addressed himself to the issues he dramatises in this novel with a mature and notably objective awareness of their complexity. It is a tribute to the balance of Cooper's thought that he could so thoroughly participate in Natty's views, could endow the guardians of orthodoxy with champions so questionable and a case superficially so unattractive and still acknowledge their justice. There is no straining to force a comprehensive reconciliation on the successive and distinctive parts of the historical process from anarchy to order. In achieving this detachment Cooper displays that *Negative Capability* which Keats defined as occurring 'when a man is capable of being in uncertainties, mysteries, doubts, without any irritable reaching after fact and reason'.[1] On a more prosaic level, Cooper chronicles the process of which T. S. Eliot wrote in *Little Gidding*:

> *We cannot revive old factions*
> *We cannot restore old policies*
> *Or follow an antique drum.*
> *These men, and those who opposed them*
> *And those whom they opposed*
> *Accept the constitution of silence*
> *And are folded in a single party.*

Of the Leatherstocking series *The Pioneers* most directly aligns wilderness and civilisation and most openly, even at the expense of narrative pace, espouses the drama of ideas. A greater proportion of all the other tales is taken up with the vigorous action of hairbreadth escapes, disasters narrowly averted and constantly renewed, which we associate with Cooper. It is just here, despite his traditional repute as a writer of adventure stories, that Cooper is most vulnerable to the criticisms of Mark Twain in his essay, 'Fenimore Cooper's Literary Offences'.[2] Twain concentrated much of his attack on *The Deerslayer*, where there is in fact a good deal more than met his searching but restricted eye. *The Last of the Mohicans* (1826) is less easily defended against the ridicule Twain directs at Cooper's perfunctory woodlore, improbable feats of arms and nebulous battles and scrimmages. In it, the intellectual content is drastically

---

[1] Keats: *Letters*, Dec. 21, 1817.

[2] See Edmund Wilson *The Shock of Recognition*, pp. 583–594i.

simplified and for the most part submerged beneath the hurly-burly of events. It doesn't quite come down to a struggle between Indians (bad) and Europeans (good), with the Anglo-French wars, the ostensible subject, only briefly on stage, but it is very nearly that. Most of the Indians are cruel and treacherous, most of the Europeans the object of admiration or pity. There are, it is true, a number of complicating factors. Chingachgook and Uncas are noble Indians—Cooper comments ironically on their natural 'liberality and candour' that 'had they been the representatives of some great civilised people (it) would have infallibly worked their political ruin, by destroying, for ever, their reputation for consistency'. During the massacre of women and children by the Indians after the British surrender at Fort William Henry, 'the armed columns of the Christian King (of France) stood fast, in an apathy which has never been explained'. Natty gives his customary extenuation of Indian practices, remarking, when Chingachgook scalps a French soldier, "Twould have been a cruel and an inhuman act for a white-skin; but 'tis the gift and natur of an Indian, and I suppose it should not be denied !' At the end of the book, too, Natty is described 'as a link between them (the Indians) and civilised life'. This has a perfectly literal meaning, but there is obviously, as well, a metaphysical one, which is not, however, kept alive throughout the novel. The criticism, in short, is not that Cooper disappoints us by flawing his image of the Noble Savage, but that, with the solitary and unexplored exception of Montcalm's ambiguous conduct at Fort William Henry, there is no counterpart to the cross-currents of principle and conduct displayed in the affairs of Templeton. On the whole, the novel rests on a simple European-Indian antagonism and even this artless conflict is worked out mainly on the level of physical violence, intrigue and counterplotting. Cooper has, so to speak, readjusted his observing lens so that the action is (at least in intention) brought up clear and sharp to the foreground, while what lies behind it remains blurred and out of focus.

We can most usefully examine in this novel, then, the details of flight, pursuit, warfare and hand-to-hand combat. There is little point in recapitulating Twain's well-documented attack on Cooper's ineptly rendered situations. A typical instance is the obscure topography of the river-island caves in which Natty and his party hide from the pursuing Iroquois. Twain's own description is both briefer and more precise than Cooper's, which is spread clumsily over some nine pages. This is what Twain says, going on to pick out 'a case of strikingly inexact observation':

'In *The Last of the Mohicans* Cooper gets up a stirring "situation" on an island flanked by great cataracts—a lofty island with steep sides—a sort of tongue which projects downstream from the midst of a divided waterfall. There are caverns in this mass of rock, and a party of Cooper people hide themselves in one of these to get away from some hostile Indians. There is a small exit at each end of this cavern. These exits are closed with blankets and the light excluded. The exploring hostiles back themselves up against the blankets and rave and rage in a blood-curdling way, but they are Cooper Indians and of course fail to discover the blankets; so they presently go away baffled and disappointed. . . . The darkness in there must have been pretty solid; yet if we may believe Cooper, it was a darkness which could not have been told from daylight; for here are some nice details which were visible in it:'[1]—and Twain goes on to quote the passage in which Alice's companions are able to see with total clarity the emotions she so abundantly registers.

It is this indeterminateness of vision which explains the featureless uniformity of Cooper's accounts of fights and battles. The prose is too clogged, the details too inexplicit, to authenticate the urgency we are merely told is there—as when, on the island, Heyward grapples with an Indian:

'In the meantime, Heyward had been pressed in a more deadly struggle. His slight sword was snapped off in the first encounter. As he was destitute of any other means of defence, his safety now depended entirely on bodily strength and resolution. Though deficient in neither of these qualities, he had met an enemy every way his equal. Happily, he soon succeeded in disarming his adversary, whose knife fell on the rock at their feet, and from this moment it became a fierce struggle who should cast the other over the dizzy height, into a neighbouring cavern of the falls. . . . At that instant of extreme danger, a dark hand and glancing knife

[1] Wilson: *op. cit.*, pp. 594g–594h.

appeared before him; the Indian released his hold, as the blood flowed freely from around the severed tendons of his wrist; and while Duncan was drawn backward by the saving arms of Uncas, his charmed eyes were still riveted on the fierce and disappointed countenance of his foe, who fell sullenly and disappointed down the irrecoverable precipice.'

It is unnecessary to linger over the evasiveness of, 'Happily he soon succeeded in disarming his adversary . . .' or the indolent visualisation of 'the fierce and disappointed countenance of his foe, who fell sullenly and disappointed. . . .' Cooper's heart may have been in the description, but his eye was defective. Criticising one of Van Wyck Brooks's 'transcriptions' of a passage from Cooper, Edmund Wilson says that Brooks 'has not merely been reflecting the glory of something that is much better in the original: he has put together his very pretty passage out of more or less undistinguished bits scattered through a great number of pages'.[1] In very much the same way, any excitement to be found in the action of the *Mohicans* is in fact supplied by the reader's own imagination, with small help from Cooper's—in these circumstances—curiously barren prose.

Cooper does not lack defenders. The current answer to the line of criticism adopted above is that it is irrelevant to Cooper's real aims. James McCormick argues that Twain's attack is 'witty but irrelevant . . . rather like a criticism of Turner for not painting in the manner of Giotto'.[2] Grossman considers that Cooper is creating 'an arbitrarily simplified world (which) . . . has no serious concern with the outside world . . .'[3] Edmund Wilson, in *The Shock of Recognition*, introduces Mark Twain's essay with the comment that Twain misses the point about Cooper and that 'there is always a poet present who redeems the abominable craftsman'.[4] On this assessment, Cooper's art is consciously impressionistic and stylised, not realist; mythopoeic, symbolist and fanciful, not strictly representational; impelled by ideas, not the ebb and flow of physical action. As we shall see, this is true

[1] Wilson: *Classics and Commercials*, pp. 229–30.

[2] John McCormick: *Catastrophe and Imagination*, p. 184.

[3] Grossman: *op. cit.*, pp. 43–44.

[4] Wilson: *The Shock of Recognition*, p. 581.

enough of the better novels—of which, indeed, *The Pioneers* is one—in the Leatherstocking series. But when these other factors are absent, as they are in *The Last of the Mohicans*, they cannot be set against the kind of criticism Twain advances, and used to excuse the dullness and insipidity exemplified above.

However, as has been suggested already, if Cooper is at his weakest in rendering motion, he does succeed elsewhere and in other ways in communicating a sombre atmosphere of violence. Many passages are superbly done even by Twain's criteria. One of them is the description of the scene after the massacre at Fort William Henry. The massacre itself is, as Cooper says, 'rather incidentally mentioned than described'. Its immediate horror in fact comes across the more effectively for Cooper's withdrawal, but it is the macabre stillness of the scene three days later that more positively satisfies the conditions in which his descriptive invention flourished:

'When last seen, the environs of the works were filled with violence and uproar. They were now emphatically possessed by stillness and death. The blood-stained conquerors had departed; and their camp, which had so lately rung with the merry rejoicings of a victorious army, lay a silent and deserted city of huts. The fortress was a smouldering ruin; charred rafters, fragments of exploded artillery, and rent mason work, covering its earthen mounds in confused and negligent disorder. .

'A frightful change had also occurred in the season. The sun had hid its warmth behind an impenetrable mass of vapour, and hundreds of human forms, which had blackened beneath the first heats of August, were stiffening in their deformity, before the blasts of a premature November. The curling and spotless mists which had been seen sailing above the hills towards the north, were now returning in an interminable dusky sheet, that was urged along by the fury of a tempest. The crowded mirror of the Horican was gone; and in its place the green and angry waters lashed the shores, as if indignantly casting back its impurities to the polluted strand. Still the clear fountain retained a portion of its charmed influence; but it reflected only the sombre gloom that fell from the impending heavens. That humid and congenial atmosphere which was wont about the view, veiling its harshness, and softening its asperities, had disappeared, and the northern air poured across the waste of water so harsh and unmingled, that nothing was left to be conjectured by the eye, or fashioned by the fancy.

'The fiercer element had cropped the verdure of the plain, which looked as though it were scathed by the consuming lightning. But here and there a dark green tuft rose in the midst of the desolation; the earliest fruits of a soil that had been fattened with human blood. The whole landscape, which, seen by favouring light, and in a genial temperature, had been found so lovely, appeared now like some pictured allegory of life, in which the objects were arrayed in their harshest but truest colours, and without the relief of any shadowing.

'The solitary and arid blades of grass arose from the passing gusts fearfully perceptible; the bold and rocky mountains were too distinct in their barrenness, and the eye even sought relief in vain by attempting to pierce the illimitable void of heaven, which was shut to its gaze by the dusky sheet of ragged and driving vapour.

'The wind blew unequally, sometimes sweeping heavily along the ground, seeming to whisper its moanings in the cold ears of the dead, then, rising in a shrill and mournful whistling, it entered the forest with a rush that filled the air with the leaves and branches it scattered in its path. Amid the unnatural shower, a few hungry ravens struggled with the gale; but no sooner was the green ocean of woods which stretched beneath them passed, than they gladly stooped at random to that hideous haven where their revolting food so freely abounded.'

The power of the passage arises from its quite complex system of contrasts. Essentially the painting of a static landscape—in contrast to the 'violence and uproar' of the place 'when last seen'—this description of macabre stillness admits also the unfeeling motions of the elements: 'the blasts of a premature November', the 'interminable dusky sheet . . . urged along by the fury of a tempest', grass ruffled by 'passing gusts' and the tossing flight of the gorged ravens. This harsh vitality—so far removed from sentimentalised Pantheism—surrounds the 'hundreds of human forms . . . blackened beneath the fierce heats of August': Cooper makes

the pathetic antithesis explicit when he speaks of the wind whistling round 'the cold ears of the dead'. As well as being appropriately cheerless, which is its simplest inspiration, the scene
carries the stronger overtones of nature indifferent to, or even
profiting by, human wretchedness. The raven feed and the soil
has been 'fattened with human blood'. The effect of such details
and phrases is sharpened by their linguistic context. The language
is studiously formal—'filled with violence and uproar . . . possessed by stillness and death'; 'veiling its harshness and softening
its asperities'; 'to be conjectured by the eye, or fashioned by the
fancy'—and draws largely on the diction of pastoral. It is certainly
with ironic intent that Cooper includes 'the clear fountain' with
its 'charmed influence'; 'the verdure of the plain' and 'the earliest
fruits of a soil', phrases whose usual associations compose an
antiphon to their immediate setting. Here, the wilderness takes
over and the pastoral beauty is tarnished. But it is tarnished by—
in the theological sense—graceless humanity as much as by
inclement nature. As Cooper directly points out, the scene is a
'pictured allegory of life'.

It is a simplification to attribute his sense of turmoil and vul-
nerability to the influence of, as 'George Steiner puts it, 'the
American setting (where) men esta blish beach-heads in climates
which are not yet ready for them or in landscapes none of whose
ragged edges have been rounded by time'.[1] American life,
although undoubtedly its forms differed and it here and there
struggled more intensely on the verge of survival, offered no
more evidences of violence, depravity and chaos than Fielding's
London. Like Cooper, who was equally of the eighteenth century,
Fielding traced the ultimate worldly stay to individual goodness
(Parson Adams, Amelia), which could be transmitted into institutions. Through these it acquired a wider social utility. The institutions themselves, though indispensable, could never be anything
but imperfect, their imperfection alleviated by the wisdom and
integrity of particular men and women. Both writers castigated
injustices without expecting human beings to implement the
chiliastic myth. Their position was that in the unending moral
struggle between private desires and general well-being, work-

[1] George Steiner: *The Americanness of American Literature, The Listener*,
July 16, 1959, p. 96.

able compromises and local victories were possible, but that the final meaning of life and its irreducible evils was inaccessible to purely mortal understanding. A position, in fact, not unlike the forlorn idealism stated by Hawthorne in *The Blithedale Romance*: 'Yet, after all, let us acknowledge it wiser, if not more sagacious, to follow out one's day-dream to its natural consummation, although, if the vision had been worth the having, it is certain never to be consummated otherwise than by a failure.'

These ideas are implicit in the Fort William Henry episode of *The Last of the Mohicans*. They are important to an understanding of Cooper, but this is really the only point in this novel at which they emerge lucidly and freely from the narrative. The particular interest of the passage to this discussion is that it illustrates the kind of dramatic situation Cooper's art could most happily appropriate. Similar examples are scattered throughout the Leatherstocking novels. The scene in *The Prairie* (Chapter 5) in which Asa silences Abiram with a sudden 'back-handed but violent blow on the mouth' carries conviction because it does not last long enough for Cooper to founder in it; so does the discovery of Tom Hutter scalped alive in *The Deerslayer* (Chapter 20) and of Asa's mutilated body in *The Prairie* (Chapter 12), both these again the grim *sequel* to violent death. For all that Cooper nowhere credibly describes an episode depending on action of any duration or complexity, his world of violence is not altogether the absurdity Twain represented it to be, limited though Cooper's expression of it was.

To examine *The Pathfinder* (1840) in detail would simply be to corroborate what the *Mohicans* makes ¦manifest enough. It too is a novel in which Cooper repudiated the drama of ideas, which he understood, for the mechanics of action and suspense, which he grasped only imperfectly. The remaining two books of the series, *The Prairie* (1827) and *The Deerslayer* (1841), renew what we might describe, in terms of the politics of Cooper's times, as the debate between Federalism and Anti-Federalism; or more generally, as we have noticed, between the contrary opinions of human perfectibility that the two parties indirectly endorsed.

As a narrative, *The Prairie*, like *The Pioneers*, is disjunctive. The core of the novel is anecdotal. Ishmael Bush and his contentious family (effectively his wife, seven sons and his brother-in-law,

Abiram White), a few mysterious hangers-on and some unspecified but evil designs, is moving from the populated areas, where he has murdered a deputy sheriff, to the remote western plains, hoping to establish himself beyond the reach of conventional society. On the way he falls in with Natty Bumppo, whom he suspects of having helped Indian raiders to steal his cattle. Having settled in on a kind of natural rock fortress in the middle of the prairie, he, his sons and Abiram set out on a hunting trip from which his eldest son, Asa, does not return. When Asa's body is discovered, shot in the back, Ishmael blames Natty but is later convinced of Abiram's guilt and takes his own reluctant revenge. He leaves Abiram tied by the neck to a tree on a high ledge from which he must eventually fall. Ishmael and his wife then disappear, not only from the novel, but, mysteriously, from life itself.

After Ishmael's return to his encampment, having found his son's body, he plays from Chapter 14 to Chapter 30 only a peripheral role. Briefly, Natty has, by a signal coincidence, which Cooper is at some pains to vindicate, met Captain Duncan Uncas Middleton, a descendant of the Duncan Heyward Natty had, years earlier, shepherded through the adventures of *The Last of the Mohicans*. Middleton is in search of his wife, Inez de Certavallos, whom Abiram had incited Ishmael to kidnap and, though they have done nothing about this, hold to ransom. Cooper is vague about this transaction and the kidnappers seem to have adopted the ineffectual strategy of moving farther and farther away from any area in which they might present their demands. During Ishmael's absence on the fatal hunting trip, Middleton and Natty free Inez, and also Ellen Wade, a distant relative of Ishmael's wife, who is engaged to another of Natty's companions, Paul Hover, a bee-hunter. They subsequently become embroiled in the warfare between the two rival Indian tribes of the region, the Pawnees and the Siouxes, the latter temporarily allied with Ishmael and his band (who remain passive observers during most of this action), the former with Natty. It is these adventures, which include a bison charge, a prairie fire, capture, escape and a pitched battle, which the chapters referred to above, comprising most of the book, recount.

The foregoing résumé shows that Cooper has made some

attempt to derive these later developments from the initial shocks which the arrival of the Bush ménage produces. We could willingly enough dispense with much of the flight, the counsellings and the subterfuges so painstakingly described, but they do not, at least, quite so arbitrarily remove us from their origin in Bush's lethargic egoism as the 'plot' of *The Pioneers* does from *its* real centre of interest. Even on the simply mechanical level, Bush's comings and goings dictate the pattern of the other events. Besides that, however, and infinitely more important, there are definite thematic links between the two parts. Natty is placed in significant relationship both to Bush and to the Indian tribes. The morality and manners of each group annotate those of the others.

Early in the novel, Cooper, in his own person, characterises the Indians as a 'wronged and humbled people' and through Natty reiterates the sentiment that they have a better right to the prairies and its game than the Europeans who have dispossessed them, often faithlessly. Of this charity we are conscious in all Cooper's renderings of the Indian, but it does not lead him to idealise them. Natty discriminates between them, so that while he identifies 'a bloody band of accursed Sioux . . . by their thieving look', he describes the Pawnees as 'a wise and a great people, and I'll engage they abound in many a wholesome and honest tradition'. The conduct of the two tribes is designed to exemplify the contrasting morals thus attributed to them. A scheme of moral law, the teachings of the 'Master of Life', is binding on all the Indians and Natty judges them by their adherence to it. Hard-Heart, the Pawnee leader, is ennobled because, in Natty's words, he 'fears the Master of Life, and follows his laws'. From what we can gather of them, these laws compose a severely Spartan ethic. The Pawnee virtues are certainly Spartan virtues, insisting on honourable conduct of war, personal bravery and endurance and, socially, relegating women to an inferior but secure status. The Sioux chieftain, Mahtoree, offends against the code of war by his repeated treachery and is particularly contrasted with Hard-Heart in his attitude to Inez. When he proposes to abandon his wife and take Inez in her place, Natty exclaims, 'The Lord forgive the heartless villain.' Hard-Heart, on the other hand, though he equally admires Inez's fragile beauty, remains, obviously with Cooper's approval, scrupulously at a distance.

Hard-Heart, like Uncas of the Mohicans—'the age, and the eye, and the limbs are as if they might have been brothers'—is the Noble Savage, but superior though he is to Mahtoree in candour and decorum, his nobility is contained within the bounds of savagery: in their final victory over the Siouxes the Pawnees do not spare the women and children of the rival tribe. Equally, among the infamous Siouxes, the council summoned to sentence Hard-Heart does reveal at least one man of honour and the ensuing battle many of courage. Cooper, that is to say, did believe in the Noble Savage, but not that his Nobility could redeem his ethic from its essentially pagan taint, nor that the special usages it supported could be valid beyond their primitive tribal basis. Sensible of European outrages, he was not led thereby to sentimentalise the Indians. For a man of his time and place he achieved a notably disinterested view both of his European and his Indian characters.

Ishmael Bush is among Cooper's most forceful studies in the character of the European pioneer. There might at first seem little to say in his favour. He and his family are vagrant, squalid, animal, bigoted and shiftless—the list might be extended. Yet they have their admirable qualities. They are staunch in danger, physically hard and enduring, phlegmatic in disaster, with the 'gigantic strength' necessary to survival in 'this changeable and moving country': 'brave, because they were inured to dangers— proud, because they were independent, and vindictive, because each was the avenger of his own wrongs.' It is this last feature that most sharply catches at Cooper's fancy, and by it that he is led once more to appraise the rule of law.

At least a suspected murderer and certainly a kidnapper, Ishmael is, in the most literal sense as well as in his general disposition, a man beyond the law. Paul Hover, who detests him, is not alone in accepting this dispassionately. Telling Natty how he had come across the body of the murdered deputy sheriff 'with a hole through the "grace of God" which he carried in his jacket pocket covering his heart', he adds sarcastically, 'as if he thought a bit of sheepskin was a breastplate against a squatter's bullet'. We recall how Bradford argued that, despite the reluctance of the English government to guarantee their security, the settlers should embark on their venture, since dangers and setbacks were inevitable anyhow, 'though they had a seale as broad

as the house flore'. Paul Hover is giving voice to the same realistic
disdain, so marked in the American tradition, for any social contract that lacks the ultimate sanction of effective authority, and
to that extent at least he is of Ishmael's party. It is between
Ishmael and Natty, however, that the issue is significantly joined,
for it is in what they seem to have in common that we find their
radical divergence of view. As Cooper says, 'Natty's opinions on
this important topic, though drawn from very different premises,
were in singular accordance with those of (Ishmael).'

Natty's opinion of the law is now much more tolerant than it
was in *The Pioneers*. He is still given to anathematising the courts
and recalls that he 'was carried into one of the lawless holes myself
once, and it was all about a thing of no more value than the skin
of a deer. The Lord forgive them! . . . they knew no better, and
they did according to their weak judgments'. But to Ellen he
acknowledges that 'the law is needed, when such as have not the
gifts of strength and wisdom are to be taken care of'. His earlier
intransigeance is manifested now in Ishmael Bush, who speaks
frequently of his contempt for 'the law . . . which says that one
man shall have a section, or a town, or perhaps a county to his
use, and another have to beg for earth to make his grave in. That
is not nature and I deny that it is law. That is, your legal law'.
Yet he calls himself 'a fair dealer' and claims that he 'always fulfills
his agreements better than your wordy dealers in contracts
written on rags of paper'. Of this, in principle, Natty is not the
man to disapprove, but Ishmael's conduct in practice departs
widely from Natty's altruistic sense of what constitutes fair play.
Where Natty, for example, recognises the justice of the 'prairie
law' by which the Indians 'claim to be the lawful owners of this
country', Ishmael simply refers his dispute with them to 'the
contents of old Kentuck', slapping his rifle in a manner that could
not be easily misconstrued'. Ishmael's principles assume a different
countenance in his application of them: force is the immediate,
not the ultimate arbiter and his only criterion is his own advantage,
in pursuit of which he turns against all other groups—and is in
the end abandoned by them all—including, in his kidnapping,
those weak and defenceless on whose behalf Natty is willing to
accept even the law he distrusts. On this reading, Ishmael represents the obverse of the individualism with which Natty keeps

faith. At the same time, Ishmael's pretensions to virtue cannot be written off as meaningless. Although his actions are so frequently infamous, we are compelled to own that he states his principles ingenuously, that he is mindful of the choice to be made between good and evil and that for his evildoing he often makes amends. Whatever his faults, hypocrisy is not among them and we discern a genuine integrity in many of his professions of faith, as when he assures Abiram that, 'When the law of the land is weak, it is right the law of nature should be strong . . . As for you, Abiram, the child has done you wrong, and it is my place to see you righted. Remember; I tell you justice shall be done; it is enough. But you have said hard things ag'in me and my family. If the hounds of the law have put their bills on the trees and stumps of the clearings, it was for no act of dishonesty as you know, but because we maintain the rule that 'arth is common property. No, Abiram; could I wash my hands of things done by your advice, as easily as I can of the things done by the whisperings of the devil, my sleep would be quieter at night, and none who bear my name need blush to hear it mentioned.' Ishmael's significance, in fact, is a complex one and much of what is doubtful in it is clarified in the trial of his 'enemies', which he conducts in Chapter 31.

In releasing Middleton, Paul Hover and Dr. Batt, the naturalist who had deserted his camp, Ishmael contrives to represent himself as the injured party. Returning Inez to her husband he admits his guilt and in what, for him, is an act of some generosity, he allows Ellen to go with Paul Hover, though he had intended her to marry one of his sons. He then charges Natty with the murder of Asa. When he accepts Natty's account of how he had seen Abiram commit the murder, frees Natty and puts the terror-stricken Abiram in his place, Ishmael attains what Baudelaire called 'la vraie grandeur des parias'. He says to his wife, who pleads for Abiram, 'when we believed that miserable old trapper had done this deed, nothing was said of mercy!' Once again Cooper comes close to the circumstances of the trial in the *Arcadia*, but here there is no fortuituous reprieve. The next chapter describes with an impressive grimness Abiram's unedifying death, 'a human form swinging in the wind, beneath the ragged and shining arm of the willow', and the horror which afflicts even the phlegmatic Ishmael. In a passage reminiscent of Poe, Ishmael imagines his victim's dying screams echoing over the 'mild loveliness' of the moonlit prairie, succeeded by 'a cry, in which there could be no delusion, or to which the imagination could lend no horror ... The name of God was distinctly audible, but it was awfully and blasphemously blended with sounds that may not be repeated'.

The sequence is quite evidently intended to be set against the account of Mahtoree's tribunal, in which the Indian chief is motivated entirely by the desire for revenge, uninhibited, finally, even by prudence and not at all concerned with his captives' guilt or innocence of specific charges. Where the Indian debate, its verdict a foregone conclusion, pursues the primitive satisfaction of the vendetta, Ishmael cannot cast off the ideal, in however aboriginal a form, of dispassionate justice. Forced into relationship with extrinsic groups, he finds that much of what he despises in the law has decided his own principles and settled the forms he must subscribe to. Like Montaigne's human being, he 'cannot rid himself of what he condemns'. Because of this his 'self-constituted tribunal excited a degree of awe, to which even the intelligent Middleton could not bring himself to be entirely insensible'; and at the end it is again Middleton who feels 'awe-struck by what he believed a manifest judgment of Heaven'. Cooper juxtaposes the two courts in order to display the superiority of the white ethic and to show how it tempers even Ishmael's anarchistic sentiments, raising him, the lawless European leader, above Mahtoree, the lawless Indian: Abiram, whose Indian counterpart is perhaps the equally degraded Weucha, is punished by his own community. Thus Ishmael's loftiest vision is bounded by Mosaic strictness, transcended, in its turn, by the more purely Christian altruism of Natty. Useful though it is to state their function so baldly, this does not represent the full range of the ideas which coalesce round them during the action of the novel; nor does it embrace their persuasiveness as, in the accepted sense, 'characters', on which their force as intellectual counters is wholly dependent.

Some of the misinterpretation of Cooper's viewpoint is undoubtedly due to identifying it with that of Natty, who has absorbed something from the beliefs of all the groups with which he associates. But Cooper did not think in terms so simplified and, though he might regret it, recognised the practical inadequacy of Natty's innocent precepts. Cooper's position is not expressed in any one character. It is implied in the pattern of contacts between the various key groups and characters and the attitudes they represent: only law and authority can establish equilibrium and at the fringes it is the vestigial reminiscences of the law which avert savagery. Cooper speaks approvingly (Chapter 15) of the Spanish colonists raised by their incorporation in the Union 'to the more enviable position of citizens in a government of laws'. This is the consummation of the social process to which all the groups must conform. *The Prairie* is particularly interesting for Cooper's shrewd and equitable account of the part played in this development by Ishmael and his kind. It is not a fruitful enterprise to construct the book an author might have written, but one can imagine a more effective *Prairie*, of the sort and length of Melville's *Piazza Tales*, written more economically around the Ishmael story. Even as it is, the action of this novel carries the ideas with considerable success.

In *The Deerslayer* Cooper resumes the themes of *The Prairie*. Substantially the same groups are represented but their ideas are more forthrightly in opposition. Cooper returns Natty to the setting of *The Pioneers* but some fifty years earlier in time. He is in his youth, an untried warrior. Chingachgook is on the verge of the marriage of which the doomed Uncas will be the issue. To secure his bride and defeat the Mingoes who hold her, he. and Natty must enter their first warpath and take human life: a loss of innocence but an assertion of manhood. The part of Ishmael Bush and his family is taken by Harry March and Tom Hutter. Hutter lives on the lake with his two daughters, Judith and Hetty (later we find out that he is not their father), in a kind of fortified houseboat. These two men display all the sordid avarice of which the frontiersman was capable, betraying what Natty calls their 'gifts' as Europeans by scalping the Indians for bounty. Of Ishmael's virtues they have only stoic acceptance of hardship. To the demands of religious faith and the supposedly benign influence of nature—it plays a major part in this novel— they are insusceptible. Pointedly, it is Harry March who, when it suits him, most dogmatically defends the law, though he is one of 'a set of men who dreaded the approaches of civilisation as a curtailment of their own lawless empire.' He asks Natty, 'if the Colony can make an onlawful law? Isn't an onlawful law more ag'in nature than scalping a savage? A law can no more be onlawful than truth be a lie'. Natty makes the obvious reply, which is important because it takes us directly to the ethical hinterland of the law, where Cooper stages the moral collisions of this novel: 'Laws don't all come from the same quarter. God has given us his'n, and some come from the Colony, and others come from the king and parliament. When the Colony's laws, or even the King's laws, run ag'in the laws of God, they get to be onlawful, and ought not to be obeyed. I hold to a white man's respecting white laws, so long as they do not cross the track of a law comin' from a higher authority.'

The Deerslayer proceeds, apart from the routine comings and goings, through a series of situations which call for purely individual and uncompromisingly moral judgments. From this point of view, the Leatherstocking novels are to be read as a gradual regression from the couching of general social and moral issues in more or less strictly legal forms: Natty's trial at the Templeton court in *The Pioneers*; in *The Prairie* Ishmael's pseudo-court. In *The Deerslayer* the characters are unconstrained by effective authority and uninstructed by the conventionalising presence of usage and precedent. Hence they must arbitrate for themselves social dilemmas which present them with a direct moral choice between self-interest and the guidance of whatever ethical sense they have. Those, like Tom Hutter, for whom the two are identified, are, of course, unconscious of any dilemma. He, quite indifferently, and Harry March, less purposefully criminal, unite in arguing their particular crisis, the propriety of a scalping raid on the Indian camp. It is Harry who carries the burden of argument and to his own satisfaction succeeds in rationalising the 'heartless cupidity' which is their real motive and which Hutter is much less concerned to palliate. Their decision brings its own retribution. They are captured and Hutter himself, in the end, is scalped.

The feeble-minded Hetty's 'situation' hinges on her deciding to visit the Indian camp to persuade the Indians, by appealing to Christian teaching as she understands it, not to harm their captives. Her innocence, in R. W. B. Lewis's words, 'is, in fact a self-delusive helplessness, a half witted conviction of universal goodness'. Lewis argues that Hetty's naïvety 'exposes her to every physical and moral danger and finally kills her'.[1] In fact, Cooper repeatedly insists that, with Hetty as with the Lady in *Comus*,

> *A thousand liveried angels lackey her,*
> *Driving far off each thing of sin and guilt. . . .*

She has the instinct which 'so often keeps those whom God has thus visited from harm'. She sleeps in the forest 'in a tranquillity as undisturbed and a rest as sweet, as if angels expressly commissioned for that object, watched around the bed of Hetty Hutter'. In the morning a bear, miraculously, leaves her unmolested and with its cubs follows 'her steps, keeping a short distance behind her; apparently watching every movement, as if they had a near interest in all she did'. There is a strong ritual element in these events. We are in the 'green wood' of Romance myth, where the animal and human kingdoms mysteriously commune.[2] It is both the prelapsarian Eden and the perilous forest—images strongly entrenched in the deeper recesses of the imagination—and it is given here unmistakably Christian associations. Cooper tells us of Hetty after her death that she was 'one of those mysterious links between the material and the immaterial world, which, while they appear to be deprived of so

[1] R. W. B. Lewis: *The American Adam*, p. 105.

[2] This is, of course, a common feature of medieval allegory. See, for example, C. S. Lewis, *The Allegory of Love*, p. 107, where he quotes from *De Planctu Naturae*, *Prosa* II, 11 ff.:

At the coming of the said virgin you would a thought that all the elements, as though they renewed their kinds, did make festival . . . The birds, moved by a certain kindly inspiration, rejoicing with the plausive playing of their pinions, showed unto the virgin a worshipping countenance . . . The fishes, even, . . . foretold by their glad cheer the coming of their lady.

Chaucer's Canacee is granted the same gift. It is common in folk-lore (the Babes in the Wood) and is attributed also to Christ. In pp. 286–7, Lewis discusses the double role of Nature as 'a fair goddess' and 'a desolate place full of wild beasts'. Drawing on this accumulation of Nature myths, Cooper is not dealing in recondite allusions, but touching spontaneously on a dominant theme which, in its many outcroppings, has variously enriched English poetry. We recognise it again in Blake's tiger 'in the forests of the night', which impels the cry, 'Did he who made the Lamb make thee?'; and in the Lion of 'Night', which lies down beside the lamb in 'green fields and happy grove'.

much that is esteemed and necessary for this state of being, draw so near to, and offer so beautiful an illustration of the truth, purity, and simplicity of another'. Hetty's significance is therefore a dual one. Quite unable to contend with the chiefs' assertion of the discrepancy between Christian teaching and the practice of nominal Christians, or to understand the barbarous world in which Indian and frontiersman alike acquiesced, she illuminates both the tragic schism between divine ideal and human actuality and the impotence of faith uninformed by knowledge of evil as well as of good. In Pascal's words, 'La justice sans la force est contredite, parcequ'il y a toujours des méchants; la force sans la justice est accusée.'

Natty, on the other hand, is inseparably caught up with the affairs of the material world and is sensible of human wickedness. His innocence, that is, does not insulate him against this knowledge, but rather has its fortitude tested against it. Released on parole by the Indians, he keeps his word and voluntarily returns to the prospect of torture and death. By doing this he confirms his integrity, as earlier, by killing the Indian, he had committed himself to the harsh demands of life. He explains to Harry March, 'This furlough is not, as you seem to think, a matter altogether atween me and the Mingoes, seeing it is a solemn bargain atween me and God. He who thinks that he can say what he pleases, in his distress, and that 'twill all pass for nothing because 'tis uttered in the forest and into red men's ears, knows little of his situation, and hopes and wants. The words are said to the ears of the Almighty. The air is his breath, and the light of the sun is little more than the glance of his eye.' This highly articulate explanation is perhaps a trifle too ornate to be altogether in character, though its Biblical tone is by no means out of keeping with the speech of a society much more familiar with the Scriptures than is common nowadays. In any case, the speech isolates two cardinal points: that the crises of this novel cut through to a directly moral choice—the issue 'atween me and God'—disengaged from society's restraints and procedures; and that Nature, in which God is said to live, is not so much an irresistible preceptor as a kind of moral reagent. When Harry and Natty first see Glimmerglass lake, Natty exclaims, "tis an edication of itself ... not a tree disturbed even by red-skin hand, as I can discover, but everything left in the ordering of the Lord, to live and die according to his own designs and laws'. Harry, however, 'thought more of the beauties of Judith Hutter than of those of the Glimmerglass'. Elsewhere, following a description of dawn on the lake, Cooper remarks that 'the whole was lost on the observers (Hutter and Harry), who knew no feeling of poetry, had lost their sense of natural devotion in lives of obdurate and narrow selfishness, and had little other sympathy with nature than that which originated with her lowest wants.' If Cooper felt the power of pantheism, it was in a manner less like Wordsworth's than like Coleridge's, which acknowledged that for most people, 'the ancient mountains, with all their terrors and all their glories, are pictures to the blind, and music to the deaf'. Nature may elevate the spirit, but only the spirit inherently thus inclined.

It has been already mentioned that Cooper used the Leatherstocking novels to comment on the tensions of his society by withdrawing slightly from their immediate formulations, unlike Poe, who projected them into a much more oblique and subjective symbolism. Nevertheless, Cooper's novels are not devoid of symbolism. The withdrawal he undertook was charged, as we saw in *The Pioneers*, with deep personal significance and involved a private emotional fulfilment which carried the settings beyond their purely social reality. The same is true of *The Deerslayer*, the most Arcadian in tone of all the novels. To the lake and its surroundings attaches something of Hetty's dual suggestiveness. It is the unviolated 'happy valley', with its 'affluent forest grandeur, softened by the balminess of June', on which the story opens. Yet it is also a real place, subject to the changing seasons, 'saturated with the humidity that constantly arose from the woods', to which the 'world of transgressions and selfishness' finds entrance past the mountains which rose around it 'like black barriers to exclude the world'. Cooper, in fact, quite consciously uses it, without washing out its sensuous properties, as a symbol of elysian innocence and simplicity, briefly invaded by the acquisitive urges of his own society. In the end the valley is liberated from strife only by the arrival of the soldiers, who, though themselves human beings as imperfect as any, supply the force without which virtue is powerless. Cooper is saying again that the state of nature means anarchy and the destruction of the feeble. Imperfect though they may be, only institutions can preserve a social harmony; and only such ideals as Natty represents can preserve institutions from autocratic abuse. The beautifully elegiac mood of *The Deerslayer*, more intense even than in *The Prairie*, where Natty dies, comes from the coupling of the freshly imagined Arcadian vision, the pastoral Eden, with the recognition that it is in fact only a partial truth—Nature too is corrupt—and that the dream could be supported only by a race of perfect human beings such as has never yet been evolved.

It is unnecessary to labour the point that Cooper never wholly succeeded in cultivating a form congenial to his ideas. He conformed too willingly to the fashions of the romance, notably, in the words of Sir Walter Scott, 'an appeal to the passion of fear, whether excited by natural dangers, or by the suggestions of superstition. . . . The force, therefore, of the production lies in the delineation of external incident'[1]: and in this, with the exceptions that we have noted above, Cooper was not at his happiest. Yet we cannot say of the Leatherstocking series, as Scott does of the romance, that it 'does not appeal to the judgment by deep delineations of human feeling, or stir the passions by scenes of deep pathos, or awaken the fancy by tracing out, with spirit and vivacity, the lighter marks of life and manners'.[2] Cooper's achievement was close to the one which Scott ascribes to Horace Walpole, 'to unite the marvellous turn of incident . . . with that accurate display of human character, and contrast of feelings and passions, which is, or ought to be, delineated in the modern novel'.[3] Cooper, most instinctively, is a novelist of ideas, specifically of the ideas on which his society subsisted. He worried intelligently and pertinaciously at the problem of expressing his themes in terms of action and character, of using the surface features of society to display its inner shapeliness. The ideas were not peculiar to America, but in America they assumed a new urgency and a new complexity, since it was a country which combined primitive conditions with modern technological and commercial progress and political sophistication. Cooper's

[1] 'Ann Radcliffe,' *Lives of the Novelists.*

[2] *Ibid.*

[3] Scott: *op. cit.*, 'Horace Walpole'.

opportunity was that this circumstance coincided with the rise of the novel as a dominant form. In attempting to make use of that form he worked on well-established European literary traditions, seeking to embody in them a range of thoughts, feelings and experiences whose effect was to broaden and alter the traditions. The shortcomings of style, construction and narrative which appear in the Leatherstocking books are defects of detail. They do not obscure Cooper's general positive achievements, nor seriously enfeeble the hold taken on our imaginations by his world and its inhabitants and the clashes of principles they represent.

Chapter Four

The Tragic Phase: Melville and Hawthorne

***

ACCORDING to R. W. B. Lewis, the dominating image in the intellectual life of mid-nineteenth-century America was that of the American as Adam, 'a figure of heroic innocence and vast potentialities, poised at the start of a new history'.[1] The image, as Lewis demonstrates, had a promiscuous vogue in newspapers and magazines. It expressed with convenient simplicity certain optimistic notions about American society and its political destiny. This optimism had varied causes. Despite the financial crises of 1819, 1837 and 1857, the national economy was expansively prosperous. With the rapid development of transport, land values rose. Agricultural exports increased, industry flourished. 'Population,' says R. V. Harlow, 'was increasing at such a rate, and the standard of living in the new West was rising so rapidly, that there was always a demand for more goods. As long as exports moved out of our sea ports and as long as there was any more West to settle, there seemed to be no limit to the possibilities of trade or to the productive enterprises which trade made possible.' Surrounded by these evidences of merit rewarded, 'Americans believed that Europe, already effete, was on the decline, and for the centuries to come the United States would be superior to any nation the world has ever seen.'[2] Thus the Adamic vision thrived among the commonalty on commercial statistics. Even men like Emerson

[1] R. W. B. Lewis: *The American Adam*, p. 1. See also pp. 4–10.
[2] R. V. Harlow: *The United States*, pp. 236 and 223–4.

and Whitman, for whom its meaning as a symbol of moral regeneration was paramount, refreshed their perfectionist faith by parading the evidences of material enterprise. 'Banks and tariffs,' said Emerson in *The Poet*, 'the newspaper and the caucus, methodism and unitarianism, are flat and dull to dull people, but rest on the same foundations of wonder as the town of Troy . . .'

In the atmosphere of the times, to attach the moral faith to the industrial success story was not so incongruous as might at first appear. It was democratic fervour and democratic principles which had shaped the Union and to the inspiration and structure of this mystical entity was ascribed both national and individual well-being. 'It is to that Union,' Webster declaimed 'we owe our safety at home, and our consideration and dignity abroad. It is to that Union that we are chiefly indebted for whatever makes us most proud of our country. That Union we reached only by the discipline of our virtues in the severe school of adversity. It had its origin in the necessities of disordered finance, prostrate commerce, and ruined credit. Under its benign influences, these great interests immediately awoke, as from the dead, and sprang forth with newness of life. Every year of its duration has teemed with fresh fruits of its utility and its blessings; and, although our territory has stretched out wider and wider, and our population spread farther and farther, they have not outrun its protection or its benefits. It has been to us all a copious fountain of national, social, and personal happiness.'[1]

America had experienced the elation of—apparently at least—rejecting the corrupt weight of the European past with its burden of guilt and so beginning anew. It had framed and implemented a radically new system of government. And now success had been empirically certified. Eliminating the frontier grossness so crudely conspicuous to Dickens and others, these diverse simples crystallized into the radiant image of American innocence, American temporal and geographical disengagement, as a massive power at once transcendental and material. While all this clearly has its precedent in the America of the Puritans, its resurgence was markedly more secular. The general drift of Emerson's confidence, benignly inclusive of city and countryside, commerce

[1] Daniel Webster: *Reply to Hayne*, January 26 and 27, 1830.

and art, good and evil, was towards the position that, as he said in *Self-Reliance*, 'Nothing is at last sacred but the integrity of your own mind'. Between man and an unclouded spiritual vision, a full realisation of his potentialities, lay the obstacles of history, tradition and, not least, what Emerson patronisingly called 'the dear old doctrines of the church'. Formalism, orthodoxy, were the brand of turpitude; change, growth, progress, heterogeneity the insignia of the 'Supreme Mind'. No longer the Puritan God, the 'Supreme Mind', the 'Over-Soul', so far as we can discern through Emerson's misty deliberations, is the pantheistic Nature of Wordsworth. In Emerson's version, the individual human soul is supreme, its aspirations perpetually accomplished, superseded, accomplished again: 'See the investment of capital in aqueducts made useless by hydraulics; fortifications, by gunpowder; roads and canals, by railways; sails, by steam; steam by electricity' (*Circles*). The amelioration has a metaphysical as well as a worldly significance, for 'Every occupation, trade, art, transaction, is a compend of the world, and a correlative of every other . . . If the good is there, so is the evil; if the affinity, so the repulsion; if the force, so the limitation' (*Compensation*). The theme of Nature is balance, the emphasis being not that evil exists but that it is always cancelled by good. Discongruities and adversities are merely 'the solid angularity of facts' which 'Time dissipates to shining ether.' Analogies of reparative scale are common in the essays. Inconcinnities merge, 'as no mountain is of any appreciable height to break the curve of the sphere' (*The Poet*). All the variety of earthly circumstance is like the line of a ship following a zigzag course which seen from a distance 'straightens itself to the average tendency' (*Self-Reliance*). The flux of life resembles the sea 'whose waters ebb and flow with perfect balance' (*Compensation*). Reconciliation is sought not through some timeless infinity but in mortal time. Thus the future becomes the incentive to the present, not the past its guide; human aspiration, not hyper-physical divinity, the universal centre. Emerson, in fact, retains the consolations of religion while eliminating its essential postulate of a spiritual resource beyond the human capacity.

It would be wrong, however, to leave so glossily conformist an impression of the American scene. Many extreme Democrats advanced a socialist analysis of the evils of industrialism, put

Utopia well in the future and made it contingent upon a programme of reformist legislation. Others proposed a complete reconstruction of a society in which, the Fourierite Albert Brisbane said in his *Social Destiny of Man* (1840), 'monotony, uniformity, intellectual inaction and torpor reign; distrust, isolation, conflict and antagonism are almost universal . . . Society is spiritually a desert'. The conflict was increasingly a class conflict. For every Whig ballad celebrating the idyllic life of the factory worker there was a Democratic counterblast. For every attribution of benevolence to the business combines there was agitation against the plight of the working men on whom their wealth and power were based.[1] Fundamentally, however, what was going on was a re-appraisal of the philosophies of Jefferson and Hamilton, both of whom openly feared and mistrusted the urban proletariat. In the new America it could no longer be ostracised. Somewhat hesitantly, the Democrats took up its cause, advocating political equality and legislation enforcing such reforms as a minimum wage and a shorter working day. Mediation of this kind was, strictly, uncanonical but it had received qualified sanction in *The Wealth of Nations*, part of the groundwork of Jacksonian thought. It is pertinent that Arthur Schlesinger should say of Adam Smith that he 'formulated on the economic level the same sentiments which Jefferson put into glowing moral and political language'.[2] The Democrats, in fact, were beatifying the industrial labourer as Jefferson had the freeholder and, by keeping him conscious of grievances to be righted and the political patronage he had to confer, securing him a title in the national progress. The Whigs had a similar aim but a different approach. They glorified the opportunities of the workers within the existing economic structure. Their argument, as stated in 1838 by the Harvard professor Edward Everett, was that 'the wheel of fortune is in constant operation, and the poor in one generation furnish the rich of the next'. The Hamiltonian virtues of enterprise and assiduity would reward the worthy. Schlesinger, whose bias is strongly Jacksonian, acknowledges that these precepts

---

[1] Evidence of the conflict, of ideas in political strategy, is given by Arthur M. Schlesinger in his *The Age of Jackson*. For the items cited here see particularly pp. 271–5 and 334–44.

[2] Schlesinger: *op. cit.*, p. 315.

found 'enormous support in the hopes of American life and a certain support in its realities'.[1] Manifestly, there were sad discrepancies between the Adamic prospects and the realities of American life. However, the angry swirl of political contention over the laggard facts was not, at bottom, antagonistic to the general hopefulness. What it really did was to balance the reckoning by its reminder that, on a closer view, poverty, misery and injustice existed and were less easily dismissed than Emerson's soaring metaphysics would suggest.

We must recognise, then, that even as early as the eighteen-twenties and -thirties, America was both clear-headed about its circumstances and enraptured by its possibilities. There was an incessant conflict between idealisation and realism, between reforming zeal and a more passive but nonetheless convinced optimism, between the political thought that came out of the Revolution and the need to extend its relevance. Though we do not, nowadays, slip easily into Emerson's serene optimism, it was by no means just escapist fantasy. It drew on solid possibilities and at least some of the existing facts. Less selectively regarded, the facts promoted an effort to re-think the theories of Jefferson and Hamilton, reconciling them to a more diversified economy and a protean society. At this stage, there was little doubt that the effort would succeed, but in the increasingly ugly later years of the century, and particularly after the Civil War, the certainty weakened and disenchantment became more insistent than optimism: a shift of emphasis, not a shatteringly fortuitous calamity; a re-instatement, in place of primally innocent man, of 'the old Adam'. An added complication was the fact, as we have seen in Chapter Two, that American society had not detached itself from the Thomist frame, through which showed the new vistas of the radicals' prognosis. Emerson himself, Lewis reminds us, recognised 'two polarised parties: "the party of the Past and the party of the Future", as he sometimes called them'.[2] Where Emerson,

[1] Schlesinger: *op. cit.*, p. 273. In fact there is considerable evidence that much of Jackson's support came from would-be capitalists and entrepreneurs who hoped for a relaxation in the legal controls over the formation of new businesses. See Richard Hofstadter, 'William Leggett and Jacksonian Democracy', in *Understanding the American Past*, ed. Edward N. Saveth, pp. 227–8 and 233–4.

[2] Lewis: *op. cit.*, p. 7.

espousing the latter, was able to say, in *Circles*, 'I simply experiment, an endless seeker, with no Past at my back', the novelists who were his contemporaries did not so blithely shake off their heritage. Their historical sense abated the headiness of the presumptive advance from immaculate conception to millennial apotheosis. Their irksome craft bound them to past disciplines and this aesthetic restraint, indeed, may well have fostered a modicum of more general faith in the value of communication with the past. Certainly, the American novelists of the period are given, on the whole, to scepticism and conservatism.

It is Lewis's thesis that the American novel of this period based a new type of hero on the Emersonian ideas of the liberated soul contending triumphantly with unprecedented opportunities in a renascent moral environment. Later, Lewis argues, disillusionment pursued the Adamic parallel to its tragic issue in the Fall. In fiction, the pattern is incorporated as the archetype of American experience—in, for example, Melville's *Billy Budd*. 'Cooper,' Lewis writes, 'differed radically from . . . Melville in his refusal to perceive any evil, overt or hidden, in the magnificent world of space, or in any of its creatures.'[1] As we have seen, Cooper's is a much tougher view than that. His forests harboured dragons as well as St. Georges, and we cannot, on the strength of Natty and the young Chingachgook, identify his opinions with those of the neo-pastoral journalists and essayists. As a writer, Cooper was conversant with the European traditions; as an observer of society he recognised that its stability depended on an accumulation of precedents stretching far into the past. At its centre was the rule of law, in which the spirit of Natty's unsophisticated probity must remain active. But there is never, in Cooper, any question of a society composed of Natty Bumppos. In the Leatherstocking series, the sense of evil, though muted, is there, and the human labour Cooper admires is the struggle against evil and the development of institutions that will constrict it. He would have endorsed Jacques Barzun's commendation 'of the long, arduous growth and superior merit of an institution to which we owe our ease and privileges as thinking beings. The law is a model of intellectual work, and it is a work of words. It is a profession easy to ridicule by its externals and it is criti-

[1] Lewis: *op. cit.*, p. 99.

cisable, like other institutions, for its anachronisms. But as an attempt of the *esprit de finesse* to mould coherent conceptions of the true and the just on the restless multiplicity of human life, it is a triumph of articulateness and exactitude'.[1] Cooper's novels trace the early stages of the growth. He works in the mundane world of shifts, contrivances and capricious motives, of dilemmas that must be clearly understood and expressed if they are to be adjudicated, not with the ambiguities and the elided meanings of Melville. To put it crudely, Cooper is an eighteenth-century realist, not, like Emerson, a late nineteenth-century optimist, nor, like Melville, a late nineteenth-century pessimist.

In a novelist like Cooper we can see how the ascendancy of this secularised Pelagianism, with all its emphases and accretions, extended from politics to aesthetics. On the political level, the story of Adam and the Fall embodied, in the form of myth, the antagonistic ideas of Jefferson and Hamilton on natural goodness and natural depravity. As it was at first interpreted, it fostered the delusive faith in a society founded on the purity of a complete rupture with the past, specifically, with any carry-over from its European origins. Like the politicians, Cooper saw a new society in the making, but he did not believe that it could dispense with the traditional restraints, nor that it had evolved human beings devoid of evil. In attempting to make use of the tensions implicit here as the material of his art, he found equally that the past was indispensable: hence the literary reminiscences we have noticed in his work. Some words of Sir Herbert Read suggest the aesthetic problems that emanated from the political developments whose complexities we have investigated.

'We might with pleasure turn oftener to the literary charm, the historical interest, the delicate fantasy with which Hawthorne evokes the New England scene, the New England past, the New England character. It is all so authentic; and if in his devotion to it Hawthorne sacrificed the finer graces of ancient culture and the surer power of established tradition, who shall say what the alternative would have cost in moral questionings—the alternative being, as Henry James was to demonstrate, expatriation? It is perhaps not a general question at all—not a question about

[1] Jacques Barzun: *The House of Intellect*, pp. 247-8.

which the critic has a right to generalise. We can only observe the dilemma, observe that Hawthorne and Henry James avoided it in different ways, and wonder whether a gain in aesthetic values is full compensation for a loss in moral virtue. That there was a third, and a desperate, solution is proved by the case of Poe, who impaled himself on the horns of the dilemma. He could neither accept for good or ill the provincialism he lived among, nor make the necessary effort to escape from it.'[1]

This comment illuminates the disputed region where the American writer had to settle upon his commitments. One questions, however, its assumption that the only alternative to voluntary expatriation was some form of aesthetic impoverishment; and its stopping short of an intimation that Poe's solution —'desperate' certainly—was not, aesthetically, fruitless. As for Poe, it has been shown earlier that the unique formal turn he gave to his apprehensions of extravagances and abnormalities of behaviour would have been impossible without the astonishing collaboration he established between the Romantic lyric impulse, his personal feelings as a spiritual déraciné, and the eighteenth-century tradition in the novel. The issues raised by the expatriate testimony have already been touched on. At this stage we must add to the catalogue of the social deficiencies charged against Americans an immaturity also of moral vision.

Dissatisfaction with an infantile rather than a saintly innocence as the basic American habit of mind goes as far back as Jonathan Edwards, who tried to re-kindle the fiercely emotional adherence to the doctrine of original sin. Edwards represented the laxer Unitarianism as a moral liability; nineteenth-century critics lamented the artistic impotence of a society that had either largely repudiated the idea of innate human depravity, or fancied that by some vast exercise in Civics it could, like bad drains, be eliminated. This critical disquiet is very fully documented[2] but

---

[1] Sir Herbert Read: *Collected Essays in Literary Criticism*, p. 275.

[2] James had his say on the matter. He re-echoed ideas already expressed by Irving, Cooper and Hawthorne. Among the critics, Edward Tyrrell Channing took the gloomy view (in the *North American Review* in 1819); Emerson (in *The Poet*), Lowell (*On a Certain Condescension in Englishmen*) and Bryant (*Poetry in its Relation to our Age and Country*), the more hopeful. See also Henry

the assumptions it attacked are most appositely illustrated, breaking our chronology, from the fiction of Henry James. The clash between the American and the European attitudes—or what he considered them to be—is, of course, James's major theme. A novel in point is *The Ambassadors*. Its 'plot' is so thin as to be almost invisible and may be briefly outlined.

Lambert Strether, an elderly American, comes to Paris at the request of a wealthy friend, Mrs. Newsome, a widow whom he expects to marry. He is to find out why her son is staying in Paris and showing such reluctance to return to the family business. Chad, the son, is suspected of a scandalous liaison with an aristocratic Parisian adventuress. Strether meets the son and finds him enormously improved, in assurance, ease of manner and understanding. Eventually he meets the lady, Madame de Vionnet, and her daughter, both of whom he finds charming. He decides that the attachment is virtuous and himself becomes so enamoured of this way of life that he persuades Chad not to go home, though this must destroy his hopes of marrying Mrs. Newsome. Mrs. Newsome's married daughter, her husband and the husband's sister then come to do the job in which Strether has failed. They refuse to accept Strether's account of the situation and succeed in persuading Chad to return with them. Accidentally meeting Chad and Madame de Vionnet on a riverside excursion, Strether realises that they intend to spend the night together at a country inn. But he does not condemn them. He tries to dissuade Chad from abandoning his lover but Chad is non-committal and we realise that he will desert her. Strether returns to America but not, we gather, to the life he left on coming to Europe.

In the course of the novel James writes of 'the extraordinary process of which his own (Strether's) absurd spirit had been the arena'. The action of the novel, that is, records, as it occurs in Strether, that dual process which D. H. Lawrence called 'the rhythm of American art activity . . .

Adams, 'The American People in 1800' in Saveth, *op. cit.*, pp. 205–6; F. L. Mott: *A History of American Magazines*, Vol. I, pp. 183–190 and 635–7; J. C. McCloskey: *The Campaign of Periodicals after the War of 1812 for National American Literature*, PMLA, 1935;, pp. 262 ff.; and R. Blankenship: *American Literature as an Expression of the National Mind*.

1. A disintegrating and sloughing of the old consciousness.
2. The forming of a new consciousness underneath.'[1]

Lawrence, of course, referred to the forming of a new American consciousness and incidentally neglected the persistence of the old and its effect on the structure of the new. What we have in *The Ambassadors*, however, is the retreat, in Strether, of the new, the American set of values, confronted by the European. Strether's 'old consciousness' is the social values, the manners and the morality of Woollett, his native town, 'our innocent and natural manners', as they are called. Against this he feels the tug of European beauty, European culture, the gracefulness of the society and the setting, glamorous because unknown. We find him responding to it, for instance, among the splendours of Madame de Vionnet's house, which represents the ease, the security, the charm of European life and the tranquilly accepted past which still lives in and gives meaning to it. But Strether's is neither an instantaneous nor a total abandonment of his position. It is a series of delicate responses, adjustments, withdrawals, effected by his experiences on his 'received' ideas, opinions, attitudes. We see them only gradually unfolded, displayed as Strether assimilates them, not fully explained until he has absorbed them and explained then only in so far as Strether understands them himself. There is a number of centrally important scenes, each marking some point at which a group of impressions received earlier coalesces and he undergoes a change of mood or makes a decision' or revaluates his position; when a whole accumulation of feelings suddenly discharges its significance at the level of conscious thought. As James says of Strether, 'He couldn't even formulate to himself his being changed. It had taken place, the process, somewhere deep down.'

One incident particularly relevant here is the arrival of the Pococks in Paris. This episode reveals the flux in Strether's mind at mid-passage between his emancipation and the drab restrictions of Woollett, their power still strong in him. Seeing the Pococks, Strether realises how uneasy in fact he has been that they may have come to declare immediately their disapproval of what he has done—or failed to do; and with what a sense of deprivation,

---

[1] D. H. Lawrence: *Studies in Classic American Literature—Edgar Allan Poe.*

despite his new love for the life of Paris, this would have afflicted him. He notices in Sarah Pocock a resemblance to her mother and 'The woman at home, the woman to whom he was attached, was before him just long enough to give him again the measure of the wretchedness, in fact really of the shame, of having to recognise the formulation, between them, of a "split". He had taken this measure in solitude and meditation; but the catastrophe, as Sarah steamed up, looked for its few seconds unprecedently dreadful— or proved, more exactly, altogether unthinkable; so that his finding something free and unfamiliar to respond to brought with it an instant renewal of his loyalty. He had suddenly sounded the whole depth, had grasped at what he might have lost.' This resurgence of an earlier set of loyalties is temporary. His conversation with Jim Pocock and Jim's obtuse failure to observe or at any rate to comment on the transformation worked in Chad cools Strether's returning warmth of feeling for the American values and judgments. So does Jim's glowing but naïve enthusiasm for Paris, so different in quality from Strether's renaissance—he is 'vulgar', his delight expressed in 'innuendo as vague as a nursery rhyme, yet as aggressive as an elbow in his side'. Jim's approving Chad's remaining in Paris is really valueless, as he has quite obviously dissociated himself from any part in passing judgment on Chad and Strether—'Jim Pocock declined judgment, had hovered quite round the outer edge of discussion and anxiety, leaving all analysis of their question to the ladies alone.' His subjection to what 'was essentially a society of women' checks Strether's renewal of sympathy for the Woollett world and he wonders 'if what Sally wanted her brother to go back for was to become like her husband'. He is further hardened in his new faiths by being made to see that Mrs. Pocock's apparent amiability is merely neutrality, the almost involuntary dissimulation people practise while the true feelings formulate beneath the surface gestures. 'They don't lash about and shake the cage,' Jim says of his wife and mother-in-law, 'and it's at feeding-time that they're quietest. But they always get there.' Yet even at the end of the sequence, Strether is still anxious for some assurance that Mrs. Newsome—and with her the community that claims him—has not rejected him.

American society, then, is presented, *in absentia*, as a matriarchal prison, irredeemably insensitive to art and confined by the nar-rowest sub-Puritan ideas of right and wrong behaviour, the obverse of the 'natural manners' whose 'innocence' is bought at the expense of urbanity and, at a deeper level, of the compassion which comes from understanding of human frailty. Strether's discovery in the delightful Madame de Vionnet of a talent for refined dishonesty and duplicity does not throw him back as, earlier, seeing Pocock's sister had done, into a homesickness for the ready-made *sententia* of Woollett. For the Pococks, her dis-simulation is the final warrant of the propriety of their own con-duct. In the end, Strether escapes both the bland imperception of the Pocock women and accepting Jim's condition 'as an improvement to his present state, as in fact the real redemption of it'. The American failure to recognise 'the abyss of infernal regions', as Conrad terms it, is treated in *The Ambassadors* in a mood of comic pathos, but it has a tragic potential—realised in *The Golden Bowl*. Either way, to erect a drama upon it, to counter-point this cruel innocence, James found it necessary to go outside America.

The American spiritual and social estate, in which James did, like Strether, see much to admire, he deplored for its lack of moral and sociological frictions. We have seen, however, in the earlier pages of this chapter, that conformist though American society may have seemed in its general outlook, there were schisms in abundance—and of the most stimulating kind—not far underneath. As well as the Emerson spirit, doting upon invul-nerable innocence, there was always the Melville spirit to mark the intrusions of evil, like Melville himself drawn beyond the guide-book to the suffering and misery of the Liverpool slums. Political theory ranged from deliberating the mechanics of con-stitutional law (the series of decisions written or influenced by Chief Justice Marshall) to advocacy of anarchic freedom— 'Wherever man goes,' complained Thoreau, 'men will pursue him and paw him with their dirty institutions, and, if they can, constrain him to belong to their desperate odd-fellow society.'[1] James's error was to associate intellectual tensions almost exclu-sively with drawing-rooms; with aesthetic accomplishment and aesthetic sensitivity. Jacques Barzun reminds us that this segrega-

[1] H. D. Thoreau: *Walden—The Village*.

tion encourages a private dilettantism in art, making it a rather precious status-symbol, a cult 'persuaded that all the works of man's mind except art are vulgar frauds: law, the state, machinery, the edifice of trade are worthless, they despise their own existence, because it fails in loveliness when compared with the meanest *objet d'art*'.[1] Law, the state and the others were precisely the works and obligations of intellect which consumed the energies of the American *élite*. The American rich had nothing comparable, for example, to the tradition of the European *salon* and of aristocratic patronage of the arts, intermittent though this was and undertaken often, as Johnson testified, for the most perverse and tangential reasons. It was this myth which captured James's imagination with a vision of rarified good taste and the flowering of delicate sensibilities. His obsession with technique was a tribute to the *consciousness* of aims and methods, the highly articulate sophistication he found in the European literary tradition. Together with the myth, it blinded him to the tenuity of much of the substance from which, with endless resource, he spun the intricate web of his style. The exile to Europe was not an unmixed benefit.

Cooper extracted his themes from the life around him—law, the community, the individual, in their American federation. Though withdrawn both in space and time, his novels bear directly on the conflicts of the Jacksonian era. Poe is a different case, but his work too has its social co-ordinates. Where Brisbane observed 'distrust, isolation, separation', Poe lived and re-created them. He is the voice of Manicheism, not only acknowledging but positively accepting evil as the active principle of life. He could neither agree with the benign immanence of Concord nor, with Cooper, hope to contain evil by social instruments. The disintegration of society, of the centre of authority, precedes the disintegration of the individual, neither of them to any creative fulfilment. The fulfilment was destruction itself. As was remarked in Chapter Two, Poe dealt in society reduced to its elements. In the adventures of his characters he dramatised, among other things, what he saw as the essential relationship between society and the individual, amplifying the emerging definitions, even though his was not, like Cooper's, an analysis of immediately political

[1] Barzun: *op. cit.*, p. 18.

relevance. We shall examine now the appearance of these themes, against the background that has been outlined, in the work of those other two writers who projected their environment into the forms of the novel, Hawthorne and Melville.

II

Having read *The House of the Seven Gables*, Melville in a letter commented on 'a certain tragic phase of humanity which, in our opinion, was never more powerfully embodied than by Hawthorne. We mean the tragedies of human thought in its own unbiassed native and profounder workings. We think that into no recorded mind has the intense feeling of the visible truth ever entered more deeply than into this man's. By visible truth we mean the apprehension of the absolute condition of present things'.[1] The key phrase here is 'the apprehension of the absolute condition of present things'. Its simplest reference is to the universality of the greatest artistic statements. The writer elicits from his rendering of a particular scene, character, emotion, experience—his inventive use of any of his material—a truth, an insight, of significance to his society as a whole, or even more generally. This generalisation is inherent in whatever his particular subject may be, though of a kind indistinguishable in the ordinary run of things, apprehended, if at all, vaguely and inarticulately. It arises properly from the immediate circumstance yet is valid beyond any one time or place or person. This remarkable extraction from the very particular, the very concrete, of the very catholic and abstract gives art its distinction and no doubt this is part of what Melville had in mind. He had, however, been early introduced, perhaps through his mother's Calvinism, to the emblematic Nature of the Puritans, the world of visible things seen as a covert of ulterior meanings. This too is an aspect of the 'apprehension' with which he credits Hawthorne. Taking this with the other application, it becomes clear that Melville was thinking of symbolic vision, the power to see, in the everyday commerce of events, images paraphrasing eternal *motifs* in the confused traffic between fallen man and his inscrutable God. At their most typical, these perceptions aren't concerned with arguable opinions. They are sudden and anguished communica-

[1] Letter to Hawthorne, 1851.

tions of spiritual loss and aspiration, of the paradoxical union of animal and angel in the human frame. They may lead to a catharsis—Melville's finally did—but their primary effect is to disturb the false peace of complacent acceptance or of the inadequate materialist simplifications. Melville's 'absolute condition' tends to be found further and further beyond familiar appearances and even beyond familiar interpretations of their meaning.

Like Poe, Melville rejected the familiar. Unlike him, he did not rest in the act of recantation. It might be said that in American fiction Poe was the first to lay open the diabolic, losing himself in the exploration of it. His discoveries greatly influenced the form and technique of Melville's novels: notably, in the practice of first compiling a solidly circumstanced reality, then attenuating it to symbol; and in the integration of lyric subjectivity with impersonal narrative of events and plain description of customs, manners, settings. At the nadir of Melville's despair, his metaphysic too had much the same desolation as Poe's, but Melville, though little less vulnerable, was able to return with the knowledge he had acquired in the same obscure regions of evil, suffering and failure. Poe's sense of guilt and damnation, his acquaintanceship with the anatomy of failure, were exercised in a manner almost clinical and, morally, incurious. Melville—and Hawthorne —extended the range of these capacities to the antecedent of motive, the aftergrowth of judgment and the varied patterns of divine, social and private retribution.

Their preoccupations can be, and regularly are, explained as projections of psychic confusions, weaknesses and maladjustments. As with Poe, these psychoanalytical accounts of Melville's and Hawthorne's art direct us to the deeply personal sources of their themes and attitudes and hence help to define them.[1] But

[1] Significant episodes in Melville's life were the catastrophic decline in his family's wealth and position; the dominance of his Calvinist mother; the death in 1831, of his father, who had gone mad. To these and related happenings is traced this obsession with the father-symbol and the perpetual longing for some re-incarnation of it—in *Redburn*, *Pierre*, and in *Moby Dick* the *Rachel's* tale of the lost child, abandoned by Ahab, for instance. The series of effeminately handsome youths, his passive adventures with the native women in *Typee*, the incest theme of *Pierre*, suggest an inverted and morbid sexual feeling. In seeking harmony and a truce with the harsh God of Calvinism, so the argument runs, Melville was writing out these neurotic pressures within him.

what to the psychiatrist may appear a maladjustment to be corrected, may by other values be accounted a heightened awareness, an exalted spiritual discernment of humanity's 'tragic phase', able through the medium of art to enter into the life of the community, because it is not merely a record of separateness and wholly private disintegration. 'O Nature and O soul of man!' Melville wrote in *Moby Dick*, 'how far beyond all utterance are your linked analogies! not the smallest atom stirs or lives on matter but has its cunning duplicate in mind.' Not, however, the soothing analogies of Emerson. 'For,' Melville continues elsewhere, 'as this appalling ocean surrounds the verdant land, so in the soul of man there lies one insular Tahiti, full of peace and joy, but encompassed by all the horrors of the half-known life.' And again: 'Consider the subtleness of the sea; how its most dreaded creatures glide under water, unapparent for the most part, and treacherously hidden beneath the loveliest tints of azure.' Torment and the tranquilising possibility of peace; evil and the good which it invests; surface affability and concealed ruthlessness. Melville drew these themes from conflicts inherent in his own personality but they found an oddly precise counterpart not only in Nature but in 'the horrors of the half-known life' of his society.

It was a society not unlike that of Thackeray's Osborne, who observed of Mr. Sedley that 'he was a better man than I was, this day twenty years—a better man, I should say, by ten thousand· pound'. Mark Twain ironically inverted the notion of meritorious affluence when he measured his progress by the change from having nothing to owing thousands. His witticism implies, perspicaciously, the illusoriness of these fiscal appraisements. Many of the operations of credit finance and real estate development, as Martin Chuzzlewit found, took place in a wonderland of nightmare fantasy. Credulity and self-deception combined to sustain the illusions which the land hawkers promoted. On the *Fidèle* of Melville's *The Confidence Man* 'reigned the dashing and all-fusing spirit of the West . . . in one cosmopolitan and confident tide'. On its route lay the 'swampy and squalid domain' of Cairo. The circumstances were ripe for exploitation. In the early nineteenth century, Schlesinger tells us, 'Reciprocal confidence was necessarily the keynote of a system so much dominated by personal relations. Business and private affairs were governed by much the same ethical code'. The decline was rapid. 'In 1840 Amos Kendal urged the circulation of the belief that "there is but one code of morals for private and public affairs". His very concern was a confession that two codes existed'.[1] The private code inevitably succumbed to the lures of remunerative speculation in non-existent properties. The double standard was securely established and the integrality of the individual that much more dislocated.

In this disintegration Melville could see reflected the disintegrative forces within himself. Both outer and inner worlds drew him urgently to the enigma of identity, of finding the authentic and irreducible *self*. Their society had a catalytic effect on the innately scissile personalities of Melville and Hawthorne. That there were deep-seated ruptures within was manifested in quite explicit ways. Hawthorne spent the years between 1825 and 1837 in Salem, depressed and bitter at the lack of public recognition, having himself diminished the likelihood of such acknowledgment by publishing anonymously. Though never a fanatic aspirant to reputation, he knew some of the appetite of the mysterious stranger in *The Ambitious Guest*. In this story, ambitious fancies blossom in the comfortable warmth of a mountain cottage, until the winter storm destroys it, with its inhabitants and their vain hopes and dreams, almost in retribution. Hawthorne alternatively hankered after celebrity and withdrew from its hazards. The hearty Melville described by N. P. Willis in the *New York Home Journal*—'with his cigar and his Spanish eyes, *talks* "Typee" and "Omoo"'—sheltered the brooding outcast who chose 'the lot of the solitary, accursed writer . . . without a fire, bundled up in a freezing cold room'.[2]

Melville's absorption in the ambiguities of identity is not surprising in a country which, riven by political, moral and psychic dilemmas, was seeking its identity too. The Puritans knew theirs. The generations of the Revolutionary years had a decisive understanding of the issues in what was still a clearly articulated political debate. Cooper retained a share in that decisiveness, but even in him, by far the most composed intellectually of these novelists,

[1] Schlesinger: *op. cit.*, pp. 334–5.

[2] Jean Jacques Mayoux: *Melville* (Grove Press), pp. 48–49.

there was room for misgivings. But these were fairly well controlled and did not call for the elliptical circuits of communication which Melville's profounder disquietude induced. Yet even Melville, when many of the hopes of Cooper's early years had languished, held on to the feeling that humanity was not inescapably circumscribed within the lower regions. Like the *Pequod*, it was subject to 'two antagonistic influences . . . one to mount direct to heaven, the other to drive yawingly to some horizontal goal'. Melville's perception of the dual affiliation repaired his Manicheistic disposition, gave reality and purpose to the idea of human defiance and raised his work from Poe's *accidie* to tragic dignity. With uncommon discernment, Melville saw through the adventitious and purely contemporary forms of his society's ethical transactions to their 'absolute condition'. This he located in the discontinuity of individual identity, the amorphous microcosm which, establishing no solid core of being within itself, could not define its relationship to the macrocosm. These perennial themes found vigorous expression in Melville's America and a meaningful interpretation in his work.

III

'It is with fiction,' Melville wrote in *The Confidence Man*, 'as with religion: it should present another world, and yet one to which we feel the tie.' The object of all Melville's novels was, through the fictional world, to elucidate the mysterious correspondences between the seen and the unseen that stirs, half-recognised, within it. *White-Jacket* is the novel in which he was most forthrightly concerned with ideas of man in society. Its purpose was propagandist, naval reform, and its basis, of course, autobiographical, his experiences aboard the frigate *United States*, which in the novel becomes the ironically heroic *Neversink*. In this particular topic Melville localised the ideas disseminated, in their manifold forms, throughout all the social activities on which politics impinged. His pronouncements in *White-Jacket*, published when he was thirty-one, are democratic and reformist. The novel proposes a quite categorical opposition between the ideals of charity, tolerance, benevolence and the appalling facts of the brutality and injustice of naval life: hopefully, on the whole.

Melville is not here persuaded that barbarity is a necessary part of existence. Flogging can be proscribed, the savage discipline relaxed. So Melville argues, accumulating on his side passion and evidence both.

Yet there is a contradictory strain. At one moment Melville rejoices in life and in humanity and its prospects; at another he discloses some frightful insight into human depravity. The two strains appear at different levels, the political included. The seamen for whom he urges the right to advancement he describes also as a 'rabble rout', and adds, in Chapter 35, that English officers are less disliked by their crews than American officers by theirs, because 'many of them, from their station in life, have been more accustomed to social command . . . a coarse, vulgar man, who happens to rise to high naval rank by the exhibition of talents not incompatible with vulgarity, inevitably proves a tyrant to his crew'. The only attempt Melville makes to reconcile these divergent estimates of the ordinary seamen is in his rather bogus distinction between 'the Public' and 'the People'—'let us hate the one and cleave to the other'. While in principle Melville was a man of the people, his dealings with them were as uncomfortable as Cooper's. His family background was genteel, his novels either unsuccessful or esteemed for the wrong reasons. All his heroes are marked out from and persecuted by the crowd, as the narrator's white jacket in this novel first sets him apart as freakish, then becomes the emblem of both his and the crew's ill luck. It is true that Melville was at this time surer than he was ever to be again of the popular faiths. 'We Americans,' says White-Jacket, 'are driven to a rejection of the maxims of the past . . . we Americans are the peculiar, chosen people—the Israel of our time . . . In our youth is our strength; in our inexperience, our wisdom'. What he described, to Hawthorne, as his 'ontological heroics' inform the Emersonian sentiment that, 'Each mortal casts his vote for whom he will to rule the worlds; I have a voice that helps to shape eternity; and my volitions stir the orbits of the furthest suns'. *White-Jacket* was written quickly. Its purpose was the practical one of ameliorating conditions whose recollected horror obscured everything else in Melville's mind. Though, for these reasons, not yet plaguing him with the anguish of full enlightenment, the irresoluteness is there.

This intellectual irresolution compromises the style, which in Melville's early books is naturally disposed to eruptions of facetiousness and, at times, outright fatuity. The opening is typical of Melville—the same abrupt, lively entrance we have in *Typee* and *Moby Dick*, hinting at excitements to come. But arresting though this is, the rollicking jocularity, the somewhat vacuous good humour, is sadly out of keeping with the narrator's character as it gradually appears and with the dreadful experiences he is to unfold. The long stretches of documentary exposition, with case histories and quotations from the authorities, enlarge the indictment but conflict with the claustrophobic intensity of the shipboard scenes. At this stage, Melville had not realised that the particular instance, properly handled, has a spontaneous generalising power. Many of the episodes in *White-Jacket* do have this power. It is a novel of parts so tremendously impressive that they make the foregoing criticisms seem extremely presumptuous. A case in point is the grim chapters describing the unnecessary amputation, without anaesthetics, in which the agony of Melville's shipmate becomes the gruesome entertainment of the psychotic ship's doctor, who delays the operation until his patient is fully conscious. In this Melville said all that was necessary of the inhumanity with which the seamen were treated, moving to the beautifully elegiac simplicity of the final paragraph. 'The following evening the mess-mates of the top-man rowed his remains ashore, and buried them in the ever-vernal Protestant cemetery, hard by the Beach of the Flamingoes, in plain sight from the bay.'

Cuticle, the surgeon, is a generic type in Melville's study of the varieties of guilt. He is the pseudo-healer who destroys life. In one of his morbid collections of anatomical freaks Melville sees the sign of 'some sin under which the sinner sank in sinless woe'. But Cuticle's element is sterility, a futile obsession with the means, not the meaning, of death. The *Neversink*'s Captain Claret, free of 'any personal, organic hard-heartedness', is a less cryptic figure, a plain representation of Shakespeare's 'man, proud man, dressed in a little brief authority'. His brutalities are the stupid man's rigorous applications of a code of discipline arbitrary in itself, of which Melville says that 'at the Last Day, man-of-war's men will not be judged by the Articles of War, nor by the *United States Statutes at Large*, but by immutable laws, ineffably beyond the comprehension of the Honourable Board of Commodores and Navy Commissioners'. Finally Bland, the ship's master-at-arms, is unalloyed evil personified, without either Cuticle's perverse satisfaction or Claret's incomprehension. 'Under all his deftly-donned disguises,' Melville writes, '. . . he was an organic and irreclaimable scoundrel, who did wicked deeds as the cattle browse the herbage, because wicked deeds seemed the legitimate operations of his whole infernal organisation.' Bland is the heart of the matter. He is evil by his very existence, not simply by deeds alone, which, as we are made to feel of Claret and Cuticle, reformed conditions may restrain. With this enigma Melville was not yet ready to deal and in the end not much is made of Bland. In *Billy Budd* he is reincarnated in the person of Claggart.

Towards the end of the book the narrator himself clashes with these overlords. Though he remains shadowy, there is more to him than we see on his first appearance. Like Melville, he is an Ishmael, derided and mistrusted by his fellows. Only at the end does he break through his isolation when, having barely saved himself from drowning—'as if I were ripping open myself'—he cuts off his white jacket. He resists the near-death of his stupefying rush into the sea, but not before we have seen into involuted depths of being which submit to the descent. The significance of the cumbersome jacket as an *alter ego* has been much discussed. Beyond noting that this is Melville's intention, there is not much to be said of it. The correspondence is a loose one and on only two occasions do we find the slide areas of the narrator's personality—the jacket's 'unseen recesses'—collapsing directly into the action: when he almost drowns, and when he rebels against the captain, another, but a different, will to death. Unjustly sentenced to a flogging, White-Jacket entertains the idea of rushing the captain and bearing him overboard in a self-destructive murder. With incredulous fascination he finds in his soul the urge to kill himself rather than be humiliated. In this incident lies a hint of the cleansing, sacrificial death: 'My blood seemed clotting in my veins; I felt icy cold at the tips of my fingers, and a dimness was before my eyes. But through that dimness the boatswain's mate, scourge in hand, loomed like a giant, and Captain Claret, and the blue sea seen through the opening at the gangway, showed with an awful vividness. I cannot analyse my heart, though it then stood still within me . . . Locking souls with him, I meant to drag Captain Claret from this earthly tribunal of his to that of Jehovah and let him decide between us.' Here its origin is impure—'no word, no blow, no scourge of Captain Claret could cut me deep enough for that.' Later he was to refine it and discover its true function, the real adversary Bland, a conflict which this novel evades.

As in the character of White-Jacket there is only a spasmodic junction of parts, so in the book itself. Melville was assimilating ideas, sensations, formulating basic attitudes, assembling from his experience, and inventing, those incidents which magically extend into the retiring perspectives of spiritual meaning. *White-Jacket* attempts to epitomise the issues as a pattern of unconditional antagonisms: the despotic laws of man against the compassion of Christ; death against life; evil, in all its forms, against a transcendent good, visible in man; democratic reform against reactionary *laisser-faire*. All the elements are there, but without the cross-currents and interpenetrations which, as Melville was to see, transgress these conventional perimeters. *Moby Dick* makes a great advance, suddenly attained, in both technical accomplishment and intellectual strength. Little can be said of it that has not been said before. Its direct relevance to the present study is in any case limited, but it cannot be entirely omitted from any consideration of Melville. As any commentary on Melville must insist, it is a magnificent portrayal of an actual whaling voyage, in its minutest details. We are rarely allowed to forget what it is like to be aboard a whaler, how the days pass, how the sea registers its fluctuating moods on the life of the ship, what jobs are to be done and who does them. The final sequence, describing the attack on Moby Dick, is flawless narrative. What lies beneath these features we must now, briefly, more closely consider.

In *Moby Dick* man expends his highest powers in fulfilment of a tragic fate. Father Mapple's sermon in the Whaleman's Chapel preaches the lesson, 'Delight is to him—a far, upward, and inward, delight—who against the proud gods and commodores of this earth, ever stands forth his own inexorable self.' Ahab pursuing the white whale which has mutilated him is impelled by this heroic obduracy. Writing in 1942, W. E. Sedgwick found it necessary to rebut the view of 'almost all the critics of *Moby Dick*,

that Melville intended (the white whale) to represent evil' and
Ahab indomitable human energy.[1] The correction was called for,
but since then, perhaps too little has been made of Ahab's positive
grandeur. We are told that he is a 'man of superior natural force,
with a globular brain and a ponderous heart . . . led to think un-
traditionally and independently; receiving all nature's sweet or
savage impressions fresh from her own virgin voluntary and
confiding breast, and thereby briefly, but with some help from accidental advantages, to learn a bold and nervous lofty language—
that man makes one in a whole nation's census—a mighty pageant
creature formed for noble tragedies'. Melville stresses the nobility
because it is indispensable to the tragedy, but adds, 'all men
tragically great are made so through a certain morbidness . . . all
mortal greatness is but disease.' The morbidness in Ahab is his
sterile burning for revenge. He is both the heroic leader and the
maimed killer. In seeking to destroy Moby Dick he seeks also to
destroy himself. Starbuck cries to him, 'Moby Dick seeks thee
not,' and indeed, during the chase, the white whale never takes
the initiative in attack. But Ahab's suicidal urge drives him on.
In the end he kills not only himself but, with one exception, his
crew: 'The cease of majesty dies not alone. . . .'

There is a coincidence of meaning between Ahab and the white
whale. 'I leave a white and turbid wake,' says Ahab, and the
whale is described as 'leaving a milky-white wake of creamy
foam'. Deviously, it leads Ahab on:

'It was while gliding through these latter waters that one serene
and moonlight night, when all the waves rolled by like scrolls of
silver; and, by their soft, suffusing seethings, made what seemed
a silvery silence, not a solitude; on such a silent night a silvery
jet was seen far in advance of the white bubbles at the bow . . .
And so it served us night after night, till no one heeded it but
to wonder at it. Mysteriously jetted into the clear moonlight, or
starlight, as the case might be; disappearing again for one whole
day, or two days, or three; and somehow seeming at every distinct repetition to be advancing still further in our van, this
solitary jet seemed for ever alluring us on.'

[1] W. E. Sedgwick: *Herman Melville: The Tragedy of Mind*, p. III. More
recent criticism has added very little to this fine interpretation of Melville's
thought. It is particularly good on the Crucifixion theme in *Billy Budd*.

Moby Dick belongs to 'the strong, troubled, and murderous thinking of the masculine sea'. Yet it is also sanctified, God-like, a symbol of power and fruitfulness. Its sanctity is clearly indicated in the chapter on the whale's whiteness: 'even in the higher mysteries of the most august religions it has been made the symbol of the divine spotlessness and power.' The dual nature of Moby Dick is that of the God to be read in him, who is worshipped through comminatory psalms as well as hymns of thankfulness. In the *Pequod*'s encounter with the *Jereboam* we meet Gabriel, for whom Moby Dick *is* God, the vengeful and frightening God of the Old Testament. 'And of all these things,' as Melville writes, 'the Albino whale was the symbol. Wonder ye then at the fiery hunt?' To the symbolism of Ahab and Moby Dick we can attach no one limiting meaning. Its complexity and strength grow and acquire new associations as the book proceeds. It is illuminated by Ahab's soliloquies; by his attitude to the various members of the crew and by theirs to him. The interpolated stories of the ships the *Pequod* meets have each a different revaluation of the whale. Seemingly passing remarks and incidents insinuate a comment on the two main symbols. There is an obvious ulterior significance, for instance, in Ahab's saying, on going down to his cabin in the *Pequod*, 'It feels like going down into one's tomb,' and in the fact that the coffin which Queequeg has made for himself, when he thinks he is going to die, becomes the life-buoy on which Ishmael escapes drowning at the end; that Tashtego's rescue from inside the dead whale is described in metaphors of birth. The cumulative suggestion is the Christian paradox that through death may come life. The multiple destruction of the final chase is not wholly negative. Ishmael is picked up by 'the devious-cruising *Rachel*, that in her retracing search after her missing children, only found another orphan'. With him emerges his new insight, born of his turbulent voyage and embodied in the story of it which he has narrated.

Ishmael's regeneration, however, is bought at a terrible cost and is a quite adventitious product of Ahab's obsession. Ahab has no such creative aim in his dedication to revenge 'on a dumb brute', as Starbuck puts it, 'that simply smote thee from blindest instinct'. His obsession is evil, a monstrous defiance of everything extraneous to himself, futilely heroic: ' . . . to chase that white whale on both sides of land, and over all sides of earth, till he spouts black blood and rolls fin out . . . Talk not to me of blasphemy, man; I'd strike the sun if it insulted me . . . who's over me?' Ahab is strength misdirected. He sees more deeply than Starbuck—Moby Dick is not merely 'a dumb creature'—that the world is a spiritual one, that he is part of a moral universe. But what he sees is warped by his fatal 'morbidness'. His only alternative to asserting his own distorted vision is inexpiable oblivion, indifferently sacrificing his associates with himself. As we noticed with *The Narrative of Arthur Gordon Pym*, Pym, unlike Coleridge's mariner, did not return. Nor does Ahab. In the moral scheme of the book, Ishmael is the beneficiary. Like Lear, Ahab destroys himself; unlike Lear, he does not attain self-enlightenment. It is no reflection on *Moby Dick* as a work of art to say that, superbly comprehensive study of the human condition though it is, it does not show us a tragic hero not only enduring a tragic fate but recognising in what the tragedy consists.

Some six years after the publication of *Moby Dick* Melville wrote *The Confidence Man*, a book still generally underestimated and misunderstood. Such praise as it gets is apologetic and hedged with unmerited reservations. It is very different, of course, from Melville's other novels. It lacks *Moby Dick's* control of a diversified rhetoric; its astonishing fertility of language and its use of Melville's expert knowledge of whaling, which provides the objective reality from which the symbols grow. That is, there is less of the detailed realism, the vivid sense of place, little of the strongly individualised characterisation and none of the exciting action, all of which so enliven *Moby Dick*. *The Confidence Man*, infinitely more austere, is set on a Mississippi steamer and consists largely of conversations. It begins on the St. Louis waterfront with a deaf-mute joining the horde of passengers boarding 'the favourite steamer, *Fidèle*, on the point of starting for New Orleans'. They are reading 'a placard . . . offering a reward for the capture of a mysterious impostor'. The deaf-mute writes on a slate which he carries a series of biblical texts, all commending charity: *Charity believeth all things; Charity never faileth*. Molested by the crowd, he eventually goes to sleep on the forecastle.

Shortly after the voyage has begun, the passengers crowd round a negro cripple, disputing his genuineness. A bitter one-legged man has aroused their suspicions—'He's some white operator, be-twisted and painted up for a decoy.' Asked if anyone can speak on his behalf, the negro replies:

'Oh yes, oh yes, dar is aboard here a werry nice, good ge'mman wid a weed, and a ge'mman in a grey coat and white tie, what knows all about me; and a ge'mman wid a big book, too; and a yarb doctor; and a ge'mman in a yaller west; and a ge'mman as is a sodger; and ever so many good, kind, honest ge'mman more aboard what knows me and will speak for me . . .'

In the course of the novel all these people, except the 'ge'mman in a yaller coat' and the 'ge'mman as is a sodjer', appear on the *Fidèle*. Quite soon we realise, although Melville never says so, that the fugitive impostor is playing all these roles and that he was also the deaf-mute and the negro cripple. The novel recounts his attempts to cozen the passengers he meets in his various guises. In all of them he protests the need for unqualified reciprocity of trust and charity.

Jean Jacques Mayoux remarks that 'in no other book does Melville succeed so well with such summary indications at giving an impression of the uproar of a crowd: one thinks of Jonson's *Bartholemew Fair*'. There is, as we shall see, a more important borrowing from Jonson, but the comment makes a valid point. Melville has not entirely forsaken the sensuous realism of *Moby Dick*. He constitutes his heterogeneous mob of passengers with· an exact and discerning eye:

'. . . there is no lack of variety. Natives of all sorts, and foreigners; men of business and men of pleasure; parlour men and back-woodsmen, farm-hunters; heiress-hunters, gold hunters, buffalo-hunters, bee-hunters, happiness-hunters, truth-hunters, and still keener hunters after all these hunters. Fine ladies in slippers and moccasined squaws . . . Santa Fé traders in striped blankets, and Broadway bucks in cravats of cloth of gold . . . Quakers in full drab, and United States soldiers in full regimentals . . . hard-shell Baptists and clay-eaters; grinning negroes, and Sioux chiefs solemn as high-priests.'

But despite its apparently firm physical presence—it 'jostles', 'flattened down (the deaf-mute's) fleecy hat', 'thrust him aside', 'jeers . . . pushes . . . punches'—the crowd is mysteriously deli-quescent, volatile. It is 'like Rio Janeiro fountain, fed from the Coevarde mountains, which is overflowing with strange waters, but never with the same strange particles in every part'. It sub-mits 'to that natural law which ordains dissolution equally to the mass, as in time to the member', and in Chapter IV has 'melted away'.

The *Fidèle* shares this capriciousness. Its outlines blur and reform, take on fleeting resemblances and assume new shapes. They multiply into the bewildering extensions of, 'Fine pro-menades, domed saloons, long galleries, sunny balconies, con-fidential passages, bridal chambers, state-rooms plenty as pigeon-holes, and out-of-the-way retreats like secret drawers in an escritoire . . .' Later they close into clandestine dimness. When the confidence man goes beneath deck, 'the whole place is dim and dusky . . . haggardly lit here and there by narrow, capricious skylights'. Towards the end, the light from a single lamp 'on all sides went rippling off with ever-diminishing distinctness'. The *Fidèle* is 'the daedal boat' which 'speeds . . . as a dream'. It is interesting to watch Melville progress through his different methods; the *Neversink*, a straightforward and rather lumbering allegory ('the world on a man-of-war'); the *Pequod*, fully existing at various levels of reality; and now the *Fidèle*, where Melville almost at the outset eliminates the world of reliable appearances and solid surfaces, taking us straight into a milieu of visionary imprecision. It is an appropriate setting for the novel's theme of mutability.

As the confidence man moves through his successive imper-sonations, we feel a growing insecurity; where, in these muta-tions, is the real human being? on what, in a world so full of dissimulation, can we finally depend? even on our certain aware-ness of self? The confidence man asks the merchant with whom he pretends an earlier acquaintance, 'Who knows, my dear sir, but for a time you may have taken yourself for somebody else? Stranger things have happened.' The cynical philosopher, arguing against the confidence man's philosophy of trust, warns him, 'however indulgent and right-minded I may seem to you now, that is no guarantee for the future. And into the power of that uncertain personality which, through the mutability of my humanity, I may hereafter become, should not common sense dissuade you, my dear Frank, from putting yourself?' The indeterminateness of motive and identity is further heightened by the neutrality of Melville's reporting. When, in Chapter V, he says of 'the man with the weed's' melancholy that, as compared with his earlier forced constraint in response to a generous gift, he is thus 'giving warmly loose to his genuine heart', that is not true, any more than that he is, as Melville says, 'unmindful of another pensive figure near', whose attention his expressions of grief are in fact designed to catch. In all this, Melville is going far beneath the deceptions of simple trickery, undertaken for gain. As the one-legged man pointedly demands, 'How much money did the devil make by gulling Eve?' The point of the novel is not the very limited one of satirising the sharp practices of American business. It is on this point that there is some misunderstanding. *The Confidence Man* is read as an unrelievedly cynical picture of a world populated only by rogues and their dupes, the image of a heartless and immoral capitalist society. Many of the confidence man's swindles are commercial, as when he pushes false shares. There is a sequence in which he talks at length with another trickster who sets out to cheat him by the crude method of making him drunk and winning his trust by a display of affability. And of course he fails: in a world of treachery condoned by as well as outside the law, guile can be defeated only by superior craft. But this is only Melville's starting-point. Again, he is after the 'absolute condition'.

In his introduction to the most recent English edition of the novel,[1] Roy Fuller says of the dupes that they 'may either be unpleasant characters . . . or pleasant . . . but really their unpleasantness or pleasantness is irrelevant: they are all duped, and their duping (since it shows them either as foolish or anxious about money) involves, in the scheme of the novel, their adverse judgment. Those whom the rogues cannot dupe—and here the vicious moral circle becomes fully apparent—are without exception unpleasant characters . . . . It is as though in *Gulliver's Travels* Swift had left out Gulliver'. It is true that there is no single character to represent Melville's conception of the reasonable man, but this reminds us not so much of *Gulliver's Travels* without

[1] Lehmann, 1948.

Gulliver as of Ben Jonson's comedies, where there is usually a similar vacuum. Despite this, Jonson does convey positively enough the standards by which his mountebanks are to be judged. We can see how he does this in *Volpone*, a play whose moral atmosphere is very like that of *The Confidence Man*.

Two of the characters in *Volpone*, Bonario and Celia, do seem to stand aside from the general corruption, but they are too pallid and ineffectual to redeem the energetic villainy of Volpone and the rest. Bonario, in any case, is a dubious representative of virtue. It is avarice which sends him to spy on his father when he is told by Mosca that Corbaccio intends to disinherit him. In the scene immediately before Mosca reveals this, we have heard his jaunty characterisation of the parasite. It might serve as an epigraph to *The Confidence Man*:

> *I feare, I shall begin to grow in love*
> *With my dear self, and my most prosp'rous parts,*
> *They do so spring, and burgeon: I can feele*
> *A whimsey i' my blood: (I know not how)*
> *Successe hath made me wanton. I could skip*
> *Out of my skin, now, like a subtill snake,*
> *I am so limber. O! Your Parasite*
> *Is a most precious thing, dropt from above,*
> *Not bred 'mong'st clods, and clot-poules, here on earth . . .*
> *I mean not those, that have your bare towne-arte,*
> *To know, who's fit to feede 'hem. . . .*
> *But your fine, elegant rascall, that can rise*
> *And stoope (almost together) like an arrow;*
> *Shoot through the aire, as nimbly as a starre;*
> *Turne short, as doth a swallow; and be here,*
> *And there, and here, and yonder, all at once;*
> *Present to any humour, all occasion:*
> *And change a visor, swifter, then a thought!*
> *This is the creature, had the art borne with him;*
> *Toiles not to learne it, but doth practise it*
> *Out of most excellent nature . . .*

With this effusion of agile self-explanation still in its ears, the audience hears Mosca preface his disclosures to Bonario with the following protest:

> *. . . but that I have done*
> *Base offices, in rending friends asunder,*
> *Dividing families, betraying counsells,*
> *Whispering false lyes, or mining men with praises,*
> *Train'd their credulitie with perjuries,*
> *Corrupted chastitie, or am in love*
> *With mine own tender ease, but would not rather*
> *Prove the most rugged, and laborious course,*
> *That might redeeme my present estimation;*
> *Let me here perish, in all hope of goodnesse.*

The words from 'I have done' to 'tender ease' provide, of course, an exact description of what Mosca does, contained within denial of their truth. In his self-assurance, Mosca deliberately couches his disclaimer in this form: claiming the conventional virtues he contrives also to indicate his real nature—'rise/And stoope (almost together) like an arrow'. Bonario accepts the speech at its face value—'This cannot be a personated passion.' He has heard but not recognised the truth which its words express. The audience, with both of Mosca's speeches together in its mind, sees the truth 'skip out of the skin' of the lie. Here and elsewhere Jonson uses this satiric irony, as we might call it, this significant convergence of truth and lie, reality and appearance, to unriddle the secret moral anarchy of such machinations. He does not condemn them through the court which finally sentences Mosca, for it too is corrupt—'A fit match for my daughter,' one of the judges calls him when he thinks that Mosca is Volpone's heir. The reiterated emphasis on chaos is itself a judgment and anticipates the inescapable dénouement, in which Mosca's ingenious duplicities slip beyond even his control and bring about his downfall. The author, that is, communicates his viewpoint not in any form of direct statement but through the inferences he forces us to draw by disposing his material into ironic conjunctions, as Jonson does here.

In *White-Jacket* Melville mentions *Volpone* as a play he has read and admired. Certainly he transferred to *The Confidence Man* its method of obliquely expressed 'commitment' to an ethical code. We must extract Melville's meaning from the interplay of the various professions of belief he sets before us. One of the novel's satirical points is that only the confidence man advocates that trust and charity which in a better world would be universally employed. To take this simply as Melville's expression of spleen with a world not so constituted is superficial. The confidence man invokes a world without evil and plays on humanity's inclination to think the best of itself. What Melville, in *Billy Budd*, calls the 'doctrine of man's fall (a doctrine now popularly ignored)' finds no place in the credulous ethic the confidence man maintains. For that reason it is as heretical as the 'disciple's' icy egotism and we are not to take his professions merely as an insincere statement of standards valid in themselves. On a number of occasions, Melville allows us to estimate their real validity. In conversation with his fellow-trickster, the confidence man suddenly springs on him a request for money, which is violently refused, whereupon the confidence man discloses that he has money in plenty. His companion hastily assures him, 'I relish a good joke . . . Of course, I humoured the thing; and, on my side, put on all the cruel airs you would have me.' Urbanely, the confidence man accepts the explanation and goes on to tell the story of Charlemont, a popular and successful St. Louis merchant who 'in a day . . . turned from affable to morose', shunning acquaintances and his closest friends. Failing in business shortly afterwards, he left St. Louis. Some years later, prosperous again, he reappeared and took up his old life. His friends continued to wonder what had caused the change in him before his bankruptcy. At last one of them asked him and Charlemont replied:

'If ever, in days to come, you shall see ruin at hand, and, thinking you understand mankind, shall tremble for your friendships, and tremble for your pride; and, partly through love for the one and fear for the other, shall resolve to be beforehand with the world, and save it from a sin by prospectively taking that sin to yourself, then will you do as one I now dream of once did, and like him will you suffer . . .'

With feigned amazement the confidence man cavils at Charlemont's reasoning and asks his companion 'whether such a fore-reaching motive as Charlemont hinted he had acted on in his change—whether such a motive, I say, were a sort of one at all justified by the nature of human society? Would you, for one, turn the cold shoulder to a friend—a convivial one, say, whose pennilessness should be suddenly revealed to you?' But the sequence of events has already, as the confidence man only pretends not to realise, justified Charlemont's melancholy resignation to the reality of sin and the need for atonement.

The confidence man tells another of his stories to a merchant, in his role as the man with the weed. It concerns his wife, Goneril, selfish and cruel, wantonly denying him affection and distressing him by her tender gestures to other men. Hearing that she plans to have him committed as a lunatic, he flees, and has become 'an innocent outcast wandering forlorn in the great valley of the Mississippi, with a weed on his hat for the loss of his Goneril'. The merchant later meets the confidence man in yet another guise and, still deeply moved, retails the story of Goneril. The confidence man now tries to place a comforting interpretation on the story:

'Take the very worst view of that case; admit that his Goneril was, indeed, a Goneril; how fortunate to be at last rid of his Goneril, both by nature and by law? If he were acquainted with the unfortunate man, instead of condoling with him, he would congratulate him.'

Half-convinced, the merchant shares a bottle of wine with his new friend, but abruptly bursts out, 'Ah, wine is good, and confidence is good; but can wine or confidence percolate down· through all the stony strata of hard considerations, and drop warmly and ruddily into the cold cave of truth? Truth will *not* be comforted. Led by dear charity, lured by sweet hope, fond fancy essays this feat; but in vain'. Again the confidence man restores his victim's composure and the merchant leaves the table 'mortified at having been tempted by his own honest goodness, accidentally stimulated into making mad disclosures—to himself as to another—of the queer, unaccountable caprices of his natural heart'. The merchant is a dupe because, against all his intuitive perceptions, he is induced to disown his sudden consciousness of the inscrutable promiscuity of human evil. Each of the confidence man's parts exemplifies the popular recoil from this consciousness. As the man in grey he is the sanctimonious 'do-gooder'; as the man with the travelling cap the apologist of a tottering commercial prosperity; as the herb doctor the votary of nature and the simple life. It is impossible to avoid the inference that Melville is castigating not the dearth of charity and confidence but their intemperance.

Melville further subtilises this conclusion by his treatment of the corollary themes of selfishness (the philosopher and his disciple), avarice (the miser) and misanthropy (the Missourian). None of these offers a practicable alternative. The most specific rebuke to an all-embracing cynicism comes from one of the dupes, but one in whom, Melville tells us, 'the old Adam' was strong. It is so raptly visualised, so agonisingly *felt*, that it is clearly Melville's own admonition:

'I have been in mad-houses full of tragic mopers, and seen there the end of suspicion: the cynic, in the moody madness muttering in the corner; for years a barren fixture there; head lopped over, gnawing his own lip, vulture of himself; while, by fits and starts, from the corner opposite came the grimace of the idiot at him.'

In this novel Melville defines his attitude no more explicitly than by the counterpointing of ideas which we have seen. Yet his position emerges quite distinctly. It is to excite a moral sensibility which neither rests beyond hope in the practice of sin nor evades the predicament by denying that evil exists. *The Confidence Man* portrays a society where both the desire and the ability to appreciate good and evil were, not dead, but distempered; where epiphanies went unrecognised though, like the merchant's, still granted. It is not, therefore, a society without God. In *Morality and Literature* D. H. Lawrence defines morality as 'that delicate, for ever trembling and changing balance between me and my circumambient universe . . . by life we mean something that gleams, that has the fourth-dimensional quality'. We have in this statement the two aspects of Melville's inquiry: the 'me', the individual, the unique identity, and 'the circumambient universe' —the communal life of affairs and social institutions, in which the world of the spirit, the 'fourth-dimensional quality', is immanent. With great intellectual subtlety—and an austerity unusual in Melville—*The Confidence Man* inspects the psychic opacities in the individual component of Lawrence's 'balance'. It is 'negative' only to the extent that Melville, refusing to adulterate his revelation, did not resolve his agony and present any instance of the balance in equable play. But it was from precisely this obdurate material that he was, in *Billy Budd*, to winnow out a grave tranquillity.

'Keeping his lone vigils', at the end of *The Confidence Man*, is 'a clean, comely, old man . . . untainted by the world because ignorant of it'. Either there is a degree of irony in the description or Melville abandoned the idea, for he goes on to show the innocent old man mortally apprehensive of being robbed, duped, or drowned in a shipwreck. In *Billy Budd* Melville proceeded with the idea of placing in some weighted situation such a character as the old man at first appears to be. The situation he finally built up is an amalgam of fact[1] and imaginative reinforcement. The plot of *Billy Budd*, with its theme of authority, rebellion and justice, refines on an episode recounted in *Moby Dick*, the *Town-Ho*'s story. The antagonists are the mate of the *Town-Ho*, Radney, 'hardy, stubborn, malicious', and one of its crew, Steelkilt, a noble and heroic figure who excites Radney's hatred. Radney gives him a humiliating and unjustified order. Steelkilt refuses to obey, strikes the mate, leads an abortive mutiny and, threatening vengeance, is flogged by Radney: 'in the foreordaining soul of Steelkilt, the mate was already stark and stretched as a corpse, with his forehead crushed in'. But 'strange fatality pervades the whole career of these events, as if verily mapped out before the world itself was charted'. It is Moby Dick who kills Radney when he is tossed into the sea in an attempt on the whale.

Steelkilt is a precursor of Billy Budd, Radney of Claggart, though the details of their fates are vitally different and the Claggart-Billy antithesis more clear-cut and insulated. The account of Bland's nature in *White-Jacket* might be applied verbatim to Claggart, also the ship's master-at -arms. He is distinguished in intelligence and appearance, with a curious pallor

---

[1] This is partly a matter of the historical background, which Melville gives in the Preface and Chapters 3–5 of the novel. A more intimate source was a case of mutiny on the U.S. Navy brig *Somers* in which his cousin, Lieutenant Guert Gansevoort, was involved. See Mayoux, *op. cit.*, p. 125 and Newton Arvin, *Herman Melville*, pp. 293–4. Melville himself refers to the incident in chapter 18 of *Billy Budd*.

'which seemed to hint something defective or abnormal in the constitution', and with the indefinable suggestion about him of high social rank. Behind the outer comeliness lies 'the mania of an evil nature, not engendered by vicious training or corrupting books or licentious living, but born with him and innate, in short, "a depravity according to nature"'. Billy's origins are equally impenetrable. He is a foundling. He might even, it is insinuated, be a son of the ship's captain, the lofty-hearted Vere. He is universally popular and his nature is free both of the inclination to suspect evil and the ability to do it. He is not wholly perfect. Under stress, some psychological impediment halts his speech—'a striking instance that the arch-interpreter, the envious marplot of Eden, still has more or less to do with every human consignment to this planet of earth'. Between good and evil there is a latent fellowship, a sympathetic vibration. As Radney for Steelkilt, so Claggart feels for Billy—whose nature, unlike Steelkilt's, 'had in its simplicity never willed malice'—'an antipathy spontaneous and profound'. So from 'wantonness of malice' and 'disdain of innocence'—unlike Radney wholly unprovoked—Claggart engineers Billy's downfall. On the strength of fabricated evidence he accuses Billy of plotting mutiny. Tongue-tied by his fatal stammer, Billy cannot voice an answer to the charge and strikes Claggart a mortal blow. Claggart is Bland of *White-Jacket* confronted with his prescriptive victim-Nemesis. Billy wreaks his own vengeance and suffers a retribution both destined and elected. The form of Billy's arraignment also returns us to the world of *White-Jacket*. He is condemned by the same naval discipline—though this time on an English ship—whose tribunals Melville had held up as the strict antithesis of heavenly compassion. The two are still so opposed. Instructing the court on the plea that Billy 'purposed neither mutiny nor homicide', Captain Vere says, '... before a court less arbitrary and more merciful than a martial one that plea would largely extenuate ... At the Last Assizes it shall acquit'. But the opposition now is much less dogmatically conceived.

So much criticism of *Billy Budd* treats of its eschatological meanings that the image, in this man-of-war, of more strictly worldly affairs is perhaps neglected. We can hardly agree with Newton Arvin's opinion that these matters 'say very little about the real feeling of *Billy Budd*'.[1] Overhanging the circumscribed arena of the novel's setting are the tremendous ideological conflicts of the French Revolution, in so many ways the inspiration of the American. Though he did not have Cooper's lengthy residence in Europe, Melville was a much less temperamental critic of the cataclysmic events which ushered in the nineteenth century. He comments on them directly and through Captain Vere, whose deliberations on this topic, as well as the court martial he superintends, are at the very centre of the novel. Melville's Preface looks on the naval mutinies at Spithead and the Nore as the Revolution in little. The tyrannous course of the larger uprising he deplores. It 'involved the rectification of the Old World's hereditary wrongs', but only after its tempering in 'the prolonged agony of continual war' did it combine serviceably with established forms of government. By and large, Melville approves the revolutionary settlement, though without the ardour which condones its outrages or the partiality which discounts the necessary conservative retrenchment.

This dispassionateness is the quality also of Captain Vere. In guiding the court martial to its decision that Billy must hang, he employs very much the same argument as Judge Temple: '. . . will an upright judge allow himself off the bench to be waylaid by some tender kinswoman of the accused seeking to touch him with her fearful plea? Well, the heart here is as that piteous woman'. His fellow-judges are 'well-meaning men not intellectually mature, men with whom it was necessary to demonstrate certain principles that were axioms to himself', men embarrassed by the metaphysical purport of their problem. Is it, the condition to which the heart easily reduces it, a simple clash between justice and mercy? Is it a question of legal duty over private conscience? Are they to excuse an unsavoury means, the death of Billy, by appeal to a problematical end, the security of a navy in which a lenient sentence might encourage further mutiny? Only Vere, an aristocrat of speculative mind, an officer, of the kind Melville

[1] Arvin, *op. cit.*, p. 294. On the religious allegory, Billy as Christ/Adam, Claggart as Satan, Arvin writes pp. 294–7. Further commentary on this aspect of the novel is to be found also in: Ronald Mason: *The Spirit above the Dust*, pp. 247–8; W. E. Sedgwick, *op. cit.*, pp. 240–42; and R. W. B. Lewis, *op. cit.*, pp. 148–51.

praised in *White-Jacket*, 'accustomed to social command', can see the trial as a choice between two evils, the lesser of which is the sacrifice of Billy Budd, a being 'of that generous nature that he would feel even for us on whom in this military necessity so heavy a compulsion is laid'. To this submission Billy comes. Vere tells him that he is to be hanged, but Melville does not report what passed between them. Visiting him later, however, the ship's chaplain 'had no consolation to offer which could result in a peace transcending that which he beheld', and Billy dies with the cry, 'God bless Captain Vere', on his lips. On this level of meaning, Billy is to be seen as a willing sacrifice to the existing political order, necessary to maintain it against the threat of chaos.

From all of them the law demands a compliance which is the secular counterpart of spiritual freedom within the Christian discipline. Absolute freedom is an illusion. The obligations which Vere and the other officers contract in taking their commissions mean that they are no longer 'natural free agents' and this images all the duties and obligations which bind man, within the gradations of family and society. It is the error of popular assemblies to confound these gradations, to identify freedom with equality, to disseminate privilege at the expense of responsibility, to glorify emotion over intellect. The higher wisdom of Captain Vere must advise his fellow judges. In their indetermination Melville sees the artlessness of 'most legislatures in a democracy'. Vere's momentary hesitation before he speaks to them is an impulse of the patrician impatience which 'deters some minds from addressing any popular assembly'. Melville does not condemn democracy. It is a reminder that any vital society must evolve an *élite to* administer its institutions and that its multifarious parts must work in harmony. Against this concept of democracy are set the revolutionary dogmas, 'invading waters of novel opinion . . . which carried away as in a torrent no few minds in those days, minds by nature not inferior to his own'. Vere opposes them not, like many of his peers, because they threaten the privileges of his class, but because 'they seemed to him incapable of embodiment in lasting institutions'.

From the theme of mutiny averted emerges the theme of lawlessness at large suppressed. Without emphasis, Melville recounts the capture by Vere's ship of the French warship *Athéiste*, a name 'proclaiming the infidel audacity of the ruling power'. Dying from a wound received in the action, Vere murmurs, 'Billy Budd, Billy Budd.' It is a sequel which demands the most tactful management if it is not to unsettle the delicate balance of meaning in Melville's fable of good and evil, of, as he put it in *Moby Dick*, 'chance, free-will and necessity—no wise incompatible—all interweavingly working together'. What he did not mean he specifies in the newspaper account of the episode which he reproduces. In this, Claggart has become a patriotic hero, Billy a mutinous scoundrel and his death a salutary punishment: 'Nothing amiss is now apprehended aboard H.M.S. *Indomitable*.' That nothing indeed is now amiss is not, however, the result of a fustian conflict between right and wrong with virtue triumphant. The reconciliation has come from an interlacing of energies the nature of whose course is as momentous as their final effect, the instrumentality as the consummation.

Clearly there can be no separation of the political from the theological matter of *Billy Budd*. Sedgwick concludes that in Billy's fate we are to see 'a reflection of the heavenly mystery, in which the idea of divine love, as attributed to Christ, is reconciled with the known facts of the rough justice which overrules the world'.[1] Reconciled, we might add, because the divine love too exacts penance, and the imperfect human law is the temporal stay of democratic rule against the anarchy 'at war with the world and the peace of mankind', which Vere resisted. It is curious that Melville, so much more anguished a thinker than Cooper, should for his last statement adopt Cooper's trick of generalising from the literal forensics of a loaded case. That the political element should, in this form, be present at all indicates the closeness to the heart of American thought of the theme of law, and the persistent topicality of Puritan and medieval reasoning. Melville's conceptions stretch further and more subtly than Cooper's beyond the purely sociological, but they are written out of his surroundings. We have seen something of his debt to Poe. Of Cooper's works he wrote that they were 'among the earliest I remember as in my boyhood producing a vivid and awakening power upon my mind'. That Melville survived the stresses which wrenched Poe apart is in some measure due to the Cooper pull towards social

[1] Sedgwick, *op. cit.*, p. 241.

orientations and away from the cave of Trophonius. Unlike Poe and Cooper, Melville was a familiar of both worlds and each was a factor in his reconciliation to the society whose fundamental conflicts he so surely apprehended in his writings. Melville's imagery is full of caves, pits, gulfs, descents. In one of his comparisons between the *Neversink* and society he writes that it 'resembles a three-story house in a suspicious part of the town, with a basement of indefinite depth'. Whatever the literal subject of his writings, Melville's interest is this 'basement of indefinite depth', under social man, solitary or gregarious, and under the corporate activities—law, statecraft, commerce—which the American intellect most assiduously pursued.

IV

Allegory and symbol were modes instinctive to Hawthorne. We have already seen, in *Dr. Heidegger's Experiment*, an example of their less dextrous employment. *The Great Carbuncle*, though not altogether free of the same hesitancy, does, without intrusive comment, sift a solidly compacted landscape into symbolic tenuity. Assembled at the foot of the Crystal Hills is a motley group of people whose purpose is to find the fabulous gem of the title. They are typical of Hawthorne's incongruous confections of personality and personification. First is the Seeker, embittered by long failure, who seeks 'because the vain ambition of my youth has become a fate upon me in my old age'. Dr. Cacaphodel, 'who had wilted and dried himself into a mummy, by continually stooping over charcoal furnaces', is a scientist prepared to destroy the gem to advance his researches; we are reminded of the more credible Dr. Cuticle. Completing the party are a merchant, a poet, a cynic set on demonstrating that 'the Great Carbuncle is all a humbug', and the simple Matthew and Hannah, who find the stone but voluntarily leave it in its resting place. Nowhere here does Hawthorne put across a vivacious image of reality, but the landscape is not thus summarily constrained within a pre-designed allegorical mould. It is 'a vast extent of wilderness . . . where the hills throw off their shaggy mantle of forest trees, and robe themselves in clouds, or tower naked into the sky'. As the ascent proceeds, this landscape, still massive, melts into 'naked

179

rocks, and desolate sunshine, that rose immediately above them . . . nothing breathed, nothing grew . . . the vapours welded themselves, as it were, into a mass, presenting the appearance of a pavement over which the wanderers might have trodden, but where they would vainly have sought an avenue to the blessed earth which they had lost . . . and thus annihilated, at least for them, the whole region of visible space'. This persuasively gradual diminution of reality illustrates the importance to the success of Hawthorne's symbolism of a realistic foundation. He was much more inclined than Melville not just to engage abstract ideas but to cultivate abstract personifications of abstract ideas. His best work is invariably that in which the ideas are fortified by his perception of actualities; not visual realism only but the localising of the ideas in historical situations. The social background, though not in any naturalistic manner, was essential to Hawthorne and it performs the same strengthening function as the landscape in *The Great Carbuncle*.

In the fine essay, 'Hawthorne as Poet', Q. D. Leavis writes as follows:

'I find it impossible to follow Mr. Parkes's argument that 'what is lacking in (Hawthorne's) framework of experience is any sense of society as a kind of organic whole to which the individual belongs and in which he has his appointed place. And lacking the notion of social continuity and tradition (he) lacks also the corresponding metaphysical conception of the natural universe as an ordered unity which harmonises with human ideals'. It is precisely these problems . . . that are his claim to importance.'[1]

The harmony which Parkes's 'Essay in Sociological Criticism' envisages between the natural universe and human ideals lies in the materialist credo of Dreiser that human misery, being the product of biological and environmental factors which are controllable, may be eliminated. Hawthorne, certainly, did not believe this. He did, however, place his individuals in that progression of rising and subsiding loyalties through which his society had evolved—'the way,' in Q. D. Leavis's words, 'in which a distinctively American society developed, and how it

[1] *Hawthorne as Poet* in Charles Feidelson, Jr. and Paul Brodtkorb (eds.), *Interpretations of American Literature*, p. 32.

came to have a tradition of its own'. The themes to which Hawthorne insistently returns are of Puritan inspiration—natural human depravity, guilty deeds and thoughts, punishment, atonement—and their setting is frequently Puritan society. But the Puritan was, as we have seen, a highly political as well as a theological community, in which, we are told in *The Scarlet Letter*, 'religion and law were almost identical'. Hawthorne's novels have this double alliance. The images through which he conveys theological meanings are deeply imbedded in American social experience. He is not primarily a novelist of antique manners and customs. 'One would think,' he writes in *Old News*, 'that no very wonderful talent was requisite for an historical novel, when the rough and hurried paragraphs of these newspapers can recall the past so magically.' His aim is not to recall the past in this way but to isolate its points of contact with the present, to trace the continuity of growth from colonies to nation, interpreting the problems of his own society by referring back to the tensions, whose impress was still distinct, in which they had originated.

One of the most haunting of Hawthorne's images is the forest. In *Old News* he describes the colony at the time of which he was writing as 'only a narrow strip of civilisation along the edge of a vast forest, peopled with enough of its original race to contrast the savage life with the old customs of another world'. In *The Scarlet Letter* Hester and Dimmesdale meet in the forest, Hester having borne for seven years the public guilt of her adultery, Dimmesdale, her child's father, still a revered minister, ravaged by his unconfessed sin. To them the forest seems an escape from the community from which, Hester openly and Dimmesdale secretly, they have estranged themselves: 'How dreary looked the forest-track that led backward to the settlement, where Hester Prynne must take up again the burden of her ignominy, and the minister the hollow mockery of his good name!' But the forest is really the abode of evil, imaging 'not amiss the moral wilderness in which (Hester) had so long been wandering'. 'Am I,' Dimmesdale asks on leaving it, 'given over wholly to the fiend? Did I make a contract with him in the forest, and sign it with my blood?' On his return he is greeted by Mistress Hibbins, reputed a witch—'at midnight, and in the forest, we shall have other talk together', she says to him. The forest is the retreat of witches' covens, the kingdom of the Black Man, empire of lawless instincts restrained in the daytime community. In *Young Goodman Brown* it is into 'the dark wall of the forest' that Goodman Brown, having bade farewell to his wife, makes his mysterious, ceremonial journey which 'must needs be done 'twixt (night) and sunrise'. In the forest he meets a traveller, in the semblance of his father, who carries a staff 'which bore the likeness of a great black snake, so curiously wrought that it might almost be seen to twist and wriggle itself like a living serpent'. As he penetrates more deeply, he is attended by other familiar shapes and apparitions. Then he sees, congregated in diabolic possession, all the most respected citizens of his town, vowing themselves to evil. Approaching them, he feels 'a loathful brotherhood by the sympathy of all that was wicked in his heart'. Among them is his wife, with whom, he now discovers, he is to be initiated. By a defiant effort of will he calls on heaven and finds himself alone. When he returns to the town he has lost all faith. From then until 'his dying hour was gloom'. Such, in the Satanic weirdness of this oppressive tale, is Hawthorne's forest. As Malcolm Cowley points out, it is not in the forest that Dimmesdale must seek his peace.[1] He must atone, before the assembled townsfolk, by his sacrificial confession within the community. Often, passing through these townsfolk, Hester has felt the companionship of guilt. The community does not represent good. But reparation may be made only behind this bulwark against total abandonment to the darkest impulses—the forest: it is the forest life which, as with Goodman Brown, destroys the faith that holds this together.

In setting up this antithesis Hawthorne was calling, of course, on ingenerate memories of European legend. But the forest early began to accumulate its own lore in America. For the Puritans it was forbidding because both lawless and pagan as well as physically hostile. As early as 1694, Cotton Mather wrote: 'Do *Old* People any of them *Go Out* from the Institutions of God, swarming into New Settlements where they and their Untaught Families are like to *Perish for Lack of Vision*.' Any temerarious

[1] 'Five Acts of *The Scarlet Letter*', in C. Shapiro, *Twelve Original Essays on Great American Novels*, pp. 42–43.

enough to attempt this, he said, have 'got unto the *Wrong Side of the Hedge*' and 'the angel of the Lord becomes their enemy'. The unsettled lands did have their champions. With other historians, F. J. Turner saw them as the breeding-place of a manly, individualistic democracy. They were extolled also as a valuable over-spill area which could absorb the restless, the discontented, the unemployed. Even in 1932 President Roosevelt, addressing the Commonwealth Club, could associate this memory with his immediate political difficulties: 'Our last frontier has long since been reached, and there is practically no more free land . . . There is no safety-valve in the form of a Western Prairie to which those thrown out of work by the Eastern machines can go for a new start.' But the antipathy was equally strong. The merits claimed for the wilderness of forest and prairie were not always thought to commend it. With the deeply irrational emotional distrust, reasons of policy, economics and law range themselves, throughout American history, against comfortable acceptance of the backlands. In 1786, Rufus King, opposing the encouragement of Western emigrants, urged that 'losing our men is losing our greatest source of wealth'. Gouverneur Morris argued at the Constitutional Convention of 1787 against the newer territories that, 'The busy haunts of men, not the remote wilderness, are the proper school of political talents.' In 1847 Justice Campbell said of the legislators from Western states, 'Their notions are freer, their impulses stronger, their wills less restrained. I do not wish to increase the number till the New States already admitted to the Union become civilised.'[1] The forest which broods over so many of Hawthorne's communities not only accommodated legendary spiritual evils and physical dangers but corresponded to a real social disquiet in American life. Palpably branched and thicketed, it is a tangible symbol on the purely social as well as the more abstract level.

Though the forest is inherently malignant, its most menacing property is that it liberates the evil in human beings. This is the quality round which Hawthorne's psychologising revolves. At the end of *Fancy's Show Box* he makes a general statement of principle: 'Man must not disclaim his brotherhood even with the

[1] See Frederick Jackson Turner, 'Pre-Civil War Sectionalism', in Saveth, *op. cit.*, pp. 220–24.

guiltiest, since, though his hand be clean, his heart has surely been polluted by the flitting phantoms of iniquity'—a call, incidentally, for the kind of charity, based on admission of sinfulness, which Melville found lacking in the world of *The Confidence Man*. Most of Hawthorne's novels and tales remind us of the insecure moral barrier between us and the recognised criminal who is our scapegoat. In moments of insight the barrier dissolves, as it did with the sense of brotherhood that flashed into being in the encounters already mentioned between Goodman Brown and his townsfolk, Hester Prynne and hers. We see it again in Dimmesdale's forest meeting with Hester, where his decision to take flight with her removes him to 'the wild, free atmosphere of an unredeemed, unchristianised, lawless region . . . (of) sympathy and fellowship with wicked mortals, and the world of perverted spirits'. When, in *Ethan Brand*, the lime burner meets Ethan Brand, who has committed 'the unpardonable sin', his 'own sins rose up within him, and made his memory riotous with a throng of evil shapes that asserted their kindred with the Master Sin, whatever it might be, which it was within the scope of man's corrupted nature to conceive and cherish'.

Hawthorne's obsession with sin controls all these episodes, but it was the idea of 'the unpardonable sin' that most haunted his imagination. In his notebook for 1844 he defined it thus: 'The Unpardonable Sin might consist in a want of love and reverence for the Human Soul; in consequence of which the investigator pried into its dark depths, not with a hope or purpose of making it better, but from a cold philosophical curiosity—content that it should be wicked in whatever kind or degree, and only desiring to study it out. Would not this, in other words, be the separation of the intellect from the heart?' Ethan Brand is such an investigator, having sinned by raising intellect above 'the sense of brotherhood with man'. Beyond telling us that he has made a young girl the 'subject of a psychological experiment, and wasted, absorbed, and perhaps annihilated her soul', the story does not detail the course of his Lucifer-like descent to suicide in the flames of the lime-kiln. His sin is duplicated in *The Scarlet Letter* by Hester's betrayed husband, Roger Chillingworth. By his appearance—his deformity, 'something ugly and evil in his face . . . getting sooty with the smoke'—and his pursuits—'compounding drugs and chemicals'—he is associated with alchemy and the black lore of old Europe. Yet he, in the beginning, is the wronged man and his moral decline comes only through his intimacy with Dimmesdale. His psychological inquisition of Dimmesdale, 'prying into his recollections, and probing everything with a cautious touch, like a treasure-seeker in a dark cavern', soon makes him privy to the minister's hidden guilt. Continuing his pose as Dimmesdale's leech and friend, he sets out, in revenge, to possess himself of Dimmesdale's soul, to harry him into flight which can never end in escape. When he and Hester are prepared to take ship, Hester learns that Chillingworth also is to be a passenger. Only Dimmesdale's final decision to stand fast and expiate his guilt saves him from a life of fruitless evasion and pursuit mockingly prolonged. The relationship between the two men displays Hawthorne's curiously modern sense of the expanding psychological affinity between the interrogator and his subject. But beyond that Hawthorne is fascinated, in Dimmesdale's final penance, by the demonstration of Providence's, paradoxically, 'using the avenger and his victim for its own purpose, and, perchance, pardoning where most it seemed to punish'. In the manifold degrees of evil 'within man's corrupted nature', Chillingworth, Dimmesdale, Hester, Pearl[1] and the townsfolk—clerical and lay—all occupy their subtly differentiated ranks. Complementing them are 'the truly saintly fathers' of the religious community, 'etherealised . . . by spiritual communications with the better world, into which their purity of life had almost introduced these holy personages, with their garments of mortality still clinging to them'. In them the reality of Good is revealed, but their wisdom reaches their fellow-pastors and flock alike—'afar and indistinctly, from the upper heights where they habitually dwelt'. This is the moral complex which is given coherence by its polarisation round the images of forest and town, used as a more purely indigenous alternative to James's America/Europe antithesis, and with equal variegation of shades.

'The old customs of another world', which in *Old News*

---

[1] Pearl, a child of nature, is at home in the forest. There is a sympathetic wilderness in her. 'A wolf, it is said . . . came up, and smelt of Pearl's robe, and offered his savage head to be patted by her hand.' It is interesting to compare Cooper's portrayal of Hetty in *The Deerslayer*.

Hawthorne contrasted with the forest life, were a heterogeneous collection, furnished by merchants, adventurers and renegade philosophies. The logic of selection which reduced them is Hawthorne's subject in *The Maypole of Merry Mount*. In the semi-mythical Merry Mount the pagan gods of Old England briefly renew their sway. Its colonists are frivolous Arcadians, votaries of the Lord of Misrule. The passage describing their Maypole festival seems quick with colour, movement, emblems of growth and fertility. Hawthorne's imagery, however, implies a frantic and meretricious vitality. It is 'dreamlike', its people are 'the similitude of men and women', its properties theatrical, 'jest and delusion, trick and fantasy', 'visionary', 'unreal'. A group of Puritans secretly watching likens the celebration to 'those devils and ruined souls with whom their superstition peopled the black wilderness'. When, under Governor Endicott, they attack the community, its depthless montage collapses before these 'iron men' and their 'sterner faith'. The Maypole is shattered and the settlement disbanded; the mockery life dissolves and the old gods are deposed. Hawthorne emphasises the ritual element by his references to the banished Pantheon of 'classic groves' and 'ancient fables', masque and anti-masque. Now as then, the old gods succumb not merely to superior force but to an inner necessity, a private recognition of inadequacy. During the revelry the May Lady and the May Lord have themselves undergone the metamorphosis of disillusionment. As between them a genuine love springs up, 'down came a shower of withering rose leaves from the Maypole'; they become 'sensible of something vague and unsubstantial in their former pleasures, and felt a dreary presentiment of inevitable change'. With its mirth, glitter and irresponsibility, Merry Mount is misplaced in its harsh environment and the expedient life-form dispossesses it. It is between Merry Mount and the Puritans that the issue must be joined. With the merchants and explorers Puritanism had no irresoluble quarrel; often they were its secular arm. Puritan hostility was directed at dissident sects and as these were eliminated the 'old customs' became increasingly Puritan, supporting the colonists in 'the moral gloom of the world . . . along the difficult path which it was their lot to tread'. The decay of the Puritan ethos, when it came, was like that of Merry Mount, inwardly decreed.

A serial renunciation of power emerges from the conspectus of

American history revealed in Hawthorne's tales. *My Kinsman, Major Molineux* chronicles another phase, the decline of royal power when the English throne began to appoint colonial governors. Robin, an obscure kinsman of the governor, arrives to seek his patronage on the night when he is overthrown by the rebellious citizens. The story is built round the conspiratorial tension in the town and Robin's bewilderment as he can find no one to direct him to his kinsman. Its climax is the riotous eruption of the townsfolk into the quiet streets, pushing the governor along, tarred and feathered, in an open cart. Though Robin pities the humiliated governor and feels a sense of cataclysmic disturbance, he cannot help but share in the exultation of the crowd. At the end a stranger assures him, 'you may rise in the world without the help of your kinsman, Major Molineux'. The nationalist reference is obvious, but Hawthorne's point is the tragedy of these fated transitions. The procession of citizens marches 'in counterfeited pomp, in senseless uproar, trampling on an old man's heart'. Hawthorne recounts ritual sacrifices, the fore-ordained failures of will and perception that make these necessary, not a glad revolutionary progress. After the saturnalia, reality will return with its enigmatic demands to test the new victors.

Not until the 1860's did the impact of Darwin's *Origin of Species* shatter the anodyne faiths of Victorian America and set philosophers to assimilating the idea that species were not immutable. In so far as the doctrine applies to governments and castes, however, Hawthorne had long since anticipated it and reconciled himself to the ruthlessness of the historical law of effective rule. Revolution was justified—because inevitable—when a disintegrative group became powerful enough to subvert and renegotiate the social equilibrium, destroying in the process a fossilising *élite*. It is relevant to note here that the instinctive American acclamation of the 1848 uprisings in Europe was soon muted. Newspapers began to argue that the French working classes were incapable 'of governing either for the benefit of themselves or others', and condoned the suppression of the June revolt on the ground that, 'No sacrifice less dreadful could have secured the permanent triumph of law and order.'[1] The

[1] Quoted in Merle Curti, 'The Impact of the Revolution of 1848 on American Thought', Saveth, *op. cit.*, p. 248.

Darwinian thesis was, ultimately, the empiric and conservative one of effectiveness in a given set of circumstances. Its implications were systematically worked out in Brooks Adams's *The Theory of Social Revolution* (1913). It belongs to that class of work which convenes not only the lifetime thoughts of an individual but the background speculation of decades. Adams's prime concern was the administrative capacity of the current American power group, for, 'It is in dealing with administration . . . that civilisations have usually, though not always, broken down'.[1] Administrative capacity determined the rise and fall of all the American governing castes: Puritans, royal governors, colonial aristocracy, Southern cotton planters, Northern industrialists. We shall examine his analysis further in a later chapter. At the moment it is sufficient to remark how germane to his own society this shows Hawthorne's diagnosis of past upheavals to have been. There is a necessary distinction to be made between Hawthorne and Adams. Adams did not assess government by absolute moral standards, while Hawthorne patently did. Equally, however, Hawthorne realised that in the business of government, moral impeccability is not enough. His territory was the human soul, not in isolation or in its transcendent relations only, but in the bearings of social life.

The American past was most fertile in the symbols that would communicate Hawthorne's vision. *The Blithedale Romance* is his attempt to find their analogues in the American present. Despite his disclaimers in the Preface, it is partly a satire on the experiment in primitive socialism undertaken at Brook Farm in the early 1840's by a group of New England transcendentalists. In the fictitious Blithedale, Hawthorne brings together, in his own words, 'the self-concentrated Philanthropist; the high-spirited Woman, bruising herself against the narrow limitations of her sex; the weakly Maiden, whose tremulous nerves endow her with sibilline attributes; the Minor Poet, beginning life with strenuous aspirations, which die out with his youthful fervour'. These are Hollingsworth, Zenobia, Priscilla and the narrator, Miles Coverdale. At the farm, Coverdale becomes aware of some secret relationship between Mr. Moodie, an impoverished old man living in Boston,

---

[1] Brooks Adams: 'Inferences' in *The Theory of Social Revolution*, reprinted in Perry Miller, *American Thought: Civil War to World War I*, pp. 262–3.

and Zenobia and Priscilla, both of whom love Hollingsworth. The complicated plot which unravels this—it is easily Hawthorne's most involved—leads to Zenobia's suicide by drowning and the joyless marriage of Priscilla and Hollingsworth. Hawthorne's handling of the complex intrigue is maladroit. What he intends to puzzle—that Zenobia and Priscilla are half-sisters—is easily unriddled; what he intends to explain—Zenobia's past life —remains obscure. Nevertheless the novel is, despite these narrative hiatuses, a dramatic and lucid articulation of ideas. Blithedale, though established for higher motives, is Hawthorne's contemporary Merry Mount. Zenobia's retreat to the farm culminates in death. Just before this climax Coverdale arrives to find its inhabitants, dancing to 'Satanic music', engaged in just such a masquerade—'shepherds of Arcadia and allegoric figures from *The Faerie Queene*'—as the Puritans had broken up at Merry Mount. Their well-meant endeavours to cut adrift from the evils of the world have no more reality than this. Their labours on the farm, which are supposed to integrate body and mind, 'were never etherealised into thought'. To prosper they must sell their produce and so collude with the system by which 'every son of woman both perpetrates and suffers his share of the common evil, whether he chooses it or no'. It is all 'an illusion, a masquerade, a pastoral, a counterfeit Arcadia', acted out 'as if the soil beneath our feet had not been fathom-deep with the dust of deluded generations'. The narrator's commentary on Blithedale modulates from gentle irony to melancholy recognition of the distant clangour of reality, muffled by folly. Action as well as image embodies the tragic antithesis. Zenobia's deception by the 'Arcadian affectation' of Blithedale robs even her suicide of dignity. Visualising a decorous and pretty death 'in the bosom of the old, familiar stream', she is in fact dragged from the river 'rigid in the act of struggling', her hands 'clenched in immitigable defiance'. Blithedale, too, harbours the affectation of Hollingsworth's crack-brained scheme to found an institution for the reform of criminals; in Boston lives the father of Zenobia and Priscilla, pauperised by a combination of imprudence and peculation—'the sort of crime, growing out of its artificial state, which society (unless it should change its entire constitution for this man's unworthy sake) neither could nor ought to pardon'. Hollingsworth minimises this social role of punishment because it crosses his own egotistical scheme to liberate the individual from any concept of a loyalty or responsibility transcending the esoteric group.

Boston represents man's involvement in a social contract. Shrouded in vile weather, it is 'sordid . . . and empty of the beautiful'. Yet it hums with 'the entangled life of many men together'. Meditating on his dual experience, Coverdale admits the involuntary interdependence of souls: 'We convey a property in them to those with whom we associate; but to what extent can never be known until we feel the tug, the agony, of our abortive attempt to assume an exclusive sway over ourselves': the heresy of Blithedale. The myriad corporeal sensations of Boston, its manners and its social intercourse, as recorded, for instance, in the tavern scene where Coverdale meets Mr. Moodie, recall Coverdale to 'the settled system of things, to correct himself by a new observation from that old standpoint'. As in *The Maypole of Merry Mount, Young Goodman Brown* and *The Scarlet Letter*, the escape to the forest nihilism can bring only disillusionment and barren sacrifice. The wilderness cannot be subdued otherwise than by the compromises of civilisation. The principle of Hawthorne's personal tragedies is the bereavement of transition: from innocence to experience, guilt to grace, savage to civilised community, epoch to epoch, ideal to accomplishment. His criticism of Blithedale is tempered by a forlorn idealism which might stand as a general comment on Hawthorne's philosophy: 'Yet, after all, let us acknowledge it wiser, if not more sagacious, to follow out one's day-dream to its natural consummation, although, if the vision have been worth the having, it is certain never to be consummated otherwise than by a failure . . . Its airiest fragments, impalpable as they may be, will possess a value that lurks not in the most ponderous realities of any practicable scheme.' Using the metaphor of physical equilibrium to describe a practicable order of society is perhaps misleading. It is a shifting, not a rigid balance, incorporating all kinds of tensions and conflicts and under perpetual review by the imperatives of these intractable visions.

Hawthorne's work travels by different routes to the same areas of experience as Melville's. It is more subdued in tone, different in method, less exotically varied in style, scene and action, but in its conception of 'the tragic phase' basically similar. Melville, we might say, worked by compression into some political artifact withdrawn in space, Hawthorne by extension backward in time. Both worked from the circumstances of their own era to express its 'absolute condition'.

Chapter Five

Twain as Satirist

THE great age of English satire seemingly pledged itself so deeply to classical models that one perhaps finds it difficult to conceive of satire divorced from that kind of knowledge and sympathy with the ancient traditions. As Ian Jack has shown, however, the Augustans adapted as much as adopted. The fundamental difference between Latin *satura* and English *satire* he summarises as follows: '. . . the Latin word, unlike the English, was never used to refer to passages of incidental satire in a composition of some other species. It is because the word in English has never referred primarily to a definite form of writing that it is now used indifferently for any literary work which portrays a particular person, or human life itself, in a highly unsympathetic manner. "Satire" now relates to the mode of a writer's vision, the temper of his writings.'[1] Though the objects of satire were traditional in the sense that vice and folly were essentially as they had always been, the poet's forms, methods, settings and language turned upon his own society. It was, as well as being of a retrospective cast, a strikingly contemporary poetry. And because the society it dealt with was an urban and aristocratic one, its features so closely delineated by Dryden, Pope, Swift, Fielding, we tend, again, to associate satire with elegance, artifice, and the sort of affectation these qualities breed. This is especially so because the poetry which criticised the sundry affectations was itself polished and correct.

The ideal of 'correctness', however, was a very compendious

[1] Ian Jack: *Augustan Satire*, p. 99.

one and it admitted an abundance of colloquial speech and straight talk. A description in the *Spectator* (618) of Horatian satire corroborates some of the popular conceptions of the eighteenth-century *genre*—that it is didactic in purpose and refined in manner; but to a far greater extent the description recommends humour, a robust variety of expression and a large acquaintance with the courses of actual life: 'He that would excel in this kind must have a good Fund of strong Masculine Sense: To this there must be joined a thorough Knowledge of Mankind, together with an Insight into the Business, and the prevailing Humours of the Age. Our Author must have his Mind well seasoned with the finest Precepts of Morality, and be filled with nice Reflections upon the bright and the dark sides of human Life: He must be a Master of refined Raillery, and understand the Delicacies, as well as the Absurdities of Conversation. He must have a lively Turn of Wit, with an easie and concise manner of Expression; Everything he says, must be in a free and disengaged manner. He must be guilty of nothing that betrays the Air of a Recluse, but appear a Man of the World throughout.' This clear injunction that the satirist of fashion must himself be in the thick of fashionable life might seem to run counter to the approved device, which we have seen in Chapter Three, of taking pastoral innocence and beauty as the measure of metropolitan defilement. We find this practised in Goldsmith and even in Johnson:

> *I praise the Hermit, but regret the Friend,*
> *Who now resolves, from Vice and London far,*
> *To breathe in distant Fields a purer Air.*

But in fact the eighteenth-century satirists did not find this wholesale simplification generally persuasive and it fails to persuade in Johnson's *London* because of this lack of conviction. It appears as an acknowledged convention, not, as with Wordsworth it was, an emotional or intellectual faith. A more typical figure is Pope's Man of Ross, in the *Moral Essays*, whose worthiness is distinctively social and civilised.

The idea that satire postulates a natural goodness which civilised life destroys can be misleading. An instance is the passage where Joseph Andrews arouses small pity in the hearts of the stage-coach passengers who find him beaten, robbed, and stripped of his clothes. James Sutherland reads this as pointing a contrast between 'natural human feeling and utter heartlessness, or between natural feelings and the artificial, affected feelings of the refined'.[1] The intention is more complicated than that. The lady's modesty over Joseph's nakedness is certainly a refined affectation, but the coachman's reluctance to help is not, nor is the attack which brought Joseph to this plight. The lawyer's proposal that they should help Joseph is made because 'if he should die they might be called to some account for his murder'. Now Fielding said many hard things about the shortcomings of the law, but here we see that it provides an incentive, even though a discreditable one, to right action which it is the natural impulse to avoid as troublesome. As Joseph Warton said of Pope, the satirist here withdraws from 'a series of precepts and reproofs'; the satire becomes 'more delicate, because more oblique'[2] and the condemnation at once more general and more discriminating than a symmetrical contrast between untutored virtue and sophisticated callousness.

Satire, indeed, flourishes in a society where there is a wide enough area of optimism, complacency, selfishness and frivolity to provoke it. The eighteenth-century satirist looked for no more than a reduction of this area within a society, necessarily imperfect, whose aim should be to dispose through social employments the human goodness which it supported as effectively as any less developed mode of life. The conclusion of Pope's *Epistle to Burlington* epitomises this outlook:

> *Bid Harbors open, public Ways extend,*
> *Bid Temples, worthier of the God, ascend;*
> *Bid the broad Arch the dang'rous Flood contain,*
> *The Mole projected break the roaring Main;*
> *Back to his bounds their subject Sea command,*
> *And roll obedient Rivers thro' the Land.*

Though this amendatory purpose was seriously held, its methods were more those of comedy than invective. We must, it is true, make the valuable distinction between the comedy of humour, which is tolerant, and the more ruthless comedy of wit, but the

[1] James Sutherland: *English Satire*, p. 112.

[2] *An Essay on the Genius and Writings of Pope*, I, 211.

distinction is a fine one, depending less on method than on intent. The great strength of English satire, even at its most waspish in Pope, is its custody of the comic spirit.

It would be difficult to imagine an environment more alien to English satire than that of the Mississippi valley in nineteenth-century America. The background of reference and allusion the writer could assume in his audience, the lively renascence of classical learning, the formal intricacies of social life, the elegance and splendour of such public arts as architecture, sculpture, interior decoration: all this was absent from the raw life of the Mississippi basin, and more inaccessibly so than at any other time or place in American history. Yet it is a curious fact that the writers for whom Europe was most commandingly present gave birth to no tradition of humorous satire. Of the writers we have studied, Poe's humour was a grotesque mockery; Cooper could be astringent but was more often elephantine; Melville was roaringly facetious; Hawthorne rather laboriously whimsical. In pure satire, Cooper's *Monikins* is ineffectively tortuous; the only success, apart from Lowell's somewhat pallid light verse, is *The Blithedale Romance*, pleasantly ironic, but its satiric accent undeniably tragic. So is that of *Earth's Holocaust*, in which Hawthorne adopted the Addisonian device of the parable. In this story of a multitude come to burn all the emblems of artificial life, marriage certificates, banknotes, title deeds, written constitutions, there is still none of that vivacious sense of the absurd which characterises English satire. It was in the cultural desert of Twain's native region that a distinctively American humour evolved, and with it a more fluent spirit of satire than seemed to be possible in the older states, where even disrespect was disposed to gravity.

Satire as we are most familiar with it directs its attacks against excesses and deviations in a prevailing order the worth of whose standards and the civilising value of whose institutions the satirist accepts. Satire may work, like Fielding's, through credible, realistic characters, or, as in Jonson's early comedies, through stylised 'humours' who are merely embodied foibles to be exposed; against vices thus realistically particularised or against abstract mental attitudes thus reduced to the minimum semblance of sensuous life. It may expound and praise good conduct as well as censuring bad, or work with greater indirectness, through

innuendo and irony conveying its positives in the negative denun-
ciation or exemplary illustration of evil, by methods of the kind
we have seen Jonson employ. The property common to all these
approaches is that, beyond the destructive purpose, the art springs
from a conservative temper, railing at abuses because they en-
croach on and disturb the settled order, against which they are
judged. Yet satire has been traditionally a hazardous occupation.
In the mind both of the satirist and his public it retains some
affinity with the baleful magic power attributed to primitive
satire, as in Irish and Arabian poetry. According to R. C. Elliott,
satire in these literatures was looked on as casting a spell that
literally destroyed the object of its venom: 'The principal belief,
of course, is that satire kills (or at least causes death), that magical
power inheres in the . . . derisive words of a poet whose function
is to praise as well as blame.'[1] Even in the most sophisticated
society belief in magic has an enigmatic half-life and because
satire never quite shakes off this disquieting association it remains
generally an employment admitted by provisional indulgence.

As magic languishes, however, belief in the lethal power of
satiric ridicule, inducing death by shame, is sublimated to the
more humane concept of satire as a social control, purposing
amendment rather than annihilation of the individual. Thus Pope
writes of men,

> Safe from the Bar, the Pulpit, and the Throne,
> Yet touch'd and shamed by Ridicule alone.

Here too the welcome accorded satire is a dubious one, since
even if denied magical properties its powers are considerable and
might easily transgress what is socially advantageous. Elliott
instances from the Ashanti culture of West Africa and certain
social functions in modern America examples of ridicule and
insult being permitted, within a ritualistic dispensation, for their
remedial, cathartic effect. When this happens, satire is coming
close to re-asserting its ancient claims and the very insulation
from normal activity of these occasions acknowledges the sub-
versive force of satire. It may itself unsettle the whole order by a
kind of synecdoche, an unintended extension of reference by its
audience, the accursed part transmitting the malediction to the

[1] *The Power of Satire: magic, ritual, art*, p. 47.

whole. Bishop Warburton has this to say of the possibility: 'The Spaniards have lamented, and I believe truly, that Cervantes' just and inimitable ridicule of *Knight-Errantry* rooted up, with that folly, a great deal of their *real honour*. And it was apparent that Butler's fine satire on *fanaticism* contributed not a little . . . to bring *sober piety* into disrepute.'[1] All these seditious rudiments underlie the imperturbably responsible surface of Augustan satire. Its unprecedented status in England it owed to the self-assurance engendered in society by the prosperous harmony of its parts. Though its sanative aim procured satire this wider licence, it did not eliminate suspicion of the revolutionary potential, however unpremeditated, which it possessed independently of any magical attributes. The protective devices of indirectness, irony, innuendo and allegory were, initially, the satirist's response to his equivocal position, though they came, of course, to be cultivated for their own sake. That the unexorcised menace did not pass unseen even in Augustan satire suggests one area of community between, on the one hand, its glittering achievement, so intimate with classical precedent, so subtle and abundant in invention, resting on a society so secure; and on the other, the satiric craft pursued in the primitive communities with which Twain was most familiar, having, almost *ab initio*, to work out its purposes and methods.

In Twain we are to look for a personal abridgment of this progress from untutored beginnings in an ingenuous culture to what Dr. Johnson called a 'vehicle of wit or delicacy', communicating by 'subtle conveyance'. The idea of satire as a social control Twain certainly held. In *The Mysterious Stranger* (1898) he casts it in a role very similar to that accorded it by Pope: 'Power, money, persuasion, supplication, persecution—these can lift at a colossal humbug . . . but only laughter can blow it to rags and atoms at a blast.' The image comes from Twain's later writing. Some thirty years earlier, after an unsuccessful attempt to make his fortune as a miner, he had joined the staff of the Virginia City *Enterprise*. Of life in these Western regions and Twain's response to it we shall speak again. For the moment, the crucial centre of his Western experience is that it absorbed him into the classic engagement of satire with political contention and the acrimonies

[1] *Works* (London. 1811), I, 155–6.

of covenanting into an ordered commonwealth, in his case at
the very inception.

Twain was assigned, with a colleague, to report the proceedings
of the Nevada Territory Assembly and its Constitutional Convention of 1863. This was a bicameral legislature and Twain was
the inspiration behind the founding of a burlesque 'Third House'
which elected him President. The office conferred on its incumbent
wide powers of ridicule and abuse whose provocativeness the
pseudo-formalities conventionalised and palliated. Of these
powers, judging by his report of the inaugural ceremony,[1]
Twain made exuberant use, imposing procedure, vigorously
insulting the members and deriding the pompous rhetoric
favoured by the Nevada assemblymen. The whole account ex-
ploits the tone of detached and amiable absurdity, so potent a
leaven in satire, as when he describes his sponsors leading him to
the Chair, 'Mr. Small stepping grandly over the desks, and Mr.
Hickok walking under them.' One guards against reading too
much into this frolic, but it is a notable stratagem for equipping
the satiric duty with a protocol and a ritualistic guarantee of
immunity. Though the details are obscure, the fact is clear that
it was the threat of violence excited by his lampoons in the
Enterprise that forced Twain to leave Virginia City; and in turn
to abandon his job at the San Francisco *Morning Call* when his
mockery of the corrupt police force grew too audacious.[2] The
citizens of the West, unlike Pope's rivals, were not content to
engage satirists in a battle of mere words.

The 'Third House' escapade aside, Twain's labours at the
Assembly display an informed and serious purpose. His formal
reports are no longer extant, but his personal commentaries on
the transactions are. Amid their buffoonery and personal squibs
there is an intelligent appraisal of legislative dispute common to
all the new territories, referring mainly to the proper relationship
between commercial interests and the popular assembly. Twain
records two pertinent cases. The state constitution drafted by the
Convention had a clause permitting taxation of undeveloped
mining properties. On this issue, while recognising the right of
the state to benefit from industrial expansion, Twain sided with

[1] See Henry Nash Smith: *Mark Twain of the Enterprise*, pp. 102 ff.

[2] See Edward Wagenknecht: *Mark Twain: the man and his work*, p. 12.

the mining companies. In a dispatch to the New York *Sunday Mercury* he calls the proposed constitution 'an excellent piece of work in many respects', adding that 'it had one or two defects which debarred it from assuming to be an immaculate conception', the tax proposal being foremost. 'It will take,' he says of the mining property, 'two or three years to get it in a developed and paying condition, and will require an enormous outlay of capital to accomplish such a result. And until it does begin to pay dividends, the people will not consent that it should be burdened and hindered by taxation.'[1]

That it was not his principle merely to emancipate the entrepreneurs appears from his condemnation of the Nevada legislature's granting a monopoly to the California State Telegraph Company. The settlement of transport and communication costs was a major political concern at the time and a rich field for chicanery by legislators and speculators alike. The theory of state control was an attractive one, though unpalatable to many. A delegate to the Illinois constitutional convention of 1869–70 had to struggle on behalf of his innocuous point that 'power to limit the rates of charges of common carriers as the public good may require is a governmental power which no legislature can irrevocably abandon or bargain away to any individual or corporation'.[2] Thus propounded, the principle is admirable, but states were not above using their prerogatives as unscrupulously as the Nevada Assembly did. Twain's dispatch of April 5, 1864, elaborates his views:

'They (the Telegraph Company) double the tariff allowed by law, and a man has to submit to the imposition, because he cannot afford the time and trouble of going to law for a trifle of five or ten dollars, notwithstanding the comfort and satisfaction he would derive from worrying the monopolists . . . And that is not the worst they have done, if common report be true. This common report says the telegraph is used by its owners to aid them in stock-gambling schemes . . . It is properly the District Attorney's

[1] See Smith, *op. cit.*, p. 122.

[2] Quoted by John D. Hicks in 'The Development of Civilisation in the Middle West', p. 88; in Dixon Ryan Fox (ed.), *Sources of Culture in the Middle West*.

business to look after these telegraphic speculators, and that officer ought to be reminded of the fact. The next Grand Jury here will endeavour to make it interesting to the Telegraph Company.'[1]

Implicit in this passage is 'probably the most characteristic political idea of the American people', in the words of Benjamin F. Wright, '. . . distrust of elected officers, legislative and executive . . . This distrust is manifested in the detailed character of our constitutions, in the difficulty of amending them, in the principle of separation of powers with its correlative, checks and balances, and in judicial review of legislative and executive actions'.[2] Wright's thesis is that this scepticism, which was not merely a dissenting recoil from the exactions of government, was as influential in the frontier as in the Eastern states. At this stage of his career Twain unmistakably had his share of both its creative and its negative virtue. His protests against these abuses of governmental privilege hypothesise the ideal of a sensitive reciprocity of obligation, not an absolute cleavage, between the legislature and business enterprise, with the process of civil law to arbitrate in the public interest. He accepts, that is, the propriety of stable institutions and the ideal of a just society towards which they work—the satiric, not the revolutionary or melancholic bent.

We can the more readily detach these ideas from his writings for the *Enterprise* because when he wanted to pillory misdemeanours which he considered serious he relinquished flippancy for a relatively earnest manner. There is none of the transition of mood at which Pope was so adept, no inclination to adapt levity to the serious burden of criticism. Flippancy is reserved for the manifestly farcical circumstance and though often it makes sad reading, at times it displays a briskly extravagant fancy. When the voters of Nevada rejected the draft constitution and at the same time ratified the nominations to State office, Twain embellished the verdict by proposing to tell the disappointed functionaries: '. . . what are we to do with these fellows? . . . Now if you know any small state, lying around anywhere, that I could get a contract on for the running of it, you will oblige me by mentioning it in your next. You can say that I have all the machinery on hand

[1] See Smith, *op. cit.*, p. 122.

[2] 'Political Institutions and the Frontier', p. 19, in Fox, *op. cit.*

necessary to the carrying-on of a third-rate State; say, also, that it is comparatively new, portions of it never having been used at all; also, that I will part with it on pretty nearly any terms, as my constitution is prostrated'.[1] Though the execution is undistinguished, the subject and the irreverent tone promise better. Twain had still to strengthen his command of style and technique and to enrich his comic gift by bringing it to bear, paradoxically, on 'some graver subject'.

His contributions to the *Enterprise* evince that 'Insight into the Business . . . of the Age' recommended by the *Spectator*, as well as the satirist's fundamental confidence in the civilising forms and institutions of his society. They were rude and unrefined, but they represented what Pope's Bar, Pulpit and Throne represented. Twain's intimacy with them, as a combination of licensed jester and straight reporter, gave him a satiric purchase and persuaded him, for the moment at least, that they were an effective social machinery, capable, where imperfect, of being shamed by satire into amendment. What has been previously described as his 'personal abridgment' of the progress of satire united a growing resourcefulness of manner with a quickening erosion of this belief. When he wrote *Life on the Mississippi* in 1883 he was able to praise the life of the upper river because its people 'are educated and enlightened . . . they fortify every weak place in their land with a school, a college, a library, and a newspaper; and they live under law'. By 1891, legislatures, and by inference all expressions of the communal will, no longer seemed to him likely repositories of some distilled, collective wisdom, refined by time and precedent: quite the reverse. Recalling his journalistic experiences, Twain says that he 'thus learned to know personally three sample bodies of the smallest minds and the selfishest souls and the cowardliest hearts that God makes'.[2] This particular relapse of faith is symptomatic. The disenchantment it typifies was to attend all the affirmatives Twain tried to read from the corporate establishments and the public faiths of nineteenth-century American society. In the mystique of the frontier, of the South, of industrial progress, in the counsel of the law and contemporary ethical systems he discovered little of that tacit assurance of a settled

[1] See Smith, *op. cit.*, p. 207.

[2] In a letter written 1891, quoted in Wagenknecht, *op. cit.*, p. 6.

order whose importance to the dialectic of satire has been indicated.

II

The bargemen of the Mississippi, as Twain characterised them in *Life on the Mississippi*, were 'rough and hardy men; rude, un-educated, brave, suffering terrific hardships with sailor-like stoicism; heavy drinkers, coarse frolickers in moral sties like the Natchez-under-the-hill of that day, heavy fighters, reckless fellows, every one, elephantinely jolly, foul-witted, profane, prodigal of their money, bankrupt at the end of the trip, fond of barbaric finery, prodigious braggarts; yet, in the main, honest, trustworthy, faithful to promises and duty, and often pic-turesquely magnanimous'. With a few obvious deletions and a little emendation, the passage would describe the public image of the frontiersman in the America of the later nineteenth century. It was, as here, a multiple image, of contrasts curiously super-imposed. Some, as we have seen, emphasised the immorality and connected it variously with spiritual gracelessness, material shift-lessness and political anarchy; others, from the reputation of magnanimity, endurance and generosity deduced pastoral inno-cence, agrarian self-reliance and democratic freedom. Both stereotypes were remarkably persistent but there can be little question that as the century advanced the latter established its ascendancy. Even this was not a unified image. It embraced the ideal of a remote, sequestered settlement, simple in tastes and modest in ambitions, tranquilly taking its rhythms from the seasons and the seasons' tasks; and conversely, the hardly com-patible ideal of a self-multiplying community, dedicated with driving energy to material growth and progress. The favourable image is thus polarised about the great instinctive allurements of the haven and the journey, repose and exploration, fulfilment and desire; and each was the necessary redemption of the other. What basis these archetypes had in immediate fact we shall now examine, for Twain grew up in the way of life that precipitated them.

As well as the bucolic there were now industrial frontiers—the Nevada mines are an example. The confluence of this develop-

ment with the major wave of transcontinental migration complicated pioneer life by embroiling it in a mammoth population
shift and an industrial revolution. From this alone it would seem
that the dynamic, thrustful frontier is the more authentic general
figure. Yet in the contemporary manifestoes lauding the frontier
in these terms, there is no stir of novelty, no disposition to un-
couple their idiom from the genteel archaisms of romantic sentimentality. Bret Harte's miners—and Harte at least recognised
their existence—were trumpery Natty Bumppos in different
clothes. The core of all the apologias was the venerable agrarian
myth and the vocabulary associated with it. In the early years of
the Republic there was a degree of substance in its picture of a
self-sufficient yeomanry absolved from the taint of avarice by its
elemental *rapport* with nature and the soil. The founders of the
nation had, without embarrassment, reasoned in terms of money
and prosperity because, like Jefferson, they saw these as desires
to be realised through the disinfectant medium of husbandry; or,
like Hamilton, through commerce and industry subject to
Federal *dirigisme*. Hamilton's theories had a short run, but city
merchants and politicians continued to compound for their supposedly disreputable activities by deferring to the moral superiority of agriculture, still the predominant national employment.
Even when this dominance succumbed to the spread of industry,
commerce and urbanisation, the moral content of the myth was
inherited intact. So, writes Perry Miller, 'few Americans would
any longer venture, aside from their boasts, to explain, let alone
to justify, the expansion of civilisation in any language that could
remotely be called that of utility'.[1]

This is not altogether true. As we shall see, a more strictly
utilitarian doctrine was on the way, conceding the predominance
of economic over altruistic motives and ratifying the feats of
industrial capitalism. But the agrarian pioneer and the primordial
frontier for long provided the moral overlay. As the haven
symbol it equipped the American imagination with an ideal to
set against the pursuit of riches and material rewards. In this sense
it was often a consciously regressive force, a wholly impracticable
injunction to contract out of the modern age and revert to rustic
simplicity. As the journey-symbol it gave the scramble for wealth

[1] *Errand into the Wilderness*, p. 207.

a gloss of respectability by representing it as an errand in which the desire for personal advancement was incidental to the sense of missionary purpose. As for the literary competence of these ideas, it is clear that they might provide a satiric touchstone, if they achieved any genuine admonitory sway, or succeeded in giving themselves some kind of social expression in the charters and institutions of the newer territories.

There is ample corroboration of the simply picturesque attractions of the pioneer environment. 'The tall corn pleased the eye,' R. L. Stevenson wrote in *Across the Plains*; 'the trees were graceful in themselves, and framed the plain into long, serial vistas; and the clean, bright, gardened townships spoke of country fare and pleasant summer evenings on the stoop.' A county town in the Mississippi valley, for all its makeshifts—streets dusty or muddy in season—had form and design: 'Here the courthouse, built usually in the monumental style of the Greek Revival, symbolised the dignity of the law in a society governed by its own citizens ... The village skyline was dominated by the steeples of Protestant churches'.[1] This architectural pre-eminence of court and church was significant of a hierarchy of values not confined to these more settled communities. As John D. Hicks says, 'these pioneers lent their support to the establishment of schools and colleges, of churches and lyceums, of historical societies and libraries ... they did not, merely by virtue of the succession of moves which had brought them to the West, forget the traditions to which they were naturally heir ... their next concern after ensuring survival was to reproduce in their new life the institutions they had known in the old'.[2] Twain's native town was a frontier community of this kind and Hannibal, of course, is the original of Tom Sawyer's St. Petersburg, Pudd'nhead Wilson's Dawson's Landing and, in *Huckleberry Finn*, in its most embryonic form, the Phelps's plantation. Dixon Wecter has remarked of it that Twain's 'genius always swung like a compass towards his fourteen years' childhood and adolescence in Hannibal',[3] a pulse of feeling, we might add, so often charged with nostalgic tenderness that it supposes sympathetic recollection. The visual presentation, in this

[1] Ralph Henry Gabriel: *The Course of American Democratic Thought*, p. 5.

[2] *op. cit.*, p. 80.

[3] Quoted in Walter Blair, *Mark Twain and Huck Finn*, p. 9.

mood of amiable recall, is intended to suggest a definite moral
as well as physical ambience. Dawson's Landing is 'a snug little
collection of one- and two-story frame dwellings . . . Each of
these pretty homes had a garden in front, fenced with white
palings and opulently stocked with . . . old-fashioned flowers;
while on the window-sills of the houses stood . . . terra-cotta pots
in which grew a breed of geraniums whose spread of intensely
red blossoms accented the prevailing pink tint of the rose-clad
house-front like an explosion of flame'. It is a town with 'shade
for summer and a sweet fragrance in spring . . . sleepy and comfortable and contented'.

The qualities which the description insinuates are tranquillity,
timelessness, a sedate propriety of conduct—the town 'was
growing slowly—very slowly, in fact, but still it was growing'—
steeped, like so many of Twain's halcyon scenes, in the warmth
of an undying summer. His political fable, 'The Great Revolution
in Pitcairn', (1878), makes explicit the association between the
atmospheric and the moral serenity. By political subterfuge, an
American adventurer, Butterworth Stavely, has himself elected
Emperor of the peaceful island of Pitcairn. He institutes a series
of 'reforms' aimed at giving the island military power and an
imperialistic programme. In time, he arouses the islanders' resentment, first expressed by a social democrat who 'stabbed at him
fifteen or sixteen times with a harpoon, but fortunately with such
a peculiarly social democratic unprecision of aim as to do no
damage'. That night Stavely is deposed. The island reverts to 'the
old healing and solacing pieties', and the condition it is described
as enjoying when the story opens—Hannibal apotheosised: 'The
habits and dress of the people have always been primitive, and
their laws simple to puerility. They have lived in a deep Sabbath
tranquillity, far from the world and its ambitions and vexations
. . . Once in three or four years a ship touched there, moved them
with aged news of bloody battles, devastating epidemics, fallen
thrones, and ruined dynasties . . . and sailed away, leaving them
to retire into their peaceful dreams and pious dissipations.' Pitcairn is America, likewise born of revolution, likewise seduced
by materialistic leaders from its ancient virtues. The reclamation
of this integrity must be total, a redemptive act of faith, not an
ineffectual tinkering with reformist stratagems. At least thus far,

then, Twain did acquire from his transmuted recollections of this phase of frontier life positive standards that were satirically functional, though hardly of much political account. These were frontier town realities, but, unhappily, the evidence rebutting them is equally strong.

The inherited traditions of a vagrant culture are highly vulnerable. This condition affected the frontier. F. L. Paxson makes it clear that 'the average distance of the migrant was not many miles . . . his connexions were not those of a westerner with the East, but of a frontier farmer with a former frontier community, fifty miles or so behind him . . . there were few funds from which the pioneer could borrow the funds necessary for the capitalisation of his venture, even on the most modest scale'.[1] As communications improved, the migrant societies were not so decisively cut off as they might have been, but the fact of disruption—and its consequences—is undeniable. Against the proprieties maintained in the Mississippi town Ralph Gabriel describes we must set his account of life in a mining town like Silver City, which exhibited all the animal sexuality, gluttonising and brutality of the pioneer. 'There is scarcely a page of reliable testimony about pioneer life,' Lewis Mumford concludes, 'which does not hint at this nightmare.'[2]

Some of it we can glean from a number of Twain's anecdotes in *Life on the Mississippi*. From the archives of Hannibal itself Walter Blair assembles a wretched catalogue of alcoholism, madness, attempted rape and lynching, homicide.[3] This background shadows even Tom Sawyer's St. Petersburg, which has its share of harrowing violence, and takes control of many of the Mississippi towns Huck Finn visits in the course of his odyssey. The 'little one-horse town' in Arkansaw is, in appearance, precisely the antitype of Dawson's Landing:

The stores and houses was most all old shackly dried-up frame concerns that hadn't ever been painted . . . The houses had little gardens around them, but they didn't seem to raise hardly anything in them but jimpson weeds, and sunflowers, and ash-piles,

[1] *History of the American Frontier*, p. 228.

[2] *The Golden Day*, p. 78.

[3] *op. cit.*, pp. 54–56.

and old curled-up boots and shoes, and pieces of bottles, and rags, and played-out tinware . . . There couldn't anything wake them up all over, unless it might be putting turpentine on a stray dog, and setting fire to him. . . .'

The slatternly look of the town is coupled with a slatternliness of spirit. In this setting Colonel Sherburn shoots down the unarmed Boggs and then harangues the mob, which has come to lynch him, into dispersing:

'Your newspapers call you a brave people so much that you think you *are* braver than any other people—whereas you're just *as* brave and no braver. Why don't your juries hang murderers? Because they're afraid the man's friends will shoot them in the back, in the dark—and it's just what they *would* do . . . Your mistake is that you didn't bring a man with you . . . a mob without any *man* at the head of it is *beneath* pitifulness. Now the thing for *you* to do, is to droop your tails and go home and crawl in a hole.'

The town's is a corporate failure, a failure of institutions; specifically, frustration of the law, one of the establishments under whose custody, it had seemed to Twain in his Nevada days, a democratic social discipline might be methodised. In the Sherburn sequence, the ugliness of the town, of its citizens' habits, the savagery of the murder, are the outcome of reverberations, in Twain's mind, from a universal declension in the polity of the frontier. The failure of the pioneer policy of 'settle and sell' to encourage community interest was reflected in a general indifference to decent principles of government, which gave frontier legislatures an authority for corruption remarkable even in a country where political venality had become accepted practice. The power, and with it the prestige, of Federal government had been in progressive decline since Jackson's assaults on it. 'We have gotten over the harms done us by the war of 1812,' Twain declared in *Life on the Mississippi*, 'but not over some of those done us by Jackson's presidency.' There was no longer a national bank and hence no Federal provision for the financing of Western improvements, which in consequence was delegated to the States. In the 1860's the tendency of Supreme Court decisions had been to leave business enterprise 'without any protection from State regulation of elections, for instance, or State regulation of railroad or warehouse rates'.[1] Thereafter, as this tendency was halted and reversed, opening up to business a legally untrammelled field, the obstructive capabilities of the States were neutralised by private deals between entrepreneurs and legislatures created in the image of the unprincipled mob that ran from Sherburn. 'The unpleasantness of mob government,' Bagehot wrote, 'has never before been exemplified so conspicuously, for it never before has worked upon so large a scene.'[2] Sensitive to the epidemic signs of this distemper in morality and the arts of government, nowhere plainer than on the frontier, Twain became obsessed with the symbolism of the seedy town rather than the idealised St. Petersburg, with the unprepossessing rather than the attractive qualities of the bargemen and all their confraternity. It was this which tore at and consumed his frail, nostalgic dream. Neither in the frontier as symbolising a way of life, nor in its evolving institutions, could he continue to find his positive, diagnostic standards.

Nor did the extraneous interests the frontier was assenting to and colluding with offer to the contemporary satirical view much that was virtuous or comely. It was, for the most part, to the least appealing, the most superficial, of Eastern ideals that the pioneer addressed his efforts. If he began, as Mumford puts it, 'as an unconscious follower of Rousseau, he was only too ready, after the first flush of effort, to barter all his glorious heritage for gas light and paved streets and starched collars and skyscrapers and the other insignia of a truly high and progressive civilisation'.[3] The sarcasm is not unjustified, but sentiment aside, it is hard to see the paved streets and the skyscrapers, in themselves, as anything but an improvement on the filth and mud and squalor that took so painful a grip on Twain's imagination. When he approved 'the wholesome and practical nineteenth century

[1] T. C. Cochran and W. Miller: *The Age of Enterprise* p. 178.

[2] Quoted in David Donald, *An Excess of Democracy* (University of Oxford Inaugural Lecture, Clarendon Press), p. 18, q.v.

[3] *op. cit.*, p. 80. Benjamin F. Wright (*op. cit.*) gives a less partial account of the process, viewing tolerantly the westerners' admiration of 'the bankers and merchants and landowners back home' (p. 32).

smell of cotton-factories and locomotives ... practical, common-sense progressive ideas and progressive works', Twain was wel-coming America's technological genius as a corrective to the parochialism and the bigotries of small-town frontier life. His panegyric, in *Life on the Mississippi*, on St. Paul is conducted almost wholly in statistics demonstrating material growth. The population, the size of the Post Office and the railway station, the volume of trade and the amount of dollars it handles declare its 'newness, briskness, swift progress, wealth, intelligence ... and general slash and go'. All these feats of technology and finance have gloriously superseded the primitive endowments of an earlier cycle: '... the poor immigrant, with axe and hoe and rifle; next, the trader; next, the miscellaneous rush; next, the gambler, the desperado, the highwayman, and all their kindred in sin of both sexes'. Twain took pride in mercantile success and the dissemination of mechanical appliances because, for a time, they seemed accessory to an improved social demeanour.

For the general public, of course, they were intrinsically good and Twain undoubtedly humoured this more worldly approval. It is the basis of his reputation as an amiable wag, happily setting European sloth and incompetence against American dispatch and efficiency; European kings and nobles, affectation and rascality against American entrepreneurs and inventors, simplicity and candour. The critics have been severe with Twain on this score. He 'followed the cult of newness', says Constance Rourke, 'like a thousand comic prophets and serious exhorters who had gone before him ... without distance, and without perspective'.[1] His satire on Europe, the case runs, brushed with straw men of his own creation, set up a meaningless antithesis and accepted a worthless scale of values. This right-minded criticism ignores the fact that Twain, like many a humorist an irascible man, encoun-tered on his travels much that was genuinely irritating and humanly vented his spleen on it without any deep moral purpose; and that many of the affectations he ridiculed are legitimate objects of satire, out of which he made effective humorous capital. *The Innocents Abroad* and *A Yankee at the Court of King Arthur* are by no means so tedious as they are fashionably made out to be. But what is more to the point is that this antithesis did not,

[1] *American Humour* p. 216.

finally, satisfy Twain himself, or provide him with the gauge his satiric vision needed. In 1905 he wrote in a letter, 'Well, the nineteenth century made progress—the first progress after "ages and ages"—colossal progress. In what? Materialities . . . But the addition to righteousness? Is it discoverable? I think not.'

The 'colossal progress' spread its benefits widely but not universally. What accompanied it Twain called, in *My First Lie* (1899), the 'silent, colossal National Lie that is the support and confederate of all the tyrannies and shams and inequalities and unfairnesses that afflict the peoples'. These were the by-products of an economic system whose traditional dynamic, individual enterprise, had culminated in the autocratic monopolism of the vast cartels consolidated by the Rockefellers and Carnegies, and the 'money-trusts' of men like J. P. Morgan. Details of the incidental social injustices crowd the newspaper 'exposures' and the naturalist fiction of the 'muck-raking' era: want, inhuman working conditions, slums and over-crowded tenements, crime and prostitution caused by low wages, ruthless strike-breaking by 'a hireling standing army, unrecognised by our laws'.[1]

Of the documentary urban realism and the extravagantly angled situations of Frank Norris, Stephen Crane and Jack London we find little in Twain. Satan's grand tour of human life takes the narrator of *The Mysterious Stranger* to a 'wholesome and practical nineteenth-century' factory worked by maltreated and half-starved employees. The short piece, 'A Humane Word from Satan' enters a sardonic plea for Mr. Rockefeller: 'In all the ages, three-fourths of the support of the great charities has been conscience-money, as my books will show: then what becomes of the sting when the term is applied to Mr. Rockefeller's gift? The charge most persistently and resentfully and remorselessly dwelt upon is, that Mr. Rockefeller's contribution is incurably tainted by perjury—perjury proved against him in the courts. *It makes us smile*—down in my place! . . . by and by, when you arrive, I will show you something interesting: a whole hell-full of evaders! Sometimes a frank law-breaker turns up elsewhere, but I get those others every time.' *The 30,000 Dollar Bequest* (1904) enters that weirdly abstract realm of hypothetical gains

---

[1] Ignatius Donnelly, preamble to the Populist platform (1892). Quoted in Henry Steele Commager, *The American Mind*, pp. 50–51.

and losses not in actual property but in property values and property rights.

A man and his wife, thrifty, comfortably prosperous, are misled into thinking that an uncle intends to leave them $30,000. Immediately they begin planning how they will dispose of it, the wife investing it—theoretically—in innumerable stocks, the man luxuriating in the comforts to be provided by the interest from these entirely imaginary investments. Into the monomania of the Fosters Twain concentrates the national speculative frenzy. Values were estimated on the basis of purely conjectural developments. So from their hoard of 'clean, imaginary cash' grows the couple's social ascent, envisaged as a kind of spectral luxury: 'Mansion after mansion, made of air, rose higher, broader, finer, and each in its turn vanished away; until now, in these latter great days, our dreamers were in fancy housed, in a distant region, in a sumptuous vast palace which looked out from a leafy summit upon a noble prospect of vale and river and receding hills steeped in tinted mists—and all private, all the property of the dreamers.' It is instructive to compare with this the much more sympathetically presented visions of Richard Jones in *The Pioneers*. These dreamers lose all contact with reality—and learn, finally, that their uncle had in fact died penniless. This bitter parable ends properly when the Fosters hear of their uncle's death: 'They sat with bowed heads, dead to all things but the ache at their hearts.' Twain, however, redundantly, goes on to make the moral explicit that 'Vast wealth, acquired by sudden and unwholesome means, is a snare'.

These occasional direct forays into the topsy-turvydom of commercial enterprises are generated by a simple, an almost unthinking, emotional response to its futilities and injustices: the weak-willed are morally destroyed by the national worship of Mammon, which is wrong; the poor and defenceless are ill-treated, which is wrong; the rich and powerful get away with lying, which is wrong. But Twain was not so well equipped to deal with the rationalisations devised to extenuate these wrongs. It is through the contending propositions of this more doubtful engagement, not the satisfactions of emotional certainty, that his work bears most intently upon the 'business civilisation' of his times.

The plainest token of the fascination the law held for Twain
is the number of trial scenes in his writings. Yet the drama of
none of these turns upon the moral, philosophical and legal
arguments raised by the activities of the great corporations and
debated most crucially in the courts. The outcome of Twain's
trials is decided by a startling revelation, a surprise witness, an
ingenious application of some scientific novelty. In *The Mysterious
Stranger*, Father Peter is acquitted because the date stamped on
the coins he is supposed to have stolen is later than the year of
the alleged robbery. In *Tom Sawyer*, Muff Potter is acquitted
because Tom eventually comes forward to give his eye-witness
account of the murder. In *Pudd'n'head Wilson*, the fraudulent
Tom Driscoll is exposed, and the charge of murder proved
against him, on the evidence of the natal fingerprints collected
by Pudd'n'head Wilson. *Huckleberry Finn* was originally intended
to have as its climax 'Jim's trial for the murder of Huck, a crime
never committed'.[1] The elaborate hocus-pocus, the pseudo-
consequentialness, is an odd evasion in Twain. He was in fact
deeply absorbed in the metaphysical underpinnings of the legal
commentary on the corporations' blanket appeal to the principle
of economic individualism. More corrosively than the evidence
of slums, brutalised workers, squalid factories, this intellectual
inquiry attacked the roots of his faith in the probity of commercial and technological advance.

The most important critics of the association between business
interests and the law were men of conservative temperament disturbed by the near-sighted extremism of the new industrial *élite*.
Prominent among them was Brooks Adams. The post-Civil War
capitalist, as Adams sees him in *The Theory of Social Evolution*,[2]
thinks 'in terms of money . . . more exclusively than the French
aristocrat or lawyer ever thought in terms of caste'. In developing
railroads and highways, for instance, an enterprise clearly in the
domain of public interest, he is 'too specialised to comprehend a
social relation, even a fundamental one like this, beyond the
narrow circle of his private interests. He might, had he so chosen,
have evolved a system of governmental railway regulation, and
have administered the system personally, or by his own agents,

[1] H. H. Rogers: *The Role of Literary Burlesque*, p. 199.

[2] The quotations from Adams in this paragraph are taken from pp. 203–230.

but he could never be brought to see the advantage to himself of rational concession to obtain a resultant of forces'. Consequently, he considers that the function of the state is to protect his interests irrespective of the welfare of other sections. He retains lawyers, 'not to advise him touching his duty under the law, but to devise a method by which he may elude it; or if he cannot elude it, by which he may have it annulled as unconstitutional by the courts'. Thus, 'in the United States alone of Western nations . . . great issues of public policy were exposed to the hazards of private litigation'.[1] For the corporations the hazards were rapidly diminished. Their wealth was used to influence both legislatures and public opinion and to secure a near monopoly of legal talent. In addition, after about 1875, the Supreme Court began almost mechanically to countenance the arguments of the corporation lawyers against any legislative inhibition of business autonomy. In a simple economy, where the competing parties have some genuine equality of opportunity, *laisser-faire* is not an unreasonable policy. The corporations, however, were gradually reducing competition by absorbing it, while they continued to invoke the principle as a weapon, now, against governmental regulation of wages, for example, or statutory support for the right of employees to strike or to organise defensive amalgamations of labour. We need not dwell here on the riot, bloodshed and oppression that followed from the Supreme Court's practice of annulling the mildest social welfare legislation and from the torrent of strike-breaking injunctions. More to our purpose is the reasoning that governed these decisions.

A basic hypothesis was that as business prospered, so did the nation. Its corollary was that in order to prosper, and hence to spread its civilising influence, business must be left to work unhampered along whatever lines it naturally took. That it might thereby conflict with public good was thought impossible. Any opposition to it was defined not, in the phrase of Louis Brandeis, as 'the contentions of the people', but as sectional agitation, which, should it achieve effective legislative form, would disrupt the natural play of forces in a free economy. Justice David J. Brewer was therefore able, addressing the New York Bar

[1] Commager, *op. cit*, p. 362.

Association (1893), to assert that the function of the courts in relation to the state was limited 'to seeing that popular action does not
trespass upon right and justice as it exists in written constitutions
and the natural law'. Although the term is unchanged, the
'natural law' to which Justice Brewer referred had, over the years,
acquired with new associations a new orthodoxy of interpretation.
Some dispersion of its meaning was inevitable in a juridical
tradition which had always indulged the enthusiasm for absolutes
expressed in Justice Story's *Address to the Suffolk County Bar*
(1829). He recommended speculation 'upon the origin and
extent of moral obligations; upon the great truths and dictates
of natural law; and upon the immutable principles that regulate
right and wrong in social and private life'. Story in fact inferred
many of his 'immutable principles' from his exhaustive and
scholarly study of precedents. But he also retained the belief that
they were derivable fundamentally, extra-historically, from the
manifestation of divine will in the natural order of things. In the
thinking of Story's day, the universe was still partly that of
Puritan theology, but in the main it was the perfect mechanism
of Newton. The rules of human conduct derived from and
articulated to this methodical structure were to promote the
same concord and inevitablity in the social order, as free of unpredictable conflict as the movements of the stars.

These concepts inspired the liberal tenets—life, liberty and the
pursuit of happiness—of the Declaration of Independence. In the
early judicial reviews of Constitutional law they were the means
of conferring legal status upon the claims of the individual in
society to rights and privileges and of measuring his claims
against those of private property and those of an individual as
an agent acquiring property. The state, that is, was the custodian
—through its legal system—of rights which were the natural
possession of the individual, not in the gift of society. Judge
Nathaniel Chipman's *Sketches of the Principles of Government*
(1793) states the position concisely. As individuals in society we
have 'the right to use our own powers and faculties, natural and
acquired, for our own convenience and happiness. The use, however, must be in a just compromise with the convenience and
happiness of others, agreeable to the laws of social nature, and
such combinations and regulations are clearly derived from those

laws. Under the last head comes the general right of making acquisitions. The exercise of this right, therefore, is subject to particular modifications.' Thus we arrive at the paradox that natural law confers rights independent of society upon the individual; and that social regulation is indispensable to the just exercise of these rights. Thus, too, the legal apparatus of society is designed, ideally, to function as a substantial protection to the weak.

By writing these oracular concepts so irrevocably into the Constitution, and by admitting the principle of judicial review, the nation had assured long life to the nebulous authority of the natural law. After the Civil War it was transferred, or extended, to the clause of the Fourteenth Amendment which required that any enactment should be discharged by 'due process of law'. The phrase was used very much as 'natural law' had been to signify some higher body of rights and principles which guided judicial opinions. As B. F. Wright explains, 'the adoption by the Supreme Court of this extremely broad and equally vague interpretation of due process of law has had the very practical effect of making possible a tremendous increase in the number of Acts declared unconstitutional'.[1] The reason for this increase is that the natural law most of the judiciary now had in mind had responded to turns in the general understanding of 'nature', 'the universe' and 'society'. For example the importance of 'property rights'—now, more often than not, associated with corporate bodies—had been elevated to a higher plane than purely 'individual' rights. This change was contingent upon a lower estimate of inherent individual worth, in a universe where rational design, equitably composed of all its separate members, seemed less obviously the working principle than it had in Newtonian nature.

Guiding the interpretation of due process was a new natural law, the product of the nature elucidated by Darwin—or, rather, of Darwinian theory as applied to social affairs by American thinkers. The elaborate ramifications of this exercise we need not pursue. In general its achievement was reminiscent of the satisfactory conclusion of Hegel that the dialectic he discerned in history had reached its final synthesis in his own age and state. Darwin's principle of natural selection decided in society, as in

[1] Benjamin F. Wright: *American Interpretations of Natural Law*, p. 305.

nature, the life-forms best fitted to survive the struggle against their unco-operative environment. No moral imperative hindered the extinction of obsolescent species; so, clearly, there could be no wisdom in trying, for reasons of charity, to moderate the destruction of the less competent that inevitably went with the rise in society of their better endowed contemporaries. Equally clearly, natural selection in the social field operated on the basis, in Veblen's phrase, of 'pecuniary aptitudes'. The most rigorously logical organisation of these theories was that of William Graham Sumner.

Sumner's thesis was that societal welfare is the only useful standard of value and that it is to be measured by 'economic power, material prosperity and group strength for war'.[1] For the idea of absolute moral values he substituted the idea of the *mores*, which were rules of conduct evolved by usage as the fittest to secure general welfare, inexorably changing with changed social conditions. So far as the individual in society is concerned, 'What the mores always represent is the struggle to live as well as possible under the conditions. Traditions, so far as they come out of other conditions and are accepted as independent authorities in the present conditions, are felt as hindrances.'[2] As the mores are evolved specifically to further societal welfare, the more thoroughly the individual conforms to them, the more surely will he serve, at once, both his own ends and those of society in general. The activities best able to accumulate 'economic power' and the rest are those of commerce and industry: 'Industry is carried on by talent, which is select and aristocratic' and so is hostile to 'the political ideals of liberty and equality'.[3] Consequently some degree of protection must be afforded these ideals, though they are really 'educational motives . . . moral incentives . . . not every-day rules of action for specific exigencies'.[4] Nevertheless, the legislator is needed:

[1] William Graham Sumner: *Folkways* (Boston, 1906), p. 100.

[2] Sumner: 'Religion and the Mores' in *War and other Essays* (Yale 1911), p. 143.

[3] Sumner: 'Economics and Politics' in *Earth-Hunger and other Essays* (Yale 1913), p. 323.

[4] Sumner: 'Definitions of Democracy and Plutocracy', *ibid.*, p. 291.

'He becomes the guardian of public or common interests, especially in regard to franchises, privileges, and compulsory powers. Here the delicacy of his functions becomes apparent, for he creates and grants privileges and overrides private rights and individual will in the name of public interest . . . we do not see how the public necessity and convenience can be served without giving this power to the legislature.'[1]

But the concession is reluctant and limited. The legislature is an overtly political force, artificially introduced into society with the declared purpose of modifying and retarding the course of free development. The danger of state intervention is that, in the sensitive constitution of society, any action purposing control of a single element in it must 'spread far through the organisms, affecting organs and modifying functions which are, at the first view of the matter, apparently so remote that they could not be affected at all . . . It is this elasticity and plasticity of the organs of society which give the social tinker his chance, and make him think that there are no laws of the social order, no science of society; no limits, in fact, to the possibilities of manipulation by "The State". He is always operating on the limit of give and take between the organs'.[2] In addition, 'the State' by its very existence constantly prevails upon rival factions to seize control, for their private ends, of the manipulative apparatus it has set up. Sumner distinguishes between the abstract 'power of capital', which is beneficent and had in former ages always worked for good, and the plutocracy of his own day, 'the most sordid and debasing form of political energy known to us'.[3] Unlike the genuine merchant or industrialist, the plutocrat, 'having the possession of capital, and having the power of it at his disposal, uses it, not industrially, but politically; instead of employing labourers, he enlists lobbyists . . . operates upon the market by legislation, by artificial monopoly, by legislative privileges; he creates jobs, and erects combinations, which are half political and half industrial'.[4] The solution is to diminish the attractiveness of the state by

[1] 'Economics and Politics', *ibid.*, p. 319.

[2] Sumner: 'Democracy and Plutocracy', *ibid.*, pp. 283, 285.

[3] 'Definitions of Democracy and Plutocracy', *ibid.*, p. 295.

[4] *Ibid.*, p. 298.

enfeebling its powers 'to minimise to the utmost the relations of the state to society'.[1]

In the end, Sumner's conclusion from these arguments was pessimistic. He could not, he says, 'see how, under existing conditions . . . economics and politics can be reconciled so that industry can prosper and law can be respected, both at the same time'.[2] He was, in fact, unable to conceive of an impartial state or one wise enough to formulate measures with foreseeable consequences; nor could he conceive of the plutocracy experiencing an accession of wisdom that would persuade them to abandon their coveting of political control. Of all Sumner's ideas, this pessimistic conclusion was the one that gained least currency. What the age took from Sumner was the general tenor of his argument, which gave formidable intellectual approval to the personal qualities of drive and initiative, to the association between business enterprise and national well-being, and which favoured any action that preserved the *status quo*. These were the principles constituting the natural law to which the judges referred in their anti-welfare state, anti-strike decisions. The Supreme Court was a nexus between the abstractions of the new social philosophy and the actualities of industry and politics. Sumner, like Aristotle in the *Poetics*, did not so much originate principles as organise them from the events taking place around him. He gives us the most complete philosophical statement; the courts provide, for us as for the Americans of that time, the most striking conjunction between intellectual theory and the mundane world of wages, profits, strikes, living conditions. For all that it was unchartered and unsystematic, this singular union of business, law and philosophy both created and, each in its own way, expressed the intellectual dogmas of its time. Without some understanding of it we cannot appreciate the fiction of the period, all of which, whether accepting or rejecting, was oriented round these ideas. So far as Twain's satire is concerned, their effect was to strike at his use of the forward march of commerce as one of his positives.

It is easy to magnify the miseries of this period, and to impute to the social Darwinites a sinister community of purpose that

[1] *Ibid.*, p. 300.

[2] 'Economics and Politics', *ibid.*, p. 300.

did not, in fact, exist. We may reasonably suppose that most Americans lived, in moderate comfort and contentment, beyond the orbit of these exchanges, though rarely altogether indifferent to them. Certainly the successes of the 'robber barons' aroused no comprehensive popular unrest: 'Because,' Richard Hofstadter argues, 'it was always possible to assume a remarkable measure of social equality and a fair minimum of subsistence, the goal of revolt tended to be neither social democracy nor social equality, but greater opportunities.'[1] Looking back on the period, we are bound to conclude that its capitalism was, however wastefully, a success, that it did not blight the national fibre and that, when it had fulfilled itself, it did submit to compromise with the forces of reform. Nevertheless, to the sensitive and articulate mind of the artist, living through the experience, the elements of misery and chaos were uppermost. That the general public acquiesced in even the most questionable expedients intensified the hopelessness.

Twain, according to Bernard de Voto, 'fiercely championed the democratic axioms; they are the ether of his fiction and the fulcrum of his satire.'[2] This account leaves unregistered the perplexities that are most interesting in Twain. As early as 1875 he was at least thoughtful about, for instance, the logic of democratic suffrage. In 'The Curious Republic of Gondour' he described a sliding scale of votes rising from one for 'every citizen, however poor or ignorant', to plural votes for accumulation of wealth and property and apportioned to the stages of advance through the educational hierarchy. The last was best endowed: 'Therefore, learning being more prevalent and more easily acquired than riches, educated men became a wholesome check upon wealthy men, since they could outvote them . . . so the learned voters, possessing the balance of power, became the vigilant and efficient protectors of the great lower rank of society'. This scheme, then, penalises the mercantile and industrial classes because their motives are primarily self-interested—in Twain's eyes, inevitably so, because he accepted the idea that character and ethical principles are conditioned by the social environment, the

[1] *The Age of Reform*, p. 10.

[2] 'Introduction to Mark Twain' in Philip Rahv (ed.), *Literature in America*, p. 211.

habits of the group, the ambitions of the individual. The self-interest of the commercial class might, in neutral circumstances, be 'enlightened'; but many egos the light failed to penetrate, and any direct conflict between the claims of self and accessory duties was settled in favour of immediate personal benefit.

At this time Twain was reading Darwin's *Descent of Man* and Lecky's *History of European Morals.* Lecky agreed with the moralists who say that man intuitively perceives and aspires to an absolute, objective good, but Twain's sympathies were with the thinkers who converted Darwin's biological observations into philosophic dogma. In a marginal note on his copy of Lecky, he has this to say: 'All moral perceptions are acquired by the influences around us; those influences begin in infancy; we never get a chance to find out whether we have any that are innate or not.'[1] The accent of the gloss is that of the rationalist dogma which he absorbed from his times. Sumner, in 'Religion and the Mores', gives more formal expression to exactly the same idea:

'They (i.e. human beings in society) are trained in the ritual, habituated to the usages, imbued with the notions of the societal environment. They hear and repeat the proverbs, sayings, and maxims which are current in it. They perceive what is admired, ridiculed, abominated, desired by the people about them. They learn the code of conduct—what is considered stupid, smart, stylish, clever, or foolish, and they form themselves on these ideas.'

The remarkable unanimity of these two passages indicates the inroads made on Twain's beliefs by the philosophical assertions most faithful to 'the very age and body of the time'. Yet he had not, in fact, Sumner's stoical acceptance of his own logic. His confusion appears in a note on Huckleberry Finn's celebrated battle with his conscience over the problem of Jim, the runaway slave. All Huck's training urges him to give Jim up, but deeper feelings revolt against the treachery. It is to this passage that Twain alludes in his Notebooks:

'Next I should exploit the proposition that in a crucial moral emergency a sound heart is a safer guide than an ill-trained conscience. I sh'd support this doctrine with a chapter from a book of mine where a sound heart and a deformed conscience come

[1] See Blair, *op. cit.*, p. 138.

into collision and conscience suffers defeat . . . It shows that that strange thing, the conscience—that unerring monitor—can be trained to approve any wild thing you *want* it to approve if you begin its education early and stick to it.'[1]

In the marginal comment on Lecky, 'moral perceptions . . . acquired by the influences around us' meant all moral perceptions. Here, Twain distinguishes, rather artificially, between 'conscience'—the sense of right and wrong developed by the community—and 'a sound heart'—innate recognition of an objective good. Despite his rationalist professions, Twain, inconsistently, held to a conviction that the human consciousness did embrace this hardy instinct, which saw Huck through his moral crisis. But where Fielding and Cooper saw individual goodness made effective in society through institutions, Twain could see no establishment congenial to it. The proponents of the 'business ethic' did not persuade him that there were no standards other than those of self-advancement and self-preservation; but they did persuade him that no others could prevail. At one level, undoubtedly, his satire favours the new (steamboats, railroads, cities, rationalism) against the old (small-town life, physical inconvenience, tradition, conservatism in both Europe and America). But he is driven back to this one positive, the standard set by an innate human disposition to what is just and good. It is beset, on the one hand, by an equally aboriginal disposition to narrow self-interest, and on the other by social institutions, which accommodate themselves to the more truculent drive. About these poles he orders the satire of his major works, in which his inventiveness of phrase and humour, while it never deserts him, serves increasingly melancholy findings.

III

Huckleberry Finn chronicles the three lives of its hero: the sinner unwillingly reformed, the fugitive on the river, the prodigal transiently returned. In the first, Huck's character begins to take shape through his commentary on the people with whom he is chiefly associated. Living with the Widow Douglas and her sister, the querulous Miss Watson, he undergoes their complementary

[1] See Blair, *op. cit.*, pp. 143-4.

spiritual diets. While Miss Watson threatens him with hellfire, Widow Douglas tempts him with the rewards of heaven. Both appeals leave Huck impassive: 'I couldn't see no advantage about it—except for the other people—so at last I reckoned I wouldn't worry about it any more, but just let it go.' Nor do the conventional comforts of shelter, bed and clothing reconcile him to the conventional restrictions of education, manners and morality. When he runs away, it is Tom Sawyer who persuades him to return: 'Tom Sawyer he hunted me up and said he was going to start a band of robbers, and I might join if I would go back to the widow and be respectable. So I went back.' Content in his own illusions, Tom can compromise with the world of adult standards, whose jurisdiction he never really challenges. Unlike Huck's defections, Tom's remain always a fantasy kept strictly within the bounds of recall. When he organises games of piracy and adventure for his followers his answer to every objection is, 'I've seen it in books, and so of course that's what we've got to do.' Turnips become 'julery'; hogs, ingots; a Sunday school picnic, an encampment of 'A-rabs' and elephants. Huck's literal mind never suspends its disbelief—'I judged that all that stuff was just one of Tom Sawyer's lies. I reckoned he believed in the A-rabs and the elephants, but as for me I think different. It had all the marks of a Sunday school.' Nevertheless, for all his scepticism he continues to refer his doings to what Tom might think of them.

Finally we see Huck falling again under the authority of his wastrel father, who has come back because he knows of Huck's windfall. This is the most interesting of the preliminary relationships. His father is brutal, slovenly, alcoholic. He epitomises all the bigotries of his backwoods squatter class, cursing Huck for the education he has acquired, a 'free nigger' because 'they said he was a p'fessor in a college . . . they said he could *vote*'. He thrashes Huck regularly and terrifies him in the nightmare scene of his dipsomaniac frenzy. Yet Huck finds life with him nearer his tastes, on the whole, than life with the widow: 'It was kind of lazy and jolly, laying off comfortable all day, smoking and fishing and no books or study . . . But by-and-by pap got too handy with his hick'ry, and I couldn't stand it.' So Huck arranges his escape. Without any sentimental qualms he kills a pig and lets it bleed on the shanty floor so that the inevitable pursuit 'won't ever hunt the river for anything but my dead carcass'.

In these episodes Twain establishes his satiric *persona*. Huck is ordinary human clay, averse to duties, responsibilities, indifferent to the welfare of others; humourless, aside from the rather heartless prankishness of a small boy, and a sardonic appreciation of adult hypocrisies. With his father he has seen and experienced cruelty and is tough and callous enough himself, so his view of the river life he is to record is not that of cloistered inexperience or a temperament readily shocked. Under these self-protective layers is the generous spirit that responds to the widow's distress over his backslidings, not because he is won to 'virtue', but because her sorrow grieves him. This is Twain's Gulliver, a more consistent figure than Swift's. He is endenizened in many worlds: the respectable society of the widow and her sister, the fantasy world of Tom, the superstitious mythology of Jim, the lethargic shanty life of his father. Content in none, he survives in them all to become the observer of and participant in the wider Mississippi world, which is familiar to him but always freshly seen. He cannot influence its courses but his qualities peculiarly fit him to transmit the significant details by which the reader may judge; and on occasion to supplement these with his own judgments. If for nothing else, Huckleberry Finn is memorable as a brilliant fusion of realistic character and efficient aesthetic device.

The main part of the book describes Huck's journey with Jim, Miss Watson's runaway slave, along the Mississippi. Twain's experience as a pilot on the Mississippi, when he got to know it professionally, defined the river for him. The romantic observer, transfixed by its pictorial beauty, stops short of its reality. The only transcendental inference prompted by its immensity and magnificence, Twain tells us in *Life on the Mississippi*, is arid and insipid—'majestic, unchanging sameness of serenity, repose, tranquillity, lethargy, vacancy—symbol of eternity, realisation of the heaven pictured by priest and prophet, and longed for by the good and thoughtless!' To describe his own response he uses the simile of a doctor to whom 'the lovely flush in a beauty's cheek' means 'a "break" that ripples above some deadly disease. Are not all her visible charms thick with what are to him the signs and symbols of hidden decay?'

This is the Mississippi of Huckleberry Finn. Lionel Trilling and T. S. Eliot see it as an elemental god representing values opposed to those of the riverside towns which Huck visits. In this interpretation the narrative scheme, alternating between the raft taking Huck and Jim down the river and the seedy communities of the shore, implies a moral pattern. The river is an idyllic haven from the violence and crudeness of the land. With the power of vengeance by flood and desolation it is a reminder, of which Huck is sensible, of human pettiness, and a symbol of supernatural judgment. Huck's goodness of heart, which estranges him from the cruelties of shore life, binds him to the outcast Jim and the disregarded river-god. This neat design is not wholly groundless, but it corresponds to very little in what we know of Huck or in the river as the novel depicts it. The thieves, in Chapter XII, propose to let the river kill the accomplice who has tried to double-cross them. It is Huck who tries to save him, and here his feelings coincide with the widow's—'I judged she would be proud of me for helping these rapscallions, because rapscallions and dead beats is the kind the widow and good people takes the most interest in.' The river transports Huck and Jim in honest companionship but accepts indifferently the arrival of the two unsavoury ruffians, the 'king' and the 'duke', who take over command of the raft and use it as a base for their shabby confidence tricks. Twain did not intend life on the raft to portray a social order essentially more satisfying than any of the others Huck experiences; nor to represent the river as in some mystical way set apart from the civilisation it serves. The only 'god' in the book is the magnanimity Huck (usually) and Jim take with them wherever they go; and to which, now and then, there is a sympathetic echo in the people they meet.

We have already seen, in the Boggs-Sherburn sequence, some of the ideas Twain expresses in this central part of *Huckleberry Finn*. Another of the critical episodes is the Wilks story. The king and the duke have learned from a garrulous traveller of the death of Peter Wilks in a small Arkansaw village. The circumstances make it possible for them to pose as the dead man's two brothers. By duping the entire village (all expectantly awaiting the brothers' arrival) and in particular three nieces, who with the brothers are Peter's heirs, they hope to make off with the whole legacy. They introduce themselves with a histrionic show of grief, which, says Huck, 'was enough to make a body ashamed of the whole human race'. Although warned by the village doctor everyone accepts the impostors. Their plans prosper until Huck, moved by the spontaneous kindness of the three nieces, takes a hand—'I felt so ornery and low down and mean, that I says to myself, My mind's made up; I'll hive that money for them or burst.' He hides the cash legacy in Peter's coffin and reveals the plot to the eldest niece, together with a complicated plan for securing his own and Jim's safety and the downfall of the tricksters. In the event, they are exposed by the arrival of the real brothers (who have great difficulty in establishing their claim) and narrowly escape with their lives. This brief account emphasises the uppermost meaning of the story, knavery (the king and the duke) successful against trustfulness (the nieces and the village) until circumvented by a less credulous good nature (Huck). This is part of the interpretation Twain intended it to bear, but it has divergent undercurrents of meaning.

The opposition between the village and the swindlers is not, morally, any more clear-cut than that between Sherburn and his townsfolk. Worked on by the king's make-believe sorrow, the assembled villagers indulge their own maudlin sentimentality, hardly less insincere. Huck's comment is, 'I never see anything so disgusting,' and his repugnance implies that it is not by the tricksters' behaviour alone that 'the whole human race' is reproached. Nor are they so much innocent as gullible. When the real brothers arrive, their good faith is patent, except, as Huck says, to 'a lot of prejudiced chuckleheads'. Earlier, the king has asked the duke, 'Haint we got all the fools in town on our side? and ain't that a big enough majority in any town?' The judgment is clearly Twain's and towards the end of the story he extends the indictment. The villagers (now a lynch mob, 'excited and panting') rush with the rival claimants to exhume the dead Peter and test their conflicting descriptions of the birthmark on his chest. As the duke recounts the climax later, he and his companion were saved by the crowd's morbid avidity at the opening of the coffin —'the gold done us a still bigger kindness; for if the excited fools hadn't let go all holts and made that rush to get a look, we'd a slept in our cravats tonight . . .'

The only community actions we see in the village are the cloying shows of grief and the mob hysteria. All through these chapters the villagers are 'the gang', 'the crowd': they 'flocked down' to meet the swindlers, gathered outside the Wilks's house so that 'the street . . . was packed', 'crowded up', 'crowded around', 'whooping and yelling . . . swarmed into the graveyard'. Their emotions are depersonalised, unhealthy, contrasted with the private grief of Mary Jane, 'crying there all by herself in the night'. Witnessing this moves Huck to divulge the plot to her. She agrees to follow his plan, though her immediate desire is revenge—'we'll have them tarred and feathered and flung in the river.' This primitive chastisement has been gradually closing upon the king and the duke. In a later chapter the threat is executed and the episode given its deferred sequel:

'. . . here comes a raging rush of people, with torches, and an awful whooping and yelling, and banging tin pans and blowing horns; and we jumped to one side to let them go by; and as they went by, I see they had the king and the duke astraddle of a rail —that is, I knowed it *was* the king and the duke, though they was all over tar and feathers, and didn't look like nothing in the world that was human—just looked like a couple of monstrous big soldier plumes, Well, it made me sick to see it; and I was sorry for them poor pitiful rascals . . . and I warn't feeling so brash as I was before, but kind of ornery, and humble, and to blame, somehow—though *I* hadn't done nothing.'

Like the widow and the 'good people' he sides with 'the rapscallions and dead beats' in their humiliation. His baffled sense of complicity in the guilt of this and all the other mobs is the saving human grace. We respect his vicarious suffering because, as we have seen, he is indulgent neither of evil-doing nor of flabby sentiment. The difference between him and the majority is his admission that he too is compromised. In the Wilks plot, he will not interfere until he sees some 'safe way . . . to chip in and change the general tune'. As it happens, it is chance, not his action, which finally discovers the king and the duke. Twain is coming very close to saying that the feeling Huck displays is estimable not because it can be expected to have very much effect on the

ways of society, but simply in itself. Huck understands this only
in part. He is the infallible observer, not the definitive interpreter
and his direct commentary supplies only part of Twain's viewpoint. To see it whole we must look at the emotions, the action
and the characters in the configurations Twain imposes on them.
Unlike Melville he makes use of a character who embodies an
edifying standard of conduct. But the total expression of his
viewpoint requires also the method exemplified in *The Confidence
Man*, of conveying meaning by the unvoiced comment of one
scene on another placed in significant relationship to it. As a
demonstration of Twain's command of the whole subtle armoury
of satire, the Wilks story may stand for all the episodes of Huck's
journey.

The moral Twain draws, then, despite the high spirits of some
of the action, differs radically from the reconciliation mooted at
the end of the parallel scene in Hawthorne's *Major Molineux*. Yet
Twain's belief in human goodness, in the urge at least to attempt
reparation, comes through with comparable force. The conflict
between these two attitudes is responsible for the hesitancy with
which he rounds off the novel by returning Huck to society.
Huck has espoused Jim's cause after a lengthy and ironical agony
of conscience: what his training made him consider evil is in
fact good and his natural compassion leads him to the ethically
correct decision of helping Jim's flight. Reunited with Tom on
the Phelps's plantation, Huck's final problem is to rescue Jim, now
imprisoned there. Nothing could be simpler than this in the circumstances, but Tom, with his love of romantic complication,
dismisses Huck's very direct proposals. As a result, some half-
dozen chapters are given over to Tom's preposterous expedients,
which, as Huck says in a flat-voiced, tail-piece comment, were
'worth fifteen of mine, for style, and would make Jim just as
free a man as mine would, and maybe get us all killed besides'.
But Huck's interest is more acutely aroused by Tom's willingness
to help Jim at all. The earlier irony is briefly recapitulated. Tom,
in Huck's eyes, has 'a character to lose'. He is 'bright and not
leather-headed . . . and not mean, but kind', yet he enters upon
an enterprise which Huck still feels to be scandalous. Tom protests
that he knows what he's about. Not until the end do we learn
what he did know: that Miss Watson, in her will, had set Jim

free. The tortuous 'rescue' was unnecessary and did not involve Tom in social heresy.

Most of the critics condemn this ending out of hand. It reduces Huck once more to the stature of a low comedy clown, dependent again on Tom's authority, despite his own new matureness. It turns its back disastrously on the mood of tragedy and violence of the river sequence. It evades the problem of Jim's final position in society by having the unsympathetic Miss Watson quite arbitrarily relent. Because Tom's plans are so tiresomely spun out it fails even as burlesque. T. S. Eliot has justified it on the ground that 'it is right that the mood of the end of the book should bring us back to the beginning'.[1]

More specifically, we may object against the critics' charges that it is quite consistent with Twain's purposes that Huck should be the same at the end of the book as at the beginning. His experiences do not initiate him into anything previously unfamiliar to him. It is the character with which he embarks on the journey that fits him for it and this character the journey simply confirms. At the end he is the same blend of compassion and knowingness, still with the deference to Tom's judgment he has never escaped. Miss Watson's change of heart, equally, is consistent with the view of society Twain utters in the body of the novel. He is saying again that, in society, good is more likely to arrive by chance than by design. Huck's labours for Jim are purposefully benevolent but his freedom is achieved by an act Twain doesn't even try to make credible, an unpredictable quirk of human nature. As in Twain's fictional trials, justice is done by a kind of sleight of hand. What is wrong with the ending of *Huckleberry Finn* is not this wry but entirely legitimate conclusion. The trouble is that Twain backed away from it, blunting its edge by embedding it in the farcical comedy of Tom's schemes. Though the final chapters are excellent burlesque and very funny indeed, they provide the wrong context for Twain's real conclusion. They are, rather, a concession to his feeling, still vigorous, that so long as such generosity as Huck's can survive, so, despite appearances, does hope remain. The mood of the action of the closing chapters is

[1] The arguments summarised in this paragraph, and the case against the contentions of Lionel Trilling and T. S. Eliot are to be found in Leo Marx, 'Mr. Eliot, Mr. Trilling and Huckleberry Finn', in Rahv., *op. cit.*, pp. 212–28.

one of joy and confidence, of tension released, inappropriate because immoderate. The failure of the ending is a want of proportion in workmanship, not a flaw in design.

On the very last page, Huck, like Natty Bumppo, decides 'to light out for the Territory'. Unlike Natty, he does not leave behind him any conviction that the good he represents has found an outlet in the society he is abandoning. In Twain's later career these misgivings, which in *Huckleberry Finn* he had tried to suppress, got the better of his erratic optimism and wrote the desolate message of *The Mysterious Stranger*. The mysterious stranger is a supernatural being calling himself Satan, in his human form taking the name of Philip Truam. The story of his visits to the medieval town of Eseldorf is told by the boy who becomes his companion, Theodor Fischer. His narrative tells how Satan entertains Theodor and his friends with his miraculous powers and, on their insistence, intervenes in the lives of some of the townspeople to ensure their happiness. The boys find to their horror that Satan 'didn't seem to know any way to do a person a favour except by killing him or making a lunatic out of him'. The story consists of a series of episodes accounting for this, linked by Satan's commentary, which demonstrates the impotence of good, the preponderance of misery, the abjectness of human ideals, and which finally brings Theodor to a despairing realisation of the futility of life.

Satan, who is Twain's prolocutor, paradoxically argues the instinctive kindliness of human beings. 'In any community, big or little,' he tells Theodor, 'there is always a fair proportion of people who are not malicious or unkind by nature, and who never do unkind things except when they are overmastered by fear, or when their self-interest is greatly endangered . . .' And elsewhere, yet more positively, he asserts, the 'vast majority of the race, whether savage or civilised, are secretly kindhearted and shrink from inflicting pain'. The faith of *Huckleberry Finn* seems to be roundly re-affirmed, but it is done with the ironic intention of making more pathetic the lesson that these benign impulses are always frustrated. The second of Satan's pronouncements follows upon a scene in which the blacksmith, the butcher and the weaver have incited the townsfolk to lynch a woman suspected of witchcraft. The natural feelings which Satan praises

are swamped in the collective passion aroused by the three pug-
naciously intolerant leaders. Such, says Satan, is the way of the
race, 'governed by minorities, never by majorities. It suppresses
its feelings and its beliefs and follows the handful that makes the
most noise. Sometimes the noisy handful is right, sometimes
wrong; but no matter, the crowd follows it . . . in the presence
of the aggressive and pitiless minority they don't dare to assert
themselves.'

Satan, we notice, concedes that 'sometimes the noisy handful
is right'. In a sense, the mob that set out against Sherburn was
'right' but its means degrade its end. Never in all Twain's por-
trayals of the mob does it throw up an untainted leader, because,
embodying its will, he must embody its malice. Either, like the
Eseldorf blacksmith and his accomplices, the leader picks on a
defenceless scapegoat, or, like Buck Harkness, he sees his following
disintegrate against the force of a stronger antagonist. Sherburn's
bravery, personal and solitary, is more impressive than the un-
adventurous brutality of the mob, but he is no less ruthless and
selfish. There is no hint anywhere in Twain of Swift's heroic
leader-figure, directing the mob to legitimate and useful ends;
his few patricians show strength, but never virtue. His instincts
were hostile to the aristocratic idea and to this *The Mysterious
Stranger* adds his now conclusive dismissal of the democratic
hypothesis of popular wisdom: to be effective, the good inherent
in the individual members of the community must be concerted,·
but they are most readily concerted in violence and prejudice and
at the behest of men, barbarous themselves, who can draw on
these qualities.

The Eseldorf witch-hunt is a parable, of course, of the sporadic
collapses into mob law of American democratic rule. There is,
however, a further, more devious analogy between the theocratic
city-state of Eseldorf and the constitutional republic of America,
in the dogmas to which their respective hierarchies refer their
acts of government. Twain intended the novel as a comprehensive
attack on the Christian doctrine of the Moral Sense, which,
according to the churches, is the manifestation of God in man,
his infallible guide to right conduct. As the narrator understands
it, it is the gift of a merciful God, enjoining men to a humane
and charitable life. Hence his horror when Satan, having created

a miniature town obliterates it and its inhabitants. Satan—who despite his name is not, we are told, the fallen angel—explains that their dismay is meaningless to him, for he is ignorant of sin. He is 'of the aristocracy of the Imperishables. And man has the *Moral Sense*. You understand? He has the *Moral Sense*. That would seem to be difference enough between us, all by itself.' Satan's passionless destruction of the little town and his indifference to human life reflect the true character of the Christian God, whose works have the heartlessness, in human terms, which we mistakenly attribute to the devil. Only by positing such a God can we reasonably account for the Moral Sense as it operates in fact, as distinct from Theodor's childish understanding of it. Again, Satan instructs him. An animal, he says, 'does not inflict pain for the pleasure of inflicting it—only man does that. Inspired by that mongrel Moral Sense of his! A sense whose function is to distinguish between right and wrong, with liberty to choose which of them he will do. Now what advantage can he get out of that? He is always choosing, and in nine cases out of ten he prefers the wrong . . . he is not able to see that the Moral Sense degrades him to the bottom layer of animated beings and is a shameful possession.'

The human race, uneasily poised between beast and angel, by a half-unconscious sophistry uses the moral sense to colour their basest acts, while simultaneously representing it as the springhead of their highest principles. In the life of Eseldorf it supplies the authority by which the church, its custodian, disciplines the saintly Father Peter for spreading the heresy 'that God was all goodness and would find a way to save all his poor human children'. The bishop suspends him from his priestly duties, an unwitting avowal of the tacit hostility between the egotistical promptings of the moral sense and the arguments of charity with which, by convention, it is associated. Its real principle always, is self-preservation, in this case, maintenance of the *status quo*, with the church as the indispensable mediator between man and a vengeful God. By a final paradox, the bishop's harshness is differentiated from the true character of the heavenly dispensation (as represented by Satan's acts) only in being considered policy, not amoral indifference.

As an allegory of the Supreme Court's solicitings of the Natural Law all this is strikingly exact. The Moral Sense is an analogue of the Natural Law. The discrepancy between the tenderness attributed to the Moral Sense and the iniquitous acts it is used to condone is duplicated in the contrast between the convenience and equity theoretically guaranteed by the Natural Law and the inequalities and injustices it was in practice called upon to sustain. Moreover, as Twain's church, through the Moral Sense, lays claim to divine approval of its judgments, so did the Supreme Court take its stand upon Justice Brewer's 'right and justice as it exists in . . . natural law' to give countenance to what was in fact, as Louis B. Boudin puts it, the particular 'economic or political assumption or predilection which determines the judge's opinion as to what is desirable or undesirable in legislation'.[1] In each case we have a remote, powerful and prejudiced hierarchy devoted to securing the *status quo* by appealing to an authority allegedly extrinsic and beneficent. There can be little doubt that the polity of Eseldorf reflects Twain's appraisement of the philosophy and the practices dominant in the polity of his own nation.

The most curious feature of Twain's satire is the impression it leaves of the satirist himelf gradually quitting his lines of defence —or attack—and accepting as true, or at any rate valid for his own times, the case made out by the people and the principles that arouse his ire; yet retaining withal an irreducible antipathy to them. Twain became, so to speak, a disciple of Sumnerism without losing his distaste for what it asserted. The dangerous and destructive force of satire adverted to by Bishop Warburton could claim no more striking victory than Twain's satire had over his own positives. In the end he clung only (and, by the standards he had adopted, illogically) to his faith in the basic decency of human beings. And even this had decayed, qualified, as we have seen in *The Mysterious Stranger*, by the exception that there are few, if any, men whom the sense of decency will deter from unkindness 'when they are overmastered by fear or when their self-interest is greatly in danger'. Its obstinate power of survival we must credit to Twain's early days and frontier experiences. Despite the formidable evidence of the cruelty and brigandage of the frontier —and despite the fact that Twain was not the least vocal witness to it—it seems to have left with him an enduring recollection of

[1] *Government by Judiciary*, p. vii.

the easy comradeship possible to men in elementary social groupings. His early writings look to the commerce, technology and education which were expanding American boundaries to ensure the transference of this private magnanimity to the necessarily more intricate establishments of a modern industrial society. But his expectations were disappointed by the ready capitulation of the public at large and of august bodies like the Supreme Court to the most extreme demands of the acquisitive spirit. Institutions, he came to believe, were founded and perpetuated themselves upon the worst instincts of man—which, it finally seemed, were likely to dominate the feeble pulse of good in any circumstances.

Twain's earliest satiric position, as a journalist in Nevada, recalled, in the ways we have seen, that of the bardic satirist. By the time he wrote *The Mysterious Stranger* his attitude was, if anything, closer to that of the primitive artist, though no longer with any sense of an accredited, if perilous, status. Though he now commanded the delicate skills of the most sophisticated satire he did not, as his eighteenth-century counterparts, for example, did, attack from a fundamentally assenting position at the heart of society. He was a Cassandra, forlornly anathematising society from a position, ideologically, on its fringes, uneasily conscious of being totally at odds with the undertakings of his fellow-citizens. With the eighteenth-century satirists he has in common only technical accomplishment and his wit and humour. This survey has said little, directly, of Twain's humour, for the reason that it is not a subject open to profitable discussion. It remains true that if jokes fail to amuse no amount of commentary will make them funny. However, we may take up here the contention that Twain is not really a humorist at all, that his genius is for the savage, grotesque and macabre. Much of his humour certainly derives from situations of that kind. But he can also laugh without acrimony at human oddness. He has the genial perception of incongruities and absurdities and the grasp of pure nonsense which constitute humour. No further argument is needed than the example of Huckleberry Finn. The humour of this character comes from the discrepancy between Huck's adult feelings (in the best sense) and the hiatuses in his knowledge and experience; between his shrewdness and his naïvety. We see it in his confused rejoinders to Joanna's queries in the Wilks's house about his

supposed life in England with the king; in his wonder at the tawdry adornments of the Grangerford parlour; in his nicely judged
malapropisms. The same sympathy with which Twain observes
and records the character of Huck tempers his condemnation of
the king and the duke, so that he is able to take an objective
delight in the king's more sententious claptrap and, in their final
punishment, to pity them. In addition to wit and pungency Twain
had the charitable humour which is a matter not of subject but
of attitude.

It was Shaftesbury who felt that, 'the only Manner left, in
which Criticism can have its first Force among us, is the *antient
COMICK*'.[1] Twain, we may reasonably suppose, would have
agreed with him. He derived a dual benefit from the comic
spirit. It provided him, as Shaftesbury suggests, with a serviceable
mask for serious intentions; and through the greater part of his
career, in the absence of a religious faith like Melville's, preserved
him from both arrogant petulance and complete despair. Only at
the end did this latter power fail him. Satan's final revelation to
Theodor is unconditionally nihilistic. Twain sweeps away entire
all the endless human debate on the meaning of life. Free will,
predestination, determinism, natural selection, the religions and
the sciences, all are meaningless. There is neither right nor wrong,
good nor evil, for the universe itself is vacant and unreal; 'It is
true, that which I have revealed to you; there is no God, no
universe, no human race, no earthly life, no heaven, no hell. It
is all a dream—a grotesque and foolish dream. Nothing exists
but you. And you are but a thought—a vagrant thought, a useless
thought, a homeless thought, wandering forlorn among the
empty eternities.'

That Twain should have been driven to this extreme, so far as
the fault was society's and not an impenetrable psychic disable-
ment in Twain himself, we may put down to the failure of the
conservative tradition in his time. It was the interests we normally
think of as conservative which, while posing as guardians of the
status quo, were in fact administering a vast social upheaval, to
the immediately disproportionate advantage of the few. Conservatism was not maintaining but radically altering the structure
of society. In addition, it abandoned its traditional habits of

---

[1] *Characteristicks*, I, 259. See Jack, *op. cit.*, p. 104.

thought to take up the travesty of the genuinely radical theories of Darwin expounded by men like Herbert Spencer. As Henry Steele Commager says, 'Darwin and Spencer exercised such sovereignty over America'—in the form of extreme *laisser-faire* philosophy—'as George III had never enjoyed'.[1] Popular reform movements, as well as the great mass of the people, were equally spell-bound by this ramshackle 'system', so that there was no emphatic counter-principle to shape their efforts. Thus the normal battle lines were muddied and confused. Nevertheless it is the classes having the power to influence opinion and direct society that must bear the heaviest responsibility. Their failure is most marked in the disturbance of the historic balance in the American political tradition between the rights of property and the rights of the individual.[2] In the course of the century, by the astonishing confluence of philosophic theory, the run of Supreme Court decisions and the concentration of political and economic power in the corporations, individual rights had come to be identified with property rights, to the detriment of the former. All the great establishments of society concurred in this massive shift of emphasis and in the body of thought that brought it about. In consequence they laid aside the duty, which previously they had assumed so ably, of arbitrating by positive and impartial action between right and wrong in social and private life, giving instead what was in effect a series of retrospective sanctions to the operation of economic forces beyond their understanding and control. In this labyrinth of intellectual confusion, political bewilderment and random material progress, Twain, with the results outlined above, groped for the certainties in which Cooper, and even Melville and Hawthorne, had been able to persist.

[1] Commager, *op. cit.*, p. 87.

[2] G. W. McCloskey's *American Conservatism in the Age of Enterprise* is an extremely able, though somewhat prejudiced, review of the period from this standpoint.

Chapter Six

Edith Wharton and the Realists

THE sins of modern capitalism are often ingeniously charged against the traditional Protestant, and especially Puritan, encouragement of thrift and hard work, which seems about as reasonable as laying the blame for adultery on marriage. Perry Miller has shown that the American Puritans 'believed in government regulation of business, the fixing of just prices, and the curtailing of individual profits in the interests of the welfare of the whole'.[1] In 1639, for instance, John Cotton condemned as 'false principle' the assertion that 'a man might sell as dear as he can and buy as cheap as he can'. It was to this tradition that Hamilton was heir, and this tradition. which the administrations of Twain's lifetime notably failed to preserve.

The last years of Twain's career coincided with the beginning of Edith Wharton's. Divided from Twain by class, environment and upbringing, Mrs. Wharton spent her formative years in the nation's passage to the social, political and philosophical innovations discussed in the preceding chapter. She inhabited the same intellectual world as Twain. Where he, however, saw it consolidate itself into apparent impregnability, Mrs. Wharton witnessed the recession of its power which followed a renascence of governmental energy and a new cycle of juridical thought. Well within Twain's lifetime, the Interstate Commerce Act (1887) and the Sherman Anti-Trust Law (1890) had presaged these developments. But they had been, to begin with, almost wholly ineffec-

[1] *The Puritans*, p. 5.

tual, neither pressed by the executive nor supported by the courts. Theodore Roosevelt initiated no legislation with the potential of these measures, but his presidency showed that they might be more than an inconclusive grandstand play to appease reformist sentiment. In 1902, over the private appeal of J. P. Morgan, he began suit against the Northern Securities Company, a railroad merger. In 1904 the Supreme Court upheld the dissolution of this monopoly. Though combination in fact continued, the action had unmistakably established the principle of Federal supremacy over the corporations; and revealed a critical swing in the leanings of the Court.

The most urgent force behind this swing was the conservative, sceptical mind of Justice Oliver Wendell Holmes, whose germinal study, *The Common Law*, was published in 1902. On his elevation from the Massachusetts to the Federal Supreme Court in the same year, he carried the practice of his theories to the ultimate legal authority, first of all in dissents, minority judgments which were in time to compose the new orthodoxy. The effect of his judicature, briefly, was to detach jurisprudence from the fossilised 'natural law' by which his predecessors had converted private conviction into public decision; and to widen the concept of that social advantage which it was the business of the law to foster. The Lochner case dissent of 1905 gives a succinct statement of principle:

'This case is decided upon an economic theory which a large part of the country does not entertain. If it were a question whether I agreed with that theory, I should desire to study it further and long before making up my mind. But I do not conceive that to be my duty, because I strongly believe that my agreement or disagreement has nothing to do with the right of a majority to embody their opinions in law. . . . A constitution is not intended to embody a particular economic theory, whether of fraternalism and the organic relation of the citizen to the state or of *laissez-faire*. It is made for people of fundamentally differing views, and the accident of our finding certain opinions natural and familiar or novel and even shocking ought not to conclude our judgment upon the question whether statutes embodying them conflict with the Constitution of the United States.'

The revolution in accent needs no emphasis. Holmes was the cardinal figure in restoring to the American judiciary the dignity, the acumen, the forwardness of judgment it had so surprisingly lost, though only, after all, for a comparatively brief period in the nation's history.

By thus renovating the postulates on which legal science rested, Holmes made it possible for government to undertake legislative experiment without arbitrary hindrance and so attempt to give precise expression to the sense of the people whose collective will they represented. In *The Republican Roosevelt* John Morton Blum describes the process now gathering way to return American government from inertia to the more positive management which its tradition embraced: 'A simple and poor society can exist as a democracy on a basis of sheer individualism. But a rich and complex industrial society cannot so exist; for some individuals, and especially those artificial individuals called corporations, become so very big that the ordinary individual . . . cannot deal with them on terms of equality. It therefore becomes necessary for those ordinary individuals to combine in their turn, first in order to act in their collective capacity through the biggest of all combinations called the government . . .' The tendency towards oligopoly of the American economic order did of course continue, but now more circumspectly and without the ruthless confidence it had taken from social Darwinism at its zenith; the reformist impulse found a place within as well as without. As Commager has remarked, Americans 'could not consistently accept determinism . . . they were logically and psychologically precluded from believing in a progress to which they made no contribution and which was divorced from their control'.[1] Sumner had not been able to 'see how economics and politics can be reconciled so that industry can prosper and law can be respected, both at the same time'. It now began to seem that the reconciliation was not, in fact, beyond achieving. Twain and Edith Wharton observed the same period in different perspectives: his conclusion is cynical and pessimistic; hers, in the series of New York novels, gradually less censorious of the rising *élite* of wealth. It may be partly because she knew the tight security of the New York mercantile and professional *élite* that she was

[1] *The American Mind*, p. 90.

able to keep a firmer hold than Twain on equanimity of judgment and observation. But at least as important was the fact, simply, of being able to look back from a greater distance on the changes she had lived through, of seeing that they too were mutable.

The novels that concern us are *The House of Mirth* (1905), *The Custom of the Country* (1913) and *The Age of Innocence* (1920). Their interior chronology is worth attention. They are all set in the compact 'beau monde' of New York, *The House of Mirth* in the eighteen-nineties, *The Custom of the Country* somewhat later at the turn of the century. Between them these two survey, as it affects the private fate of their characters, the accelerating drift, in Sumner's terminology, from settled traditions of conduct to the unconventional mores of a new group, risen to wealth and power by different paths and seeking now the eminence of their predecessors in the world of art and fashion. *The Age of Innocence* returns to the seventies, when the old mercantile upper class was unchallenged arbiter of taste, manners and morality. A brief sequel to the main action advances to the period of *The Custom of the Country*, or a little beyond. The chronological scheme Mrs. Wharton adopts is reminiscent, it will be remarked, of Cooper's in the Leatherstocking series, the final novel withdrawing farthest into the past and ending with a brief excursion to the 'present'. From this vantage ground Mrs. Wharton gives what we must regard as her final judgment on the merits of new and old, as compared with each other and with the European society variously represented in this and the other novels. Like the Leatherstocking books, Mrs. Wharton's New York novels are best read in the order in which they are written, but not only for the pathos, at the end, of the different pasts so lovingly evoked in the knowledge that they are irrecoverable. It is *The Age of Innocence*, with its double focus on the past, which resolves the theme of social change running through all the novels.

As viewed by the realist school, social change was a portentous affair of left or right wing revolution springing from the sensational inequalities of wealth depicted in their novels. Appalled by the sufferings of the industrial poor, by the corrupt alliance of business and politics, these novelists, having documented the miserable underside of American prosperity, predicted a desperate workers' insurrection or a plutocratic dictatorship. Ignatius

Donnelly's *Caesar's Column* (1891) is an anti-Utopia set in 1988, when capital is presumed to live in futuristic opulence over a sub-world of labour repressed by terror and brutality. As Donnelly saw it, this plutocratic super-state resulted from the same programme of calculated oppression that was causing the labour grievances of his own times: the slum dweller was the victim not of relatively impersonal forces but of a deliberate conspiracy of wealth. Jack London's *The Iron Heel* (1908) similarly—and quite impressively—foretells social revolution as the inevitable outgrowth from a tiny *élite's* conscious policy of securing luxury to itself by despoiling the mass of workers who produce its wealth. This is an interpretation of events which does credit to the hearts, if not the heads, of these political novelists, whose inspiration is strongly emotional and whose realism strongly naturalistic, selecting its material from within the pale of poverty and squalor that worked upon their feelings. (See Appendix B.) They represent extreme forms of a temper to which Edith Wharton was not unsympathetic. By no means all her writings deal with the little world of the New York aristocracy. Her own realism, in the reporting of the social scene, comprehended events and settings bitter and sordid enough, strictly in the naturalist convention. She is, as Edmund Wilson has said, 'always aware of the pit of misery which is implied by the wastefulness of the plutocracy, and the horror of fear of this pit is one of the forces that determine the action'.[1]

Summer (1917) sets out into the rural proletariat of the back country of Massachusetts. The mountain settlements, from which the heroine, Charity Royall, has been rescued by adoption, are one of the old fastnesses outside the law, like Hawthorne's forest given over to elemental forces. Brooding over the remote village of North Dormer, the mountain catches all the summer storms, which, 'torn up and multiplied . . . sweep back over the village in rain and darkness'. Going back to visit an offshoot from the colony of squatters, Charity takes shelter from a storm in one of the hovels, 'heavy with the smell of dirt and tobacco', into which the rain 'sent a stream through the patched panes and ran into pools on the floor'. Its occupants—'the face of the sleeping man so sodden and bestial'—are 'swamp-people living like vermin in

[1] 'Justice to Edith Wharton', in *The Wound and the Bow*, p. 181.

their lair'.. This community Charity's guardian, Lawyer Royall, describes as 'a gang of thieves and outlaws living over there, in sight of us, defying the laws of their country', going on to explain 'in somewhat technical language how the little colony of squatters had contrived to keep the law at bay'. Charity vacillates between an atavistic recall to these people, the rudimentary sophistication of North Dormer—which, 'compared to the place she had come from . . . represented all the blessings of the most refined civilisation'—and Bovaryesque longings for lofty romance and the great outer world of 'railway, trolley, telegraph, and all the forces that link life to life in modern communities'. In the end, disappointed by a young urban dilettante, she marries her guardian, reconciling herself happily enough to his 'grave friendliness' and the parochial round of the village. It is an answer we shall find again in Mrs. Wharton, not unlike the humdrum but virtuous resolution of differences between the Chamberlaynes in *The Cocktail Party*, which,

> *In a world of lunacy,*
> *Violence, stupidity, greed . . . is a good life.*

Summer puts naturalism to the service of aesthetic rather than propagandist ends. The wilderness of the mountains is both contemporary and timeless, a realistically observed backwash of the twentieth century and the primordial haunt of barbarism. As compassionate as the Londons and Donnellys, Mrs. Wharton is infinitely less strident in her use of comparable material, setting it in a more broadly dimensioned social cosmogony, less concerned to condemn than to interpret.

In *The House of Mirth* the decline of Lily Bart's fortunes takes her far beyond the normal purlieus of her modish class to the world of the urban poor. The final 'pit of misery' is, for her, a threat only and Mrs. Wharton's purpose was not to describe the abyss in the manner of the radical novelists. But the threat is sharpened by, and the abyss, though it remains off-stage, powerfully hinted in, Lily's new familiarity with the life a precarious stage or two above it. As the scene of Lily's death, it calls more for an atmosphere of failure and despair than for physical details, but we are given as well, in vivid glimpses, the mean side streets, the seamy apartments, the monotonous toil which contribute their dreary aura to the mood. In these ways, Mrs. Wharton's art touches on but is not constricted within the chosen field of the orthodox naturalists. She reads no message of revolutionary convulsion from the miseries she observed as keenly as they, nor does she limit realism to the scrutiny of the lowest strata: life would continue much as it had always done, with some rising above, some surviving in and some defeated by their circumstances, whatever might be their social level. Nevertheless, we may conclude, Mrs. Wharton displays vestiges at least of the naturalist manner and benefited from the general movement, in which the naturalists were the most extreme participants, to push the boundaries of fiction beyond the genteel conventions. Her mind was too inquiring and her conscience too quick not to welcome such an extension of the material considered proper to the form.

Yet in the novels for which she is best known her realism operates mainly on a level far above the social badlands of orthodox naturalism and does not necessarily home on the sordid and the ugly, as though facts could be of that order alone. While her realism, further, does include plain verisimilitude, precise reporting of physical detail—furnishings, buildings, dress, customs —it was realistic, if we may thus interpret the term, in the profounder way of grasping and conveying the core of beliefs, assumptions, precepts, which lay behind the outward forms of manners and behaviour: rather as Taylor wrote his poetry out of the logic which held Puritan society together, but without accepting hers as Taylor accepted his or, like Twain, at once loathing it and allowing its infallibility. In Mrs. Wharton we shall find a dispassionate critique of the society which bred and followed the teachings of Sumner and it is in her rendering of the social penetration of Sumnerism, rather than in the surface authenticity of the *roman de moeurs*, that her realism consists. It is, then, with the foregoing points in mind that we are to read the three novels mentioned above.

II

The House of Mirth presents Lily Bart, we realise at the very outset, in evolutionary terms which are partly metaphorical banter but partly, too, seriously hermeneutic. Seeing her in Grand Central Station and struck by her glowing elegance in the drab concourse of passengers, Lawrence Selden feels 'how highly specialised she is', suspects, even, 'that a great many dull and ugly people must, in some mysterious way, have been sacrificed to produce her'. The playfulness of the figures should not obscure the truth they are intended to convey, that Lily has, indeed, been evolved, her qualities appropriately specialised, by her environment and upbringing, that these have determined her aims and her adaptability within them has ensured her survival. Through the improvidence of her mother, we gather, and the business failure of her father, she has been left without money to support herself in the fashionable and prodigal world in which she had grown up. Her function in this society is to be decorative, amusing, expensive; to follow gracefully the seasonal round of pleasures; and ultimately to make an advantageous marriage. When we meet her she has, since her mother's death, been a poor relation in this world, depending on the charity of friends, longing for and intriguing towards a secure place in the charmed circle of wealth and, with increasing disquiet, realising that the necessity of marriage is becoming critical. 'You think,' she says to a friend, 'we live *on* the rich . . . but it's a privilege we have to pay for ! . . . the girl pays it by tips and cards too—oh, yes, I've had to take up bridge again—and by going to the best dress-makers, and having just the right dress for every occasion, and always keeping herself fresh and exquisite and amusing !'

Yet there is much more to Lily Bart than this. She is not wholly content with what the mores prescribe and not only kicks against the strains and embarrassments of achieving her end but queries its intrinsic value. From some mysterious source she has inherited qualities and longings alien to the philistine aristocracy with whose 'jumble of futile activities' her adventures familiarise us. As the novel proceeds, the limitations of the Darwinian imagery are annotated. 'Inherited tendencies,' we are told towards the end, 'had combined with early training to make her the highly specialised product she was: an organism as helpless out of its narrow range as the sea-anemone torn from the rock. She had been fashioned to adorn and delight; to what other end does nature round the rose-leaf and paint the humming-bird's breast?

And was it her fault that the purely decorative mission is less easily and harmoniously fulfilled among social beings than in the world of nature? That it is apt to be hampered by material necessities or complicated by moral scruples?' Lily Bart is at once a specimen of her society, a lens through which we observe it and, with her intuitions of extratribal values, herself an intermittent critic of its ways. The novel, in fact, takes up and dissents from the Sumnerian thesis that the individual's only profitable function is to conform to the mores which his society has established and which alone have educated him: the individual is less plastic than determinist theory would have him, there are absolute values by which the prevailing mores are to be judged and nonconformity and failure may testify, even in a character so far from flawless as Lily's, to the durability of these values.

In the opening half-dozen chapters, describing Lily's arrival at the country-house party of the Gus Trenors, the orchestration of these themes begins. Having met Lawrence Selden, a man of more liberal breeding than was common in his class, on her way through New York, she impulsively defies the conventions by having tea alone with him in his apartment. As she leaves, she meets Sim Rosedale, an astute vulgarian wealthy enough to aspire to 'society' but still ostracised by it, fails to conceal her indiscretion from him and also wounds his pride. It is the first of a series of lapses from the code which requires unremitting affability of her and anticipates more dangerous—and more admirable—acts of defiance at the stage of her career when even Sim Rosedale will have come to seem an eligible suitor. Arrived at the Trenors, she is at once caught up in her ambivalent feelings about her class. In an upsurge of expansive contentment, 'her companions seemed full of amiable qualities. She liked their elegance, their lightness, their lack of emphasis'. Then, at dinner, she finds that Selden's arrival and her attraction to him, indecisive because his circumstances are only moderate, have shaken the kaleidoscope of her impressions into a new pattern. Ironically she studies her fellow guests:

'How dreary and trivial these people were! . . . young Silverton, who had meant to live on proof-reading and write an epic, and who now lived on his friends and had become critical of truffles;

Alice Wetherall, an animated visiting-list, whose most fervid convictions turned on the wording of invitations and the engraving of dinner-cards . . . Jack Stepney, with his confident smile and anxious eyes, half-way between the sheriff and an heiress . . .'

The thoughts are Lily's but the epigrammatic tartness is Edith Wharton's. So too, however, is the earlier evocation of leisured charm. The novel allows us grounds of belief in both sets of impressions. Like Scott Fitzgerald, Mrs. Wharton relished what we might call the urban pastoralism of an affluent group, the languorous succession of careless festivities, the witchery of hedonistic comfort. However vulnerable morally, its gloss and glamour are undeniable. Thus until the tragedy takes control, Fitzgerald endows Gatsby's receptions with a property of halcyon enchantment in which the casual guests come and go 'like moths among the whispering and the champagne and the stars'. Thus, in *The House of Mirth*, we have the description of the meeting between Lily and Selden at the Brys' *tableaux vivants*:

'Gravel grated beneath their feet, and about them was the transparent dimness of a midsummer night. Hanging lights made emerald caverns in the depths of foliage, and whitened the spray of a fountain falling among lilies. The magic place was deserted: there was no sound but the splash of the water on the lily-pads, and a distant drift of music that might have been blown across the sleeping lake.

'Selden and Lily stood still, accepting the unreality of the scene as a part of their own dream-like sensations. It would not have surprised them to feel a summer breeze on their faces, or to see the lights among the boughs reduplicated in the arch of a starry sky. The strange solitude about them was no stranger than the sweetness of being alone in it together.'

This glittering décor, subtly unreal, in no utilitarian sense functional, it is the business of the rich to provide. Selden, who sees its superficiality and knows the barbarism and fatuity it often disguised, nevertheless 'enjoyed spectacular effects, and was not insensible to the part money plays in their production: all he asked was that the very rich should live up to their calling as stage-managers, and not spend their money in a dull way. This the Brys could certainly not be charged with doing'. Similarly the Trenors keep up their country estate, seated on whose terrace Lily sees 'a landscape tutored to the last degree of rural elegance. In the foreground glowed the warm tints of the gardens. Beyond the lawn, with its pyramidal pale-gold maples and velvety firs, sloped pastures dotted with cattle: and through a long glade the river widened like a lake under the silver light of September'. It it not for this opulence, obnoxious to the reformer, that Mrs. Wharton castigates the rich. One of the responsibilities proper to them is to cultivate such decorative arts and it is to the rich as the *elegantiae arbiter* that Lily is drawn.

Other responsibilities, of course, there are. Lily's unformulated dissatisfactions are put into words for her by Selden, during their inconclusive flirtation at the Trenors. 'I don't,' he tells her, 'under-rate the decorative side of life. It seems to me the sense of splendour has justified itself by what it has produced. The worst of it is that so much human nature is used up in the process . . . a society like ours wastes such good material in producing its little patch of purple! Look at a boy like Ned Silverton—he's really too good to be used to refurbish anybody's social shabbiness.' To erect 'the decorative side' of this life, any enterprising deviations are constricted to fit the banal taboos of the caste and the sober morality of an earlier age is diluted. *The House of Mirth* is a complex study of the syndrome. On the whole, we are left in no doubt, the *élite* is diseased. Its culture is skin deep, its pleasures sensual, its morality based almost wholly on preserving appearances, its recognition to be secured, ultimately, by wealth. For George Dorset, the opera season is 'another six months of cater-wauling', attended as a social duty. The home of Lily's guardian is a horror of monumental furniture, 'large steel engravings of an anecdotic character', and the 'seven-by-five painting of Niagara which represented the one artistic excess of Mr. Peniston's temperate career'. In the trip to Europe which Lily takes with the Dorsets, we see the expatriate group isolated from the life around them 'in the stupid costliness of the food and the showy dullness of the talk, in the freedom of speech which never arrived at wit and the freedom of act which never arrived at romance'. Rosedale, with his multiplying riches, is at last espoused by the fashionable, having placed 'Wall Street under obligations which

only Fifth Avenue could repay'. Finally, in this uninviting conspectus, when Lily is disgraced by a combination of innocent
circumstances and malicious scandal circulated by a jealous wife,
she says mockingly, 'it's a good deal easier to believe Bertha
Dorset's story than mine, because she has a big house and an
opera box, and it's convenient to be on good terms with her'.
Because, as we are later told, 'Bertha Dorset's social credit was
based on an impregnable bank account'—and a malleable husband
—her own notorious infidelities are tolerated.

The foregoing indictment, clearly, is compiled with wit.
Lily's story calls on graver tones. Her flirtation with Gus Trenor,
thoughtlessly entered on her part, lustfully on his, displays a plain
moral incapacity. Thus it is that she accepts money from him,
knowing full well that it is not an altruistic bounty. She is at once
aware of 'treading a devious way' and persuaded by the flimsy
deceit that the money is, as Trenor professes, interest from
speculations made in her name—a stratagem typical of the age,
even seduction turning the craft of the stock exchange to account.
For a period, Lily succeeds in diverting Trenor's importunities by
her deliberate misconstruction of his lumbering hints and com-
plaints, a delicate comedy of cross purposes. But she feels the
situation gradually escaping her control and Trenor finally tricks
her into coming alone at night to his New York house, where
his supplications turn to the threat of violence. Lily is saved, however, by dissuasions long unexercised but still alive in Trenor:
'Old habits, old restraints, the hand of inherited order, plucked
back the bewildered mind which passion had jolted from its
ruts.' The mores of the present defer to traditional decencies. He
lets her go, but, humiliated by his insinuations of past misconduct,
she has seen the abyss of fashionable harlotry she had been skirting.
The revelation transmutes to a lonely terror of penitence the
superb self-assurance which had made Trenor hesitate. The 'old
restraints' that held him back now deliver her to the even older
visitation of the Furies, 'who might sometimes sleep, but they
were there, always there in the dark corners, and now they were
awake and the iron clang of their wings was in her brain . . . She
opened her eyes and saw the streets passing—the familiar alien
streets. All she looked on was the same and yet changed. There
was a great gulf fixed between today and yesterday. Everything

in the past seemed simple, natural, full of daylight—and she was alone in a place of darkness and pollution. Alone! It was the loneliness that frightened her. Her eyes fell on an illuminated clock at a street corner, and she saw that the hands marked the half-hour after eleven. Only half-past eleven—there were hours and hours left of the night! . . . Oh, the slow cold drip of the minutes on her head! She had a vision of herself lying on the black walnut bed—and the darkness would frighten her, and if she left the light burning the dreary details of the room would brand themselves for ever on her brain . . . To a torn heart uncomforted by human nearness a room may open almost human arms, and the being to whom no four walls mean more than any others is, at such hours, expatriate everywhere'. It is powerfully written, stripping through the accumulated impedimenta, with which society reassures itself of its substance, to the soul cut adrift from such comfortings. Here the social comedy turns to the condition of tragedy, though as it happens Lily is able this time, like T. S. Eliot's typist, to 'smoothe her hair with automatic hand' and once more pacify the agitated soul with the routine opiates of social pleasures.

She is not, then, guiltless. Nor is she guiltless in her relationship with Selden, one of Mrs. Wharton's well-meaning but ineffectual heroes. The blame for their failure to find a way to marriage is as much hers as his. On a number of occasions they declare their love. But at the last, Lily always temporises, unwilling to repudiate the luxury a more advantageous match might afford her, and Selden lacks the force of will that would compel her to decide. He chances to see her leaving Trenor's house after the incident described above and, ironically, takes this as corroboration of the scandals which rumour has charged against her. He cancels an appointment made with her for the following day and so at this critical moment Lily is left without his support. Coincidence, his failure of trust and Lily's own interior confusions keep them apart. When Selden finally settles on a positive profession of faith it is, as will appear, too late to avert the final tragedy.

Throughout their relationship, Selden has remained ignorant of the decision which most clearly sets her apart from her fellows, The central moral issue is a bit melodramatic and contrived, reminiscent of a nineteenth-century 'problem play'.

Lily has come into possession of compromising letters written to Selden by Bertha Dorset. By using them she could both revenge herself on Bertha Dorset and rehabilitate herself in the society from which Mrs. Dorset's malice has excluded her. This, although she is herself entirely innocent of the moral lapses alleged against her, she refuses to do and, without even telling Selden, destroys the letters during her last meeting with him. In this, Lily is guided by the sense of honour which makes her use her guardian's legacy not to relieve her own distress but to repay her debt to Trenor. In the loneliness of her boarding-house room she makes the arrangements for paying off the debt, overwhelmed by her eviction to the 'social outskirts', by her tedious work as a milliner, her sleepless nights, the unanswerable problems of survival in the infinity of days stretching before her 'like a shrieking mob', by her sense of the life around her, of 'all the men and women she knew', as 'atoms whirling away from each other in some wild centrifugal dance'. The Eumenides have returned. At least half in love with the prospect of death, Lily takes an increased dose of her sleeping draught. As it takes effect her terrors slip away. She becomes dreamily conscious of 'something she must tell Selden, some word she had found that would make all clear between them'. Awakening suddenly to 'a dark flash of loneliness and terror', she sinks at last into tranquil sleep. Early in the morning, when Selden comes to visit her—'he had found the word he meant to say to her, and it could not wait another moment'—she is dead.

It seems, and is usually interpreted as, a heavy punishment for her peccadillos. Her moral scruples unfit her for the vicious social contest, her closeness to its standards alienates Selden. It would appear that her ending, an unrelieved failure of her worldly aims, does not succeed even in commemorating her worthier parts, for she has been unable to support a new life upon them. Yet the real meaning of her death is to be sought in its afterglow. As the concluding paragraphs made clear, it enshrines for Selden the victory she has won over herself by deciding to pay back Trenor. Her death consummates the act of abnegation from which, as he looks on her lifeless body, Selden 'could even draw . . . courage not to accuse himself for having failed to reach the height of his opportunity'. By it he is drawn 'penitent and reconciled to her side . . . and in the silence there passed between them the word that made all clear'. The society to which she is thus sacrificed is unworthy of her, but the value of the sacrifice is not thereby diminished, for it reaches out from the last act of her life to deny the Sumnerist morality which has brought her to this pass, to ennoble Selden's tardy resolution, to apotheosise a relationship in which 'all the conditions of life had conspired to keep them apart'. Like the other societies we have seen, this one too exacts, often ignobly, the sacrificial death which, wasteful though it may appear, serves to redeem, by the deportment of its victim, the prevailing usages which demand it.

It is the opinion of Van Wyck Brooks that Mrs. Wharton's judgment on this society is one-sided and intolerant, that she refused to admit that it was merely, in fact, 'yielding to the types from which, like all bourgeois aristocracies, it had sprung, the speculators and traders of three generations before'. 'Her standard and scale,' he says, 'were "old New York", but how far was that a superior world? All she could claim for it, when she wrote *A Backward Glance*, was a pair of "moral treasures" that she felt were lost—the "social amenity" that will never be lost because it is too pleasant and the "financial incorruptibility" one finds in any village store.'[1] The former of these virtues is, indeed, in the ways we have seen, but faintly presented in the society of *The House of Mirth*; the latter hardly at all. We do see the meritorious charitable pursuits of Gerty Farish, Lily's cousin, but on the whole it is irresponsibility, moral ugliness, the ubiquitous egotism of this world which the novel stresses, so that there is something to be said for Brooks's complaint that Mrs. Wharton's is a very partial vision, so far, at any rate, as this novel is concerned. But we are not to expect from a novel the scientific comprehensiveness we may rightly demand of a social survey. *The House of Mirth* employs the deliberate selectiveness of a *memento mori*. Its purpose is to suggest the suffocating paramountcy of the Sumnerist ethic in the personal intimacies of social intercourse, to acquaint us with its hideous strength and thereby to make all the more remarkable and all the more touching even so hesitant a rebellion as Lily's. There were, in reality, more pleasing aspects of her society than Mrs. Wharton shows us in this novel, but it was

[1] *The Confident Years*, pp. 180 and 179.

not her business to acclaim them. The fact that she did not has no aesthetic relevance. The novel is eminently successful in balancing the claims of atmosphere—a society generally imbued with selfish materialism—against the problem of finding, within such a society, sufficient moral diversity to provoke conflict that would be more than just a predatory spitefulness. Necessarily, given these conditions, the more admirable qualities are rather thinly spread. In other novels, Mrs. Wharton is more lavish with her positives. In this the forbidding worldliness is uppermost, by its own standards victorious, because it destroys the rebel. But in the person of Lily Bart, who queries everything the training of a lifetime had been designed to nurture in her, Mrs. Wharton allows, as Twain had not been able to do, the possibility of resisting the pressures of the mores, choosing at last a higher loyalty and so hardening the faith of others in the moral absolutes.

The House of Mirth gives us fleeting glimpses of a group of regional *arrivistes*, wealthy mid-Westerners determined to extort recognition from New York society. This is the group which supplies the heroine of *The Custom of the Country*, Undine Spragg, from the middle Western town of Apex. Ruthless and uncompromising, with a 'business-like intentness on gaining her ends', she succeeds, where Lily Bart has failed, in possessing herself of an unquestioned place among the fashionable, a caste now presented as in a kind of metastatic flux. Again, however, the imagery describing this flux is more Darwinist than geological, and again it evaluates as well as describes. The parties to the shift are in intricate relationship. On the outermost periphery are Undine and her kind, avid for the acquaintance of what Undine does not yet recognise as merely a parasitic fringe on a belt which, nearer the centre than her own, at some points eddies closer to the centre, at others further away. The exclusive centre, made up of the descendants of the old New York families—the Dagonets, Fairfords, Marvells—Mrs. Wharton calls the Aborigines, lumping the various gradations of *nouveaux riches* together as the Invaders, some of whom 'had already been modified by contact with the indigenous: they spoke the same language ... though on their lips it had often so different a meaning'. Their pristine virtues and vices we see in Undine's parents and in Elmer Moffett, whom the plot connects with Undine first as the rapidly divorced husband of her Apex days, then as her final matrimonial catch when, at the end of the novel, his financial dealings have magnificently prospered.

Moffett, like Undine's parents, has acquired none of the airs and graces, the protective coloration, with which his predecessors on the upward path have learned to deck themselves in their fallow hours. He still uses the dialect of his people. His unconformity of speech is amusingly pointed up when he meets Ralph Marvell, Undine's first victim and one of the 'Aborigines'. Moffett has been discussing with Mr. Spragg the vista of 'deals' he sees opening before him. Apex, he declares, 'was too tight a fit for me. . . . New York's my size—without a single alteration'. He compares himself to Undine, who 'don't beat about the bush. . . . She told me straight out what was bothering her. She wants the Marvells to think she's right out of Kindergarten. "No goods sent out on approval from this counter!"' Marvell enters shortly after this inelegant trope, asking, 'Am I awfully in the way, sir?' and begging pardon 'most awfully'. Between these two men the difference in speech signalises a fundamental difference in rearing, interests, aptitudes and ethical standards. Before Marvell's entry Moffett had been threatening to disclose the secret of his marriage to Undine, should Mr. Spragg not use private knowledge to discredit a Congressman who stands in the way of a lucrative piece of jobbery. This is the world, in which Moffett and Mr. Spragg are at home, of private blackmail, inside information and sharp practices, of whose routine of betrayal and dishonesty Marvell knows only that it exists. It is the world which provides for the Invaders he knows best, the Lipscombs, Driscolls and Van Degens, all of them more forward in sloughing their *gaucheries*, but in methods and ideals the same as Moffett. They form 'a phantom "society", with all the rules, smirks, gestures of its model, but evoked out of promiscuity and incoherence while the other had been the product of continuity and choice'. The image is of an efficient, predatory culture subduing an effete. It then appropriates the exterior rites and forms to which the incomers attribute a certain indefinable superiority in the dispossessed, who, 'doomed to rapid extinction, . . . would be exhibited at ethnological shows, pathetically engaged in the exercise of their primitive industries'. Their destruction is poignantly symbolised in the fate of Ralph Marvell. Overwhelmed by a New York heat wave, barely convalescent and, now divorced from Undine, worried by her claim for custody of the child to which she had always been so indifferent, he commits suicide:

'He bolted the door and stood looking about the room. For a moment he was conscious of seeing it in every detail with a distinctness he had never before known; then everything in it vanished but the single narrow panel of a drawer under one of the bookcases. He went up to the drawer, knelt down and put his hand into it. . . .

'He passed his left hand over the side of his head, and down the curve of the skull behind the ear. He said to himself: "My wife . . . this will make it all right for her . . ." and a last flash of irony twitched through him. Then he felt again, more deliberately, for the spot he wanted, and put the muzzle of his revolver against it.'

Once more we have a sacrifice, this time unmistakably willed, again at the behest of a society inferior to its victim.

Marvell's natural loyalties are to what he calls 'the sanction of (his) own special group and of the corresponding groups elsewhere'. His group's 'antecedents, its rules, its conventions' are more than a parade of modish etiquette. They signify, as Ralph puts it to Mr. Spragg, 'the obligation recognised between decent men to deal with each other decently'. Mr. Spragg hears this with polite incomprehension, himself recognising, in most transactions, only the primitive requirement that 'it's up to both parties to take care of their own skins'. His record of land jobbing and the monopolising of public utilities in Apex is unsavoury, yet Undine's wanting a divorce simply because of her inclination for another man is 'as shocking to him as it would have been to the most uncompromising of the Dagonets and Marvells'. This middle-class naïvety is abandoned by the more sophisticated Invaders, who have converted the discretion required of a society gallant into an omnibus indulgence of promiscuity. Van Wyck Brooks deprecates Mrs. Wharton's treatment of the Spragg parents. It is ill-conditioned and snobbish. They 'might have looked for a little more charity on the part of their creator'.[1] Yet, though she is quite merciless on Mrs. Spragg's torpidity of mind,

[1] *op. cit.*, p. 171.

Mrs. Wharton allows a kinder interpretation of her artless garrulity, her total lack of humbug, which draws her 'much closer
to the Dagonet ideals than any sham elegance in the past tense'.
And Mr. Spragg is made to appear, in fact, by no means un-
engaging. He has a sense of decency in his private rule of conduct
which raises him above his more urbanised fellows, an agreeably
laconic wit, which infuriates Undine, and he accepts stoically the
decline in his fortunes to which Undine has so lavishly contributed. Nor is Edith Wharton's antipathy to Moffett complete.
Here too is a rogue, living in the recurrent shadow of trust
investigations, now testifying for the State, now eluding it,
switching loyalties as his own interests dictate, indefatigable in
the pursuit of wealth. Yet his wealth, when he acquires it, is used
to gratify unexpected aesthetic yearnings, far beyond Undine's
range : 'she saw that the things he looked at moved him in a way
she could not understand, and that the actual touching of rare
textures—bronze or marble, or velvets touched with the bloom
of age—gave him sensations like those her own beauty had once
roused in him.' He has, as Ralph Marvell says, greatness in him,
'a kind of epic effrontery'. His business expertise reminds Ralph
of a lesson in acting he had once seen in the Conservatoire, where
a familiar role was 'taken to pieces before his eyes, dissolved into
its component elements, and built up again with a minuteness of
elucidation and a range of reference that made him feel as though
he had been let into the secret of some age-long natural process'.
Moffett can similarly dissect and reconstitute the intricacies of a
business affair, negotiating not only with the impersonal economic
factors in mind but seeing too 'how the personal idiosyncrasies
of "the parties" affected them'.

It is an impressive performance and contrasts sadly with the
ineffectualness of Ralph even in the interests that mark his supposed superiority. During his dreadful honeymoon with Undine,
before it sours beyond hope, he meditates his dramatic poem—
or will it be a critical essay? Lying on the hot Sienese hillside he
feels artistic power stirring within him—never, it is clear, to be
tapped by the man who proposes the whimsy of sitting by a
waterfall 'to lie in wait for adjectives'. He is not unconditionally
approved by his creator. Like old Mr. Dagonet, whose sarcasm
'had as little bearing on life as the humours of a Restoration

comedy', Ralph belongs inescapably not only to the virtues but to the limitations and prejudices of his class which, as he sees himself, were like 'sign-posts warning off trespassers who have long ceased to intrude'. There is truth in Ralph's cousin's comment that Moffett (with his zest and vigour), is 'the kind of acquaintance the Dagonets have always needed'. The tragedy is that in gaining such acquaintances the Dagonets and their kind have been unable to transmit to them anything of their code but meaningless runes; and have not renewed themselves from the Invaders' vitality. Old New York, Ralph Marvell feels, had been 'small, cautious, middle-class'. He had rebelled against its provincialism, but now, as he sees it die, realises that its deals were 'singularly coherent and respectable as contrasted with the chaos of indiscriminate appetites which made up its modern tendencies'. That much—and it is of consequence—is to be said in favour of old New York. But Mrs. Wharton clearly charges against its representatives a failure of responsibility and of nerve, an eremitic willingness to accept their fate as the obsolescent gods and submit to dislodgment without transmitting as a functional organism the tradition of which they were custodians.

It may be granted that the usurpers, as Mrs. Wharton presents them, offer an unpromising repository for the faiths of the class they superseded. In this novel, perhaps unfairly, she associates their deficiencies with the middle West, as most brazenly epitomising all that is uncouth in the civilisation of her America and disreputable in its business life. From what we can gather, Apex appears a dim region of civic corruption and barren pleasures, inhabited by tradesmen of a uniform social and moral shabbiness. It is a resurrection, in modern guise, of the oldest feelings about the disruptive nature of western and frontier life, now gracelessly urbanised but lawless still. Yet in going to what she obviously considered the Invaders' base camp, Mrs. Wharton, less prejudiced than her critics allow, concedes it the virtues we have seen. That its virtues were not enlarged, its vices restrained, that the communication between the new and the old was so faulty and hesitant, is accountable, in part at least, to the debility of the old, complacently withdrawn from any effective part in the administration of law, politics and business. By custom, the sons of the family read law at Columbia or Harvard, but only as the ritual prelude to a life of 'more or less cultivated inaction'. Nothing, we are told, 'in the Dagonet and Marvell tradition was opposed to this desultory dabbling with life'. Like Ralph Marvell on his boyhood holidays, the Aborigines have found and retired to 'a cave—a secret inaccessible place with glaucous lights, mysterious murmurs, and a single shaft of communication with the sky'. The image conveys both the charm and the futility of the life they have evolved, that of an aristocracy without duties. In consequence the world around them is relinquished to the Undines who, having lost the conscience which dignified the old, erect 'in layers of unsubstantialness . . . a slavish imitation of the superseded'.

The only world sure enough of itself to resist the lures of this masquerade gentility is that of Raymond de Chelles, the French aristocrat Undine marries after Ralph's suicide. In marrying into this 'Faubourg' society, Undine, dazzled by its being so exotically 'foreign', is repeating precisely her mistake in marrying Ralph, that of taking the unpretentiously exclusive for the showy imitation which is what she really wants. But unlike Ralph, de Chelles is well able to withstand Undine's thriftless demands. Here the tradition of wealth dedicated to service is still alive, its social rites grown from useful activity in politics and the management of family estates. Against this is set the rootlessness of Undine's upbringing in an America, in de Chelles' words, of 'hotels as big as towns, and ... towns as flimsy as paper, where the streets haven't had time to be named, and the buildings are demolished before they're dry, and the people are as proud of changing as we are of holding to what we have'. Mrs. Wharton, writing of Dreyfus's France, romanticises it, one may legitimately object, as much as she belittles America, but life of the kind she praises did subsist there. She could not yet see in America any such deep-rooted discernment of 'the relation of a sovereign function to the nation as a whole'[1]: only intermittent vestiges of decency and taste and an aristocracy, by her account of it in this novel, that had betrayed its trust.

This diatribe of de Chelles, who speaks in anger and disillusion, is not to be taken as giving Mrs. Wharton's considered view. She would acknowledge it part of the truth, but lacking the reserva-

[1] Brooks Adams, *loc. cit.*

tions set out in the course of the novel. To abridge her views is similarly to extinguish their subtleties, but the following statement fairly represents the argument of the two novels. *The House of Mirth* shows us a society permeated with what, for convenience, we have called Sumnerism, such good as there is in it derived from the old traditions, still to some extent effective. *The Custom of the Country*, re-interpreting the same scene, is much more critical of the old, on the grounds that it has resigned its place in the world of affairs and with it the power to direct the energies of the class now rising upon new conditions and new opportunities. In *The Age of Innocence* we see the tradition extend itself usefully into the new dispensation.

The action of *The Age of Innocence* is by far the plainest and most compact of the three novels. The plot does not ramify into the complicated intriguings of *The House of Mirth* or graduate into so many and such widely ranging settings and 'situations' as *The Custom of the Country*. In this third novel Mrs. Wharton constructs her social history tightly around a single narrative thread. As it unfolds, the attitudes of its hero reveal the role of his class in law, politics and business, a class even at this period beginning to freeze into a recoil from the wider bearings of the first two, though still active as a kind of unofficial but stringent and, within its limits, highly effective judicatory in questions of commercial morality. The central issue, however, is a private moral dilemma, which touches on the interests of the state, this miniscule and inbred state of the upper families. Its inbreeding is mapped in periodic deadpan accounts of the elaborate genealogical connexions between the Mansons, the Mingotts, the Dallasses, Rushworths Archers and the rest. From these old families come the hero, Newland Archer, and May Welland, who have just, as the novel opens, become engaged. Archer, on the whole, accepts the faiths of his class. If he is conscious of an intellectual and imaginative constriction, his criticism of this deficiency in the group is tolerant. He hopes to indulge his superior tastes privately, without questioning the collective moral authority of his peers. He is 'placidly in love' but envisages a marriage of 'passionate and tender comradeship' with the young girl whose foremost characteristic, reiterated like a Wagnerian *motif*, is an innocence 'cunningly manufactured by a conspiracy of mothers and aunts and long-dead ancestresses': but not, he is confident, as he is to be the guide to her maturing feelings, 'the innocence which seals the mind against imagination and the heart against experience'. Yet so much is Archer a creature of his environment that he shares the general shock which greets the arrival of Ellen Olenska, May's cousin. She has returned from Europe, in a miasma of scandal, after a broken marriage to a European nobleman and, according to rumour, having lived as the mistress of the man who had helped her escape her husband's cruelties. Now, received back into the family—rightly, as Archer rather preens himself on believing—she has appeared with his fiancée in the Mingott family box at the Opera, a public gesture of sponsorship which Archer cannot bring himself to countenance. The opening question of the novel is whether the fashionable families will accept her.

Gradually, and after some delicate intriguing, they do. Archer, loyal to the desires of May and her relatives, is active in helping her, anxious about her occasional sideslips into less reputable social circles, her impulsive hobnobbing with the vaguely Bohemian côterie of New York writers and artists, all actions born of her familiarity with the more liberal interests of European society. Nominated by her family to represent his firm of lawyers as Ellen's adviser, Archer gleans a secondhand acquaintance with the life she has fled. Olenski's heartless treatment of his wife offends all Archer's inherited convictions, yet what he learns conjures up as well a range and depth of experience, within one of the really old 'rich and idle and ornamental societies', surpassing anything imaginable in New York. In the documents he reads there is a hint of desperate romance, of transgressions justified in their own exotic milieu. At first sharing his senior's view that Ellen should not seek a divorce, he moves to suspecting that this expresses 'the Pharisaic voice of a society wholly absorbed in barricading itself against the unpleasant'. Yet he advises her as his upbringing directs. 'Our legislation,' he tells her, 'favours divorce—our social customs don't.' It may bear hard on the individual, it may be 'stupid and narrow and unjust—but one can't make over society'. The individual, in fact, must support his misery to serve 'the collective interest': to keep private scandal from the scurrilous attentions of a popular Press, to hold the family together, to endorse the obligations of the marriage contract, to stand against any relaxation in the strict code honoured by the class. Discreet misconduct, reluctantly tolerated, is preferable to the habit of casual re-marriage, which, once accepted, threatens the whole social organism. These, ironically, are the arguments Ellen reiterates when, before his marriage to May, Archer's sympathy has deepened to love and he asks Ellen to divorce her husband to marry him. For the reasons he has himself supplied, she refuses, seeing in the course he now suggests a 'happiness bought by disloyalty and cruelty'. This moral insight is the instruction of her American sojourn. She has learned that 'under the dullness there are things so fine and sensitive and delicate that even those I most cared for in my other life look cheap in comparison ... it seems as if I'd never before understood with how much that is hard and shabby and base the most exquisite pleasures may be paid for'. The 'exquisite pleasures' she has known in her other life are those of the more richly endowed European tradition, 'the life of art and study and pleasure ... the sober and splendid old houses she must have frequented, the people she must have talked with, the incessant stir of ideas, curiosities, images and associations thrown out by an intensely social race in a setting of immemorial manners'.

All this magically alien brilliance is bound up, for Archer, with his love for Ellen. Even after he has married May, the temptations persist. Archer sees now a grand passion triumphing over hypocritical conventions. His and Ellen's is a case beyond precedent, beyond the categories of husband, wife and mistress. 'I want,' he says, 'to get away with you into a world where words like that— categories like that—won't exist. Where we shall be simply two human beings who love each other, who are the whole of life to each other.' It is Ellen who disillusions him. Her Europe comprehends the tawdry *demi-monde* where the grand passion works itself out in seedy deceptions, the joyless underside of the social splendours. 'Where is that country?' she asks Archer. 'I know so many who've tried to find it; and, believe me, they all got out by mistake at wayside stations: at places like Boulogne, or Pisa, or Monte Carlo—and it wasn't at all different from the old world, but only rather smaller and dingier and more promiscuous.' After their final meeting alone together in the dreary surroundings of the Metropolitan Museum, Ellen returns to Europe and her husband and Archer does not follow her.

This collation of the European and American settings is intended to demonstrate not a categorical superiority in the European but a divergence in kind between the two, each with its distinctive quality. As Ellen remarks, America was not discovered 'only to make it into a copy of another country'. Its fundamental quality is that of May Welland's innocence, capable of its own penetrating intuitions. After his wife's death, Archer is told by his son what, without its ever having been voiced between them, he had always known, that his wife had followed the secret progress of his desires and that in leaving Ellen he was giving up the thing he most wanted in submission to May's unspoken plea. Like Aeneas, and for comparable reasons, he leaves his Dido, the communal loyalty overriding the personal satisfaction. In a purer form, it is the sacrifice of Lily Bart re-enacted, helping this time to preserve virtues inherent in the society, not exterior and in opposition to it. His marriage, he recognises, has had 'the dignity of a duty', lapsing from which it becomes 'a mere battle of ugly appetites'.

Around this personal drama the wider life of the society to which Archer thus pays his tribute fills out the scene. In his infatuation he thinks his own world 'damnably dull. We've no character, no colour, no variety'. Yet variety and colour enough diversify Mrs. Wharton's *dramatis personae*. The sententious charlatan, Dr. Agathon Carver, of the Valley of Love, makes a briefly entertaining appearance, moving 'his arms with large pawing gestures, as though he were distributing lay blessings to a kneeling multitude', lamenting of New York, 'how little the life of the spirit has reached it!' A New World Lady Bracknall, Mrs. Manson Mingott combines, within the 'immense accretion of flesh which had descended on her in middle life like a flood of lava on a doomed city', a regal eccentricity with the severest dignity and uprightness of conduct. In Mrs. Wharton's New York there is no dearth either of character or nuances of manners and morals. When Julius Beaufort transgresses the 'unblemished honesty' which 'was the *noblesse oblige* of old financial New York' he is uncompromisingly outlawed. His wife appeals to her family to restore his credit, but though 'a wife's place was at her husband's side when he was in trouble . . . the mere idea of a woman's appealing to her family to screen her husband's business dishonour was inadmissible, since it was the one thing that the Family, as an institution, could not do'. It is a recognition, in Hawthorne's words, that this is 'the sort of crime, growing out of its artificial state, which society (unless it should change its entire constitution for this man's unworthy sake) neither could nor ought to pardon'. Their censure, however, is the limited social one of ostracising the offender, its effectiveness clearly dependent on a business community still conducting its affairs largely as a personal matter between individuals all of whom, belonging to the same restricted group and knowing each other well, are amenable to such discipline: for the impersonal corporations and the rising wave of 'new men' it can have no meaning at all. Towards the public offices, the law and politics, whose mandate could be brought to bear dispassionately on these malefactions, Archer's class is apathetic. The law Archer practises is devoted to the commonplace transactions established over three generations of New York gentility, offering no outlet to the larger issues of polity deliberated by a Kent, a Marshall, a Story. As for politics, Archer's feeling is that 'the country was in the possession of the bosses and the emigrants, the decent people had to fall back on sport or culture'. When a journalist friend asks him, 'Why don't you all get together and be "they" yourselves?', the question strikes impotently against the simple dogma, beyond discussion, that gentlemen 'stayed at home and abstained'. Archer belongs to an aristocracy which, by the eighteen-seventies, though still bearing witness within itself to the most correct ideals of private and civic conduct, had no thought of adventuring these ideals in the rough and tumble developing outside its enclave.

It is this life which Archer has found satisfactory until its assumptions are thrown in doubt by his intimacy with Ellen. When he first suspects that he must leave her, 'his whole future seemed suddenly to be unrolled before him; and passing down its endless emptiness he saw the dwindling figure of a man to whom nothing was ever to happen'. The melancholy vision is not, in fact, to be realised. The brief epilogue shows us Archer, some years after his wife's death, recalling the courses of his life. Standing out now in highest relief is his response to the personal appeal of Theodore Roosevelt that 'if the stable's ever to be cleaned out, men like you have got to lend a hand in the cleaning'. Though his own contribution was, he recognises, trifling, 'he had had high things to contemplate, great things to delight in; and one great man's friendship to be his strength and pride. He had been, in short, what people were beginning to call "a good citizen".' Still respecting much in the observances that have died out he now understands the limitations of what he and his contemporaries had bent their energies to—'the narrow groove of money-making, sport and society to which their vision had been limited'. The evidence of new achievement he finds in the generation of his children, 'absorbed in state politics or municipal reform', intelligently re-discovering their country's past, more tolerant in their views—'there was good in the new order too'. It is not a world swept suddenly to perfection. The reformist urge has its by-products of 'fads and fetishes and frivolities'. But it is a world seeking to cultivate the unruly new estate by restoring to public service the virtues of the old, widening and making good the path on which Archer had set his feet. Beside this, Ellen and his regrets have become a 'vision, faint and tenuous', his sacrifice a choice justified by events, the possibility of sublime romance faded before the reality of a life 'filled decently'.

For a critic, like Edmund Wilson, of left-wing sympathies, the tolerance of this conclusion is symptomatic of a decline in the 'intensity' of Mrs. Wharton's vision: her period, the assumption is, could inspire little, in the mind rightly disposed, but *saevo indignatio*.[1] Van Wyck Brooks, on the other hand, feels that her censure of her country is unnecessarily severe. That this conflict of opinion should arise suggests, in itself, that the delicate shadings of Mrs. Wharton's evaluations have escaped both commentators. It is perhaps even more surprising, in the light of the interpretations advanced in this chapter, that Blake Nevius should consider her 'perhaps the least "American" of our important novelists'.[2] Quite apart from the fact that her eminently diacritical intelligence so accurately reports, as we have seen, on the shift of social motivations in her own period, it reincarnates and refers to that period

[1] This, though never so baldly stated, is the tenor of his essay, 'Justice to Edith Wharton', in *The Wound and the Bow*, pp. 174–90.

[2] *Edith Wharton: a study of her fiction*, p. 25.

the disposition of the original New World Puritans to exalt the community—where the Kingdom was to be shaped—above the wilderness—Mrs. Wharton's middle West and its recoil upon the older centres; and to impose obligations on an instructed and responsible *élite*; both these corollaries annexed by circumstances to the generic Puritan distrust of human nature—in its untrained state, as Mrs. Wharton remarks in *The Age of Innocence*, 'not frank and innocent . . . full of the twists and defences of an instinctive guile'. If we are to cite American precedents in her own medium, then her affinities are with Cooper rather than with Melville and Hawthorne. They, as we have seen, took up Poe's rather than Cooper's aesthetic legacy, with the radical difference that, however far they might, like Poe, explore the individual psyche, like Cooper they set the collective, the social good above the claims of the wanton ego. By a comparable modification, something of Poe's Trophonian divination deepens Mrs. Wharton's brilliant social observation. Her ideals, like Cooper's, were social ideals, and like him she held to them. But from time to time we come on a collapse in the reassuring continuity of companionship, habit and tradition, catch a sudden flicker in the apparently solid line of house and street and furnishings, a recognition that the community, in its transitions and adjustments, may strip the unwary individual of his customary defences: we think of Lily Bart's Eumenides and Ralph Marvell's suicide. Her final response to disasters of this kind, however, is not Poe's, who swept all externals to cataclysmic destruction: it is more like Hawthorne's, with his apprehension of the sequential nature of society, its continuous evolution of new from old.

By Mrs. Wharton's life and by her autobiographical record, *A Backward Glance*, we are left in no doubt that she found in Europe, and especially in France, an aesthetic sensibility transubstantiated into the innumerable particulars of daily living, a culture, in short, having a 'real presence', instinctively accepted, in which America was deficient. Her novels, however, are raised upon no such categorical antithesis. They moderate the antithesis in the ways discussed in this chapter and it is a necessary part of the moral conflicts they enunciate that it should be thus moderated. Mrs. Wharton prophesied no realisation of 'the American dream'—her view of human nature prohibited that—

but detached from her country's affairs a new iconography of the endless contest between lawless enterprise and the laudable toil, not, as she finally presented it, inauspicious, of holding together a tradition of civilised life. Edith Wharton's fiction reminds us sharply that novels are not reality, are successful, as Dr. Johnson said of 'imitations' generally, 'not because they are mistaken for realities, but because they bring realities to mind'. This her novels incisively do. The realities she brings to mind are selective, but provide the basis for an interpretation of her times of a balance and comprehensiveness not to be achieved simply by accumulating 'facts' in the manner of the orthodox realists, who, indeed, were even more selective, and less judiciously so. Concrete, representational realism play its part in her fiction, but more important is the realism which sees through the social paraphernalia to the moral diversity—of whose existence James was dubious—in the segment of American life she knew best. Despite her predilection for the charms—which she exaggerated—of the European synthesis of social poise, artistic accomplishment and public service, she was notably successful in evaluating within its own boundaries a society whose intellectual energies and moral sensibilities—complex enough for any novelist—operated for the most part in law, commerce and the petrifying observances of fashionable deportment. Her novels are *romans de moeurs* of European extraction but dealing with American society and cognate with the work of her American predecessors in the novel, themselves in their various ways indebted to European origins.

Chapter Seven

Modern American Fiction and its Inheritance

B Y the range of differences between the highly individual talents which settle into the accordances and homogeneities of an artistic tradition we may measure the tradition's strength. The more uniform it becomes, the closer its dissolution, and the more easily is it to be defined. The variety of forms and manners we have scrutinised in the preceding chapters bears out at least the diversity of the American tradition in the novel. Having augmented this diversity, the present age has brought the ease of posthumous definition no nearer. We are dealing with what is still very much a living and intromitting entity. A comprehensive survey of the modern American novel is impossible within the scope of this study. Still, it may with reasonable brevity be shown that certain dispositions and capacities recurrently serviceable in the past have persisted into the present. While we need not recapitulate the earlier soundings in detail, some account must now be attempted of the resemblances which echo among the writers of the past.

The quality of imagination most saliently manifested in Poe we have defined by reference to the legend of Trophonius. Of the complementary spirit, exhibited in Cooper's novels, the examplar is Theseus. He is the traveller through the perils of the wilderness to the city, the victor over the terrors of the cave, the thesmothete, his achievements as king of Athens distinctively civic and juridical. This spirit we might fittingly call Athenian, or, after the goddess of the city, Minervan, signifying thereby the idea of a community democratically ordered under a government of law and set against the dangerous experiences of trackless outland and sub-terrene labyrinth. Both these strains, it is clear, are strong in the American novel. They correspond, in the great generalisations of European aesthetics, to the romantic and the classical imaginations, variously attracted, so far as American fiction is concerned, to the contrarieties of individual and community, wilderness and city, journey and haven, lawlessness and order. As we have seen at the end of the preceding chapter, each of our novelists, within a general attachment to one or other of the two modes of vision, calls also upon its converse. At the very beginning, Taylor, the religious visionary, and Freneau, the political controversialist, set out upon these distinctive tracks. As a Puritan, Taylor's poetic subject was the tergiversations of the individual soul. Equally because he was a Puritan, he considered the individuality, the separateness, of the soul as alleviated by its belonging to a spiritual communion and a social community—the region of Freneau's verse. Though Taylor's poems focus most particularly on the interior agony, the assumptions behind them are political as well as theological. By fulfilling itself in salvation, the soul strengthens the community which is itself so organised as to advance the questing soul—the point, of course, at which Poe, likewise absorbed in catechising the psyche, parts company from Taylor. Even in Poe, of them all the most Trophonian, we find elements of the Athenian faculties. Melville and Hawthorne, familiar with the enigmas of cave and wilderness, like Theseus complete the journey to the city, whose virtues they celebrate.

As Swift arrived at a workable variation on the Augustan vogue, and Taylor on the metaphysical, so have the novelists drawn upon sub-traditions within the two major categories. Among those to which they have engaged themselves, related to their own subjects and themes, and in consequence branched off from, are the later romantic lyric, the classical 'rules of composition', pastoral and satire in their various kinds, all of these acting upon the central obligation of the novel to tell a story mirroring the tensions, forms and mores of an actual human society. The list is not exhaustive, for these developments, elucidated in the body of this work, are simply particular undertakings in a general design—comprehending all annexments of this kind—in which two matters are involved: the link between

the American novel and its society, and between the American
novel and its European antecedents. As Professor Trilling argues,
the link between literature and life is its exposition of 'formulable ideas'. It is through the very general ideas outlined in
the last paragraph, formulated by and expressing the essence
of the American experience, that the American novelists
converse with the life around them; and the most general
association between American fiction and European artistic precedents is that by 'imitating' these ideas in fiction the American
novelists have naturalised romanticism and classicism along the
lines discussed above and illustrated, in their diverse manifestations, in the earlier chapters. On the whole, the American novel
tends to express classical-Athenian attitudes transfigured and
illuminated by the intuitions and tramontane irruptions of
Trophonian romanticism. Its peculiar fusion of these two sets
the American apart from the English novel. The English novel
may be said to centre, by and large, on a society firmly consolidated into settled manners and institutions, a major part of whose
fascination is that they catch up current actualities, the complex
affairs of living beings, in the slow deposit of past customs and
procedures. Within this order the intrigue reaches its resolution.
The American novel, on the other hand, represents a society in
every way more mobile, fundamentally serial in nature, its
characteristic drama the struggle to contain its transitions, to
perpetuate in changed and changing circumstances the articles of
stability, some of them, like Thomism, inherited from Europe,
others, like the very special position of the Supreme Court, indigenous. In accomplishing the passage to new conditions the
tensions and conflicts of the narrative are resolved: thus, for
example, the establishment of Templeton, the agony of Billy
Budd and Major Molineux, the sacrifice of Newland Archer. As
we have seen, the drama is frequently localised around the poles
of the wilderness—the forest, the prairie, the middle West—and
civilisation—the settlements and cities—and in the dissensions of
commerce and government, the law and its principles. American
novelists have for the most part advocated rather classical
restraints than romantic anarchy, recognising that 'the American
dream' can be realised only in part and with the compromises and
concessions (laws, discipline, punishment) demanded by the

human condition. These themes and treatments are of equal importance to the modern American novelist.

A number of these writers, however, have at one stage or another lost their considerable talents in a sour backwash from the old utopianism, decided that as life is manifestly imperfect and chaotic, the dice loaded against the individual and perfection unattainable, then there is nothing at all to be done but cultivate one's own pleasures. Of these the best known is Ernest Hemingway. Most of his heroes are refugees from the humdrum chores by which society holds its lines against barbarity. Disillusioned by personal accidents (the unhappy childhood, the experience of war) and the general messiness of life (poverty, injustice, mass dishonesty), they turn in upon themselves, form uneasy groups of like-begotten, like-minded companions. Unresponsive to any traditional codes and faiths, they opt out of everything but narrowly personal relationships and solitary pleasures. They are beings of one-syllable thoughts, feelings, reactions. With considerable ingenuity Hemingway contrives, within their contracted universe, to suggest standards by which they may be judged, good behaviour distinguished from bad. But it is necessarily a very limited morality and, in the scenes where the characters propound it, carries even the famous dialogue into sickly twaddle. In *The Sun Also Rises*, Lady Ashley breaks off her affair with a young bull fighter, partly because she feels she might ruin his career, partly too because he insists that she should conform to his ways, not he to hers. This, she says, is 'sort of what we have instead of God'. Catherine Barkley in *A Farewell to Arms*, dying after childbirth, entreats Lieutenant Henry, 'You won't do our things with another girl, or say the same things, will you.' As Philip Young has said, Hemingway writes of people in a world either literally or figuratively at war: 'restricted grimly by the urgencies of war, their pleasures are limited pretty much to those the senses can communicate, and their morality in a harshly pragmatic one; what's moral is what you feel good after'.[1] The inadequacy of this we may illustrate best by reference to Twain, a writer with whom Hemingway is often compared, but whose morality is in fact infinitely more subtle. We think, in

[1] Philip Young: *Ernest Hemingway* (University of Minnesota Pamphlets), p. 39.

this connexion, of the use Twain makes, in *Huckleberry Finn*, of the fact that what is moral is, often, just what doesn't make you feel good, the hardy refusal to take the first and easy decision. In a lopsided way, Hemingway's heroes do follow the code of Natty Bumppo—self-sufficiency, expert craftsmanship, bravery—but lack Natty's consciousness of moral imperatives, just as Hemingway lacks Cooper's instinct of community, reaching out for expression in civic and political forms.

Reading the novels, enchanted by Hemingway's stylistic and narrative gifts, we may accept, for a time, the mystical values he attaches to heroic drinking, Herculean sexual prowess, to brute courage and bull fighting, to hunting, shooting and fishing, to—most important of all—the ability to endure, though to endure to no ultimate purpose. It is fundamentally, however, as we become increasingly aware even while we read, a sentimental attitude; childish rather than, even, child-like, the perverse refusal, having been hurt, to take any part in the corrupt system. Like Newland Archer's gentlemen, Hemingway's heroes, in their own ways, 'stay at home and abstain'. *For Whom the Bell Tolls* is, of course, politically 'engaged'—predictably, to the Loyalist side in the Spanish Civil War. But it gives no impression that political ideas speak to Hemingway as they did to Cooper, Melville and Hawthorne. It is beautifully written around the central episode of the doomed attack on the bridge, extremely exciting but, in the end, no more articulately positive than the earlier novels. The hero, Robert Jordan, has no clearer idea of the faith to which he sacrifices his life than, we must suppose, has his creator. Hemingway gives so much pleasure, is himself in so many ways an exquisite craftsman, records so perceptively the detritus of a major war and an ill-managed peace, that he almost persuades us to look no further, until we realise how restricted is his canvas, how unrelievedly emotional are his judgments, how far, in seeking, understandably, to avoid uplift, he has strayed into a quite amoral sensualism, sinking, from want of intellectual vigour, into the most insipid romanticism. The same may be said of John Dos Passos, whose America, in his collectivist novel, *U.S.A.*, is no less abject than Hemingway's.

This trilogy covers the period immediately before, during and immediately after the First World War and is American enough in having as its central interest the character of American society. Technically it displays great virtuosity. The main narrative introduces us to a variegated cross-section of characters from all ranks of society. We are given a fairly concise biography of their early years, the narrative speed slowing from time to time to deal with particular sections of their lives in greater detail. None of these stories is told straight through. At arbitrary points the story is broken off and we are introduced to yet another character or return to the story of someone we have left earlier. As the trilogy develops, the lives of some of the people cross. One of the people in the first book, for instance, Janey, is given four sections, each having her name as its title. By the end of the book, however, she has been engaged as secretary to another of the characters, J. Ward Moorhouse, and in the second and third books we have only occasional glimpses of her as she makes fleeting appearances in the sections devoted to him and to some of the other characters with whom he is associated. Again, in the last section devoted to Janey, we see her going to lodge with a Jewish family in New York, the Comptons. The second book begins in detail the life story of Benny Compton, a radical agitator. By this technique Dos Passos presents characters from dramatically different points of view, suggests the casual, haphazard relationships and meetings of modern life, the social cross-currents of American society which carry this individual to entirely new social levels and circumstances while others remain static. The characters are selected at random from all the social strata, and at random, some of them, they come together, either to cohere or to drift apart again. Janey's brother, Joe Williams, who has four sections to himself, spends a night off his ship—he is an A.B.—in Nice. Going back to his ship drunk he meets two soldiers with whom he shares a drink. Later, in a section dealing with Richard Ellsworth Savage, we gather that he was one of the soldiers, and so view the incident from another angle—the two lives cross each other for a brief moment. a meeting made more poignant by Williams's being killed shortly afterwards in a tavern brawl. These episodes are the core of the trilogy, the main stream of narrative.

Of the three other kinds of sequence which separate these fictional episodes we shall concern ourselves with only one, the series of biographies of real people, inserted at irregular intervals throughout the novel. There are twenty-seven of them. They cover the lives of American citizens in some way famous, representative or both. Seven of them, all unsympathetic, are of financiers who represent privilege, reactionary thought and political activity, egotism—Pierpoint Morgan, Hearst, Carnegie, for instance. Four deal with people occupied with left-wing politics—a martyr like Wesley Everest, a national leader like Debs or La Follette, all of them united in their hatred of capitalist society and of war. Others of the biographies deal with politicians of different shades, for the most part derogatory portraits showing how hypocrisy succeeds in public life or how ideals become corrupted over the years, as in the section dealing with President Wilson. In all of them the left-wing bias is unmistakable, presenting its highly simplified version of life, seeing things in unrelieved blacks and whites, the existing order always wrong, the reformers always right, but never effective. The tone is too dogmatic, too strident and, eventually, wearisome. It is particularly noticeable in the fictional parts, where there is hardly one likeable character. They are hypocrites, career men, corrupted by the search for money or power, people who restrain none of their sensual appetites. Even a man like Joe Williams, the unambitious sailor, to whom Dos Passos is on the whole sympathetic, is not likeable. He remains uncorrupted by the longing for either money or position, but his life proceeds at the lowest level of sensibility; he is animal-like, his days a sequence of physical appetites satisfied or disappointed. Ben Compton, who retains and suffers for his socialist ideals, fails completely in his personal relationships, soured and embittered by repeated political disappointments.

In one way or another all the characters fail. Yet this universal pessimism is to some extent refuted by the biographical sketches, for there we find men who are neither defeated nor corrupted. One biography is devoted to the Wright brothers and their inventing the aeroplane. They were simply technicians, men immersed in practical problems, wholly given to making comlicated machinery work, retaining dignity and modesty through all their success. With them we may compare the fictional Charley Anderson. He too is a technician, also interested in aircraft, who has developed a new and efficient engine starter. A company formed to exploit it brings him wealth. Tempted by offers from a rival firm he runs out on his partner; he begins to dabble in the abstractions of finance and the stock market. His drinking becomes compulsive, his sexual demands insatiable, his body gross and decayed. In the end he kills himself and a woman in a car crash and dies talking, unable to stop the endless flow of self-pity and self-justification, a wreck of the man he had been, his mechanical skills forgotten, tailing fitfully away with an unfinished sentence on the hospital bed where he dies. It is a most depressing, hopeless story—and we have the right to ask why he should be so different from the Wright brothers, why there should be no fictional counterpart to the story from real life, why, in sum, the gloom should be so universal. In a novel of this length, purporting to picture a whole society, it is a failure in aesthetic discrimination not to counterpoint the scenes of failure, self-interest and dishonesty, the betrayals, lusts and lecheries, with some echo of the virtues which the novel's documentary content admits. In what both Dos Passos and Hemingway have to say there is truth, but they exclude so very much that we cannot allow them that breadth of vision which enabled our other writers, none of them mindless optimists, to see the subtle inflections of good as well as evil in their different eras, to rest content with the compromises which are all man can be expected to make of his ideals. Other writers have surveyed the contemporary scene without such resolute revulsion. Scott Fitzgerald's *The Great Gatsby* is a case in point.

Perhaps the quality which enables Fitzgerald to view composedly so much that is distressing is his affectionate understanding of human caprices and absurdities. *Gatsby*, for instance, for all its tragic content, has a number of most amusing passages: the drunk man in Gatsby's library, reverently awed by his discovery that his host has stocked his shelves with books that are 'absolutely real—have pages and everything. I thought they'd be a nice durable cardboard. Matter of fact they're absolutely real. Pages and—— Here! Lemme show you. . . . See!' he cried triumphantly. 'It's a bona-fide piece of printed matter. It fooled me. This fella's a regular Belasco. It's a triumph. What thoroughness! What realism. Knew when to stop, too—didn't cut the pages. But what do you want? What do you expect?' This kind of entertaining extravagance is very much a part of the atmosphere which pervades the novel until the tragic over-tones expunge it. It is an urban tragedy in which 'the electric trains, men-carrying, plunge through the rain from New York. It was the hour of profound human change, and excitement was generating in the air'. This in another context, is

> ... *the violet hour, when the eyes and back*
> *Turn upward from the desk, when the human engine waits*
> *Like a taxi throbbing waiting*

Fitzgerald establishes an intimate connection between the human beings and their surroundings. As well as having a strong sensuous existence, the background can suggest symbolic depth, as though, endowed with a life of its own, it responded to the moods of the human beings we see against it. So the drab cuckold, Wilson, moves towards his bankrupt garage, 'mingling immediately with the cement colour of the walls'. Gatsby's and Daisy's 'tragic arguments fade with the city lights'. The plane flight at the beginning of *The Last Tycoon*, as well as being a perfect re-creation of the physical details, becomes also 'the extraordinary illuminating flight where (Stahr) saw which way we were going ... he came here from choice to be with us at the end. Like the plane coming into the Glendale airport, into the warm darkness'. Here and elsewhere, as in Poe, Melville, Hawthorne, the background is used to reveal unexpected significances, to reflect or tone the mood and personality of the characters, to shift from the unambiguous clarity and sharpness of its sensuous being to this discreet symbolism.

It has been objected against *The Great Gatsby* that Gatsby's rather tawdry dream of taking Daisy, from whom circumstances had separated him, away from her boorish husband, is the book's only positive good. This is to exclude the viewpoint of the narrator, Nick Carraway, like Fitzgerald himself from the middle West; but no longer the merely vulgar and bustling West of Mrs. Wharton, nor the region of Twain's tiny hamlets. For Fitzgerald the accretion of modes, habits, observances has, in the now long- settled towns and cities, precipitated an enchoric quality, both urban and pastoral, more artless than that of the East but retaining an innocence and the sense of a national spirit weakened in the cosmopolitan East. Gatsby's tragedy has a value beyond itself. In assuming responsibility for the death of Wilson's wife, killed by Daisy's reckless driving, he sets off the chain of events which culminates in Wilson's shooting him; and thereby brings Carraway the enlightenment he lacked himself and which is necessary to interpret the events. Thinking over the story he has told, Carraway meditates its significance:

'One of my most vivid memories is of coming back West from prep school and later from college at Christmas time. Those who went further than Chicago would gather in the old dim Union Station at six o'clock of a December evening, with a few Chicago friends, already caught up into their own holiday gaieties, to bid them a hasty good-bye . . .

'When we pulled out into the winter night and the real snow, our snow, began to stretch out beside us and twinkle against the windows, and the dim lights of small Wisconsin stations moved by, a sharp wild brace came suddenly into the air. We drew in deep breaths of it as we walked back from dinner through the cold vestibules, unutterably aware of our identity with this country for one strange hour, before we melted indistinguishably into it again.

'That's my Middle West—not the wheat or the prairies or the lost Swede towns, but the thrilling returning trains of my youth, and the street lamps and sleigh bells in the frosty dark and the shadows of holly wreaths thrown by lighted windows on the snow. I am part of that, a little solemn with the feel of those long winters, a little complacent from growing up in the Carraway house in a city where dwellings are still called through decades by a family's name. I see now that this has been a story of the West, after all—Tom and Gatsby, Daisy and Jordan and I, were all Westerners, and perhaps we possessed some deficiency in common which made us subtly unadaptable to Eastern life.'

It is the time-imprinted succession of such days and ways that makes an ordered community and it is the ideal this represents which, leaving the middle West of his childhood, Gatsby has lost to the surrogate dream of re-possessing Daisy. We are told explicitly at the end of the novel that Gatsby's dream, in reality, had he been able to recognise it, 'lay behind him, somewhere back in that vast obscurity beyond (New York), where the dark fields of the republic rolled on under the night. . . . So we beat on, boats against the current, borne back ceaselessly into the past'. The value of Gatsby's tragedy and of the sacrifice he makes in taking Daisy's guilt upon himself, is that it brings this illumination to the narrator.

The comprehensive genius of William Faulkner has taken up, among many other themes, one that is implied in *The Great Gatsby*—Gatsby is a bootlegger—the encroachments of organised crime and violence on ordinary life at all its social levels. This is the world most generally made known by the slickly written American detective thrillers, many of them, for avowed pot-boilers, of a quite extraordinary competence, in dialogue and construction particularly, and reaching, in the work of men like Dashiell Hammett and Raymond Chandler, a stature we cannot readily ignore. It is one mark of the maturity of American literature that its most popular form should be capable of achieving a style and expressing ideas in a manner entirely beyond its moribund English counterpart. Faulkner's most notorious essay in the genre is *Sanctuary*, but violence and hoodlumism are generally an integral part of his picture of the modern South, one of the phenomena which it has been particularly the business of twentieth-century American society to manage and of its writers to interpret: the gangsters, after all, are no other than the new Ishmael Bushes and Tom Hutters. What is most remarkable about Faulkner's long series of novels is not the decadence, violence, perversion and decay he so abundantly records in his Yoknapatawpha county, but the sense with which he leaves us of a land grown into and working to perfect that homogeneity out of which alone, he says (*Intruder in the Dust*), 'comes anything of a people or for a people of durable and lasting value—the literature, the art, the science, that minimum of government and police which is the meaning of freedom and liberty, and perhaps most valuable of all in a national character worth anything in a crisis . . .'

Intruder in the Dust tells the story of Lucas Beauchamp, a negro, who is arrested—not, miraculously, lynched on the spot—for the murder of a white man. Having white ancestors in his lineage, he has always comported himself with a pride, even an arrogance, which irks most of the white community. They long for him just once, if only for a moment, 'to admit he's a nigger', to be abject, to acknowledge an inbred inferiority. In this crisis, facing the threat of a lynch mob invading the jail, he remains as he has always been, disdaining to present any defence, though hinting, aloofly, at his innocence. The hints are pursued by a young white boy, through whose eyes we see the story unfold. He has for years been fascinated, having experienced it once himself, by Lucas's lordly manner, now, seemingly, arrived at its final and extreme manifestation. After a grave-opening, the discovery of a second corpse, proof that Lucas's gun could not have fired the fatal shot—all devices exactly of the sort Twain relished—the murderer is found to have been one of a lawless family living in 'Beat Four', a region traditionally defiant of all constituted authority. This blood and thunder story of prejudice and fratricide Faulkner uses to comment on the nature of the South, more particularly on its peculiar problem of race relations, most generally on the whole question of how the contagious nihilism of Beat Four is to be held within reasonable bounds.

As we are introduced to it, Beat Four, like the mountain settlement in *Summer*, harbours 'a race a species which before now had made their hill stronghold good against the county and the federal government too, which did not simply inhabit nor had merely corrupted but had translated and transmogrified that whole region of lonely pine hills . . . into a synonym for independence and violence: an idea with physical boundaries like a quarantine for plague so that solitary unique and alone out of all the county it was known to the rest of the county . . . as in the middle twenties people knew where Cicero Illinois was and who lived there and what they did, who neither knew nor cared what state Chicago was in'. They are the most obdurate of 'nigger-haters', but in this merely the extremists of an endemic and ubiquitous prejudice, shared at the beginning by the young boy, whom Faulkner shows growing out of it as the story proceeds, in part through the instruction of circumstances themselves, in part through his uncle's homilies on the meaning of the circumstances. Lucas's predicament is the predicament of his race, of the second-class and persecuted citizen. It is this subjection which Faulkner wishes to see relieved, but not by the North's 'simple ratification by votes of a printed paragraph', imposing from without legislation that cannot in practice be enforced because the majority of the vast region to which it applies is against it. To bring the negro into the community requires that the South should want this, for effective laws are the expression of a general consent. 'That's what we are really defending,' says the uncle: 'the privilege of setting him free ourselves. . . . We expiate and abolish it ourselves, alone and without help nor even (with thanks) advice.' The past—a past, especially, distinguished by so devastating an episode as the Civil War—cannot be easily or quickly repudiated.

Almost all Faulkner's novels admit as part of the order which, for him, the South represents, its unbreakable ligatures with the past, its consciousness, kept alive in relics of the war, in monuments, in regional anecdotes, in family histories, of the society the past was building until the war and 'reconstruction' shattered it, a society not classless but democratic, 'where a man could be the jailer or the innkeeper or farrier or vegetable peddler yet still be what the lawyer and planter and doctor and parson called a gentleman'. Out of the wreckage of that attempt even the aberration of Beat Four has found itself an organic part of the post bellum settlement. It is the South outcast and impenitent, admitting freely to beliefs and conduct which the generality at least dissimulates. It is, in the analogy Faulkner uses, the one man 'in any random thousand Southerners . . . who would himself lynch Lucas no matter what the occasion', distinct from those who dissimulate the same feeling, from those who are simply indifferent to the negro's plight and from those 'who do begrieve Lucas' shameful condition and would improve it'. It is, in short, the South's peculiar version of the lawless and intolerant elements in all communities, peculiar because Beat Four is the wilderness actually embedded in the community, answering to some atavistic need in the community itself, for that reason the harder to extirpate, its sins, for that reason also, to be expiated only by the community from whose tragic history it has grown. In these ways, the novel offers us a fascinating recension of the traditional antithesis between the barbarous outposts and the law-giving *urbs*.

Intruder in the Dust is interesting because it states thus positively much that Faulkner leaves to be inferred in the novels which have given him his name as the poet of the South transmogrified into a kind of Gothic charnel house: the demented sexual perversion of Popeye in *Sanctuary*, Percy Grimm's sadistic mutilation of Joe Christmas in *Light in August*, the cretinism of Benjy in *The Sound and the Fury*, which hints also, in Quentin's fantasy relationship with his sister, at incest. That Faulkner should so often turn to such psychological monstrosities is one token of his kinship with Poe. Yoknapatawpha County combines the sort of mundane realism with which Cooper portrayed Templeton with Poe's tortured apprehension of the ugly mysteries that may lie under the placid surfaces of daily living. At times, in Faulkner, the orderly processes of society run wild: in *Sanctuary*, to take an extreme case, Goodwin is condemned, and then lynched, for the murder Popeye committed; later Popeye, in another state, is hanged for a murder of which he is in fact innocent. Faulkner is terribly conscious of the hysteric forces which threaten to subvert society as they do the ill-starred individual; he faces the grim eventuality in which, in Yeats's words, 'Things fall apart; the centre cannot hold'. Yet he leaves us with the feeling that the only possible response to this knowledge is resistance, fed by the stubborn attachment to life which others among his characters evince: so at the end of *Light in August*, after all the suffering and destruction, Lena continues her trustful odyssey in search of Burch, the father of her unborn child; so Dilsey, in *The Sound and the Fury*, provides the uncomplaining strength on which the stricken family depends. Even when it seems most meaningless and worthless, Faulkner is saying, life has both value and meaning; where fortitude and loyalty remain, so does the hope of order. Just what he considers the order to involve *Intruder in the Dust* most plainly sets forth.

Finally, in this brief survey of the contemporary scene, we turn to James Gould Cozzens, a novelist unaccountably neglected by the critics. His subject has been the alternations of inflexibility and pliableness by which the social order retains its equilibrum, here holding out against a critical remission of inherited ways, there yielding to a pressure otherwise insupportable, assimilating change, accepting imperfections, in order to preserve its essential character. Within this play of forces the individual dramas are staged. One of his earlier novels, *Castaway*, is a frightening parable of the individual bereft of his customary supports, thrust lonely and suddenly into a world replete with all the luxurious gadgetry of modern life, lacking the skills to use it, or the spiritual strength to support his isolation. It is prefaced by a quotation from Defoe which reads:

'. . . how infinitely good that providence is, which has provided in its government of mankind such narrow bounds to his sight and knowledge of things; and though he walks in the midst of so many thousand dangers, the sight of which, if discovered to him, would distract his mind and sink his spirits, he is kept serene and calm by having the events of things hid from his eyes.'

Without further preliminary, the novel discovers Mr. Lecky alone and frightened in an enormous department store, cut off from the world and normal life for reasons never explained. Here he must feed himself and defend himself against both any intruder and the terrors richly provided by his own mind. Ineptly and laboriously he equips himself with food and weapons; savagely because inefficiently he kills a man, brutish in appearance, mysteriously familiar, encountered on one of the lower floors, dragging the mutilated body to the basement steps. In this strait he has taken on instinctively the habits of barbarism, after the deed feeling 'no more remorse than Cain, his prototype'. He drinks and broods, falling prey to childhood fears of deserted woods, adult fears of insanity and violence:

'The first was exemplified by chance solitude in what he had considered deep woods . . . Long ago, under a seamless gray sky which would probably end with snow; in an autumnal silence free from birds, unmoved by the least breath of wind, he had come to be walking at random impulse. . . .

'It might have been this receptive vacancy of thought which let him, little by little, grow aware of a menace. The unnatural light leaf-buried ground, the low dark sky, the solitary noise of his unskilled progress—none of them was good. He began to notice that though the fall of leaves left an apparent bright openness, in reality it merely pushed to a distance the point at which the wood became as impenetrable as a wall.

'He walked more and more slowly, listening, hearing nothing;

looking, seeing nothing. Soon he stopped, for he was not going any farther. Standing in the deep leaves beneath bare trees and practically dead in the catalepsy of impending winter, he knew that he did not want to be here. A great evil—no more to be named than, met, to be escaped—waited fairly close . . .

'Mr. Lecky's maniacs lay in wait to slash a man's head half off, to perform some erotic atrocity of disembowelment on a woman. Here, they fed thoughtlessly on human flesh; there, wishing to play with him, they plucked the mangled Tybalt from his shroud. The beastly cunning of their approach, the fantastic capriciousness of their intention could not very well be met or provided for. In his makeshift fort, everywhere encircled by darkness, Mr. Lecky did not care to meditate further on the subject.'

Finally, submitting to the cumulative outrage of mind and emotions, he abandons his useless fort and descends, involuntarily, to the basement, where, turning over the shattered corpse, he recognises himself. It is a tale, wholly Trophonian, of the world of Poe transposed to modern conditions, of the derangement and violence ever ready to rupture the modes, laws and customs on which security depends. It differs from Poe because Cozzens observes his horrors, not unmoved, from the cover of an erudite and rational mind, most apparent in the elucidative quality of his prose, precisely delimiting shades of feelings and ideas. He evokes, in warning, a horrid augury of the dangers of the wilderness, whose eternal menace the proud achievements of a technological civilisation may obscure; he is the monitor of his civilisation, not, like Poe, the victim of the abnormalities he records. *Castaway* extends 'man's narrow bounds to his sight and knowledge of things', discovering the 'many thousand dangers' and presenting a world with whose obverse most of Cozzens's novels are concerned, the normal courses of life, where, though the spirit of Cain may riot, it is met by the concerted opposition of a homogeneous community, in whatever obscure and convoluted ways it may express its opposition.

The principal Cain-figures in *The Just and the Unjust* are Stanley Howell and Robert Basso, on trial for the kidnapping and murder of Frederick Zollicoffer, a drug-peddler. Mike Bailey—their leader and the actual murderer—has been mortally wounded when running from the police and, thinking himself betrayed, has given enough information to implicate his accomplices. One of them, Roy Leming, has testified against the others. As the trial takes its way, the novel, absorbingly at ease in the niceties of legal procedures and concepts, expands its field of view to take in the general life of Childerstown, the quiet rustic community where the court is in session. Both the trial and the wider scene we observe mainly from the standpoint of the assistant district attorney, Abner Coates, his family for a number of generations locally and legally distinguished, his father a judge of the Superior Court, now crippled by a stroke and acting as a passive commentator on the events his son reports to him. Much of the subsidiary action relates to the work of the district attorney, on which Abner, considering his possible succession to the office, meditates thus:

'Night and day, people (and often old familiar ones) were busy with projects considered or unconsidered, which would suddenly collide with the law and become public . . . There would be forcible entries here and felonious assaults there. Someone would wantonly point a firearm; and somebody else would sell malt beverages without license. Fornication had duly resulted in bastardy, and the Commonwealth was charged with seeing that the disgruntled father supported his little bastard. Heretofore respectable, an old man would feel indescribable urges to expose himself to women, and this was open lewdness. Forged instruments would be uttered, fraudulent conversions attempted; and, in passion or liquor, somebody might seek to kill a man or rape a woman.'

Among the subordinate cases of this kind which are directly treated in the novel are situations whose complexity, in their bearings on character, morals, politics, testifies to the abundance of Cozzens's imagination: the scandal of a high school employee's indecent advances to his pupils, procedural irregularities in an assault case, the suspicion of political pressure in the investigation of a car accident, the ethical intricacies of a disputed will.

None of this, however, has the pruriency, the urge to shock, of a *Peyton Place*. The improprieties are disclosed with philosophic disrelish and to balance these, so to speak, customary disorders within the community is its orderly social life: traditional festive outings, the prosaic routines of making a living, deciding on marriage, a career, as Abner does in the period the novel covers. In neither is his choice uncomplicated. Rather smugly, he hesitates to accept nomination for the post of district attorney, because he considers it to be too much in the gift of the local party manager, whom he dislikes. These scruples of his son Judge Coates disparages:

'If you want to get away from (politicians), you'll have to get away from human society. There wouldn't be any society without them. It's attempted every now and then. Some so-called reform movement made up of people who aren't politicians sometimes wins an election. Either they learn how to be politicians pretty quick, or they don't last. . . . I've never observed a human activity in which the practice is the same as the theory.'

Childerstown, as we see it in the novel, demonstrates the justice of the observation, as any agglomeration of people will. Just and unjust are not, on searching examination, so easily distinguishable as we might hope. The inhabitants of Childerstown who crowd the courtroom regard with righteous abhorrence the men on trial, visitants from an alien world where haphazard violence is the norm. In so thinking of them, they are, to a degree, correct:

'. . . they were gangsters all right. They were the very thing. Abner thought of Howell, sick and white, standing with Max Eich in the hall by the bars of the passage to the jail. He thought of Basso's dark surly face, the empty and feeble looks of menace as Basso bitterly kept whatever absurd pact Basso had made with Basso to get back at something—his invulnerable prosecutors, his own bad luck, fate, the indifferent world; it hardly mattered, for against none of them was any recourse possible—by refusing to answer. Abner thought of Roy Leming, meek, placatory, harrowingly beyond shame or pride, on the degrading anxious seat as state's evidence . . . They furtively carried guns, and very little was enough to panic or confuse them into shooting, and then they were liable to hit someone . . . When they remembered all that their own dumbness and greed and desperation had made them go through, and yet how little of the thing they were trying to get their suffering and effort had brought them, some of them—specifically, a man like Bailey, who had the cunning to contrive, with only such poor material as Howell and Basso and Leming, the kidnapping of Frederick Zollicoffer, and the cold nerve to shoot Zollicoffer afterwards; and yet who also jumped at a knock, ran at a word, and entertained hysterical fancies about being betrayed—would indeed, what with the one and the other, kill a man in a paroxysm of malignity and terror as soon as look at him.'

But Childerstown's abhorrence contains also less admirable emotions:

'Many of those present now had been present since the opening of the trial. The oak benches were as hard as iron to their buttocks; they did not know these people who were on trial; they could hardly hear what was being said; they did not understand the procedure of the court well enough to follow the drama if it could be called one; but still they sat. They looked thirstily, drinking it in, slaking their indescribable but obstinate and obscene thirst. They looked, but never quite their fill, at Howell and Basso who were probably (terrible and titillating thought!) going to die; at Leming, who took his drugs before breakfast; at the widow of a murdered man, the whilom sharer of his bed; at Susie Smalley, the lewd object of what lewd passions; at Judge Vredenburgh in his robe whose word was law; at the clerks serving some purpose they did not know under the bench; at the jury, whose word was life and death; at the attorneys making their assured gestures, familiars of the solemn mystery in which, all jumbled together, the just entered into judgment with the unjust.'

From this web of instincts, motives and attitudes, the verdict emerges. In the face of all the evidence, Lowell and Basso are found guilty only of second degree murder and so escape, to Leming's despair, with their lives. Justice has not been done, nor has the law, in this instance, demonstrated its truths with that certainty which, because 'Certainty is the Mother of Repose', the epigraph tells us, the law aims at. In earlier writers we have seen the individual, like Billy Budd, sacrificed to preserve a principle.

Here we have the community, from unfathomable notions of right and wrong, strong enough now to absorb such jolts, sacrificing a legal principle manifestly applicable in order to save two corrupt individuals whose guilt might, just possibly, be only accessory. The verdict, at first galling to the judges, is finally accepted without rancour and vindicated by Judge Coates as illustrating the way in which lay participation relieves the strict juridical interpretations of law, binding the community more closely to the professional body charged with interpreting and administering its statutes:

'A jury has its uses. That's one of them. It's like a——' he paused. 'It's like a cylinder head gasket. Between two things that don't give any, you have to have something that does give a little, something to seal the law to the facts. . . . The jury protects the court. It's a question how long any system could last in a free country if judges found the verdicts. It doesn't matter how wise and experienced the judges may be. Resentment would build up every time the findings didn't go with current notions or prejudices. Pretty soon half the community would want to lynch the judge. There's no focal point with a jury; the jury is the public itself. That's why a jury can say when a judge couldn't, "I don't care what the law is, that isn't right and I won't do it." It's the greatest prerogative of free men . . . They may be wrong, they may refuse to do the things they ought to do; but freedom just to be wise and good isn't any freedom. We pay a price for lay participation in law; but it's a necessary expense.'

To this conclusion the narrative weaves its various narrative threads; once again it is to a court of law and the discipline of legal science that the novelist goes to evaluate the strengths and weaknesses of the society which supplies his material.

Guard of Honour is a novel of equal complexity, rather similarly constructed. In it too theory and practice collide, in this case the principle of social equality among the races with the impracticability of implementing it unconditionally on a Southern air force base during the Second World War, a dilemma which calls up the illiberalities of both the right and the left. From this episode branch out the peripheral dramas, some of them aggravating the central difficulty, some, more loosely connected, showing how the stresses of war (even, as in this location it is, a noncombatant war) affect the habitual conduct and emotions of the human beings caught up in it. Occupying a role which, though more active, is comparable to that of Judge Coates, is Colonel Norman Ross, in peace-time a judge, now bearing much of the responsibility of mediating between antagonistic groups and individuals on a difficult station. Over the three days the novel occupies he is given ample opportunity to contemplate a variety of prejudices and vanities, competence and bungling; to ponder the conditions of human greatness and of human failure, the individual fate entwined with the vast destinies of war, the part in that war of a great nation fumbling to realise its potential. Listening with judicial composure to a visiting general's account of the Quebec conference, subtly flattered at being thus admitted at second-hand to the parleys of the great, Colonel Ross becomes aware of an underlying and more personal concern:

'The listening concern heard, and it trembled, as General Nichols spoke his doubt that the big brass, the VIP's at Quebec, intended to make the best use of air power . . . When it learned that fighter planes would soon escort the bombers all the way, it blew hot and cold, considering first the new safeguard, and then the fearful danger which that decision attested . . . The identified thought presented itself for an instant in the picture of his son, Jimmy, crouched bundled up in the bomber's naked, defenseless-looking, transparent nose, the bomb-sight cup against his eye; neither he, nor the plane whose run he now controlled, able to deviate one jot, evade one inch, while the guns below, with exquisite precision, preternaturally collecting and correcting their own data, laid themselves, and kept themselves, on this creeping, sitting target.'

Such concatenations of the chilly logistics of war and politics with the countless reverberations they set up in private lives betoken the compassion which supplements Cozzens's intellectual grasp of the abstract concepts from which political decision springs. In considering *The Just and the Unjust* we concentrated, for the most part, on the political issues which the novel dramatises. It deals as well, however, with those intimacies of the human relationship which distinguish sexual passion from love. *Guard of*

Honour whose main concern is equally, in the widest sense, political, takes up also the theme of love subjected to the urgencies and separations of war.

Cozzens's is not a world inhabited by *preux chevaliers*; the best we find are decent men conscious of their responsibilities, anxious rather to fulfil them than to fail, but liable to error and temptation. In *Guard of Honour*, Captain Duchemin blandly and amorally and entertainingly pursues his *amours* and the other pleasures of the flesh; the simple Captain Andrews, believing, 'You reap what you sow. Nothing would make sense if that weren't true,' by rooted and undemanding instinct remains true to his wife; Captain Hicks, for long, and without undue effort, faithful to his, succumbing to momentary and fortuitous circumstances, consummates in a hotel bedroom, dismally and pathetically, his wholly unintentional love affair with a WAC lieutenant:

'There had been those earlier labored tears begun on the balcony that dried in action; and the seizures of moaning that came on as the toils engaged her deeper. Some whimpered, not-to-be-contained cries were wrung out of her. Last came, exhausted and easier but copious, some final tears. These might acknowledge at first only the searchings of pleasure. Continuing, it was plain they deplored more and more, helpless and too late, every circumstance that brought her here to be uncovered and looked at; to have the demented convulsions of her body noted and her mouth's hateful sounds heard.

'Seeing tears to be idle, she had stopped them after a while, and made a slight eloquent movement, a sad pleading to be free.

'Hearing her breathe, and hearing them sing downstairs, Nathaniel Hicks thought of things to say; but none of them seemed very good. Not sure what to do, he put a hand out and touched her damp cheek.'

The necessarily narrow compass of this discussion can give no adequate idea of the novel's many merits. But even in the few encounters here described, whether of private or more universal significance, we are conscious of a quality Cozzens ascribes to one of his characters, 'a stern wakeful grasp of the nature of things', reflected even, it is not an exaggeration to say, in the flexibility of his style, the intricacies of his formal prose alleviated by his ear for the living idiom, the familiar making lively contact with the cultivated. Cozzens's verdict on 'the nature of things' is most fitly summarised by a speech of Abner's father towards the end of *The Just and the Unjust*. It advocates that tolerance which recognises the fact of human frailty without condoning it or drifting into the tenuities of radical sentimentality:

'A cynic is a man who found out when he was about ten that there wasn't any Santa Claus, and he's still upset. Yes, there'll be more wars; and soon, I don't doubt . . . There'll be deaths and disappointments and failures. When they come you meet them. Nobody promises you a good time or an easy time . . . But no bets are off. There is the present to think of, and as long as you live there always will be. In the present every day is a miracle. The world gets up in the morning and is fed and goes to work, and in the evening it comes home and is fed again and perhaps has a little amusement and goes to sleep. To make that possible, so much has to be done by so many people that, on the face of it, it is impossible. Well, every day we do it; and every day, come hell, come high water, we're going to have to go on doing it as well as we can.'

This recognises all the shortcomings so distressing to Hemingway's heroes and, undisfigured by *Weltschmertz*, makes a more dignified and more useful response to them. It is the response which the American novel, considered as a whole, has always made.

Appendix A

FRANKLIN and Irving represent an interesting divergence along these lines. The division between them is not a dogmatic one, since Franklin was by no means a spectacular departure from genteel usages and had no feeling that intimacy with English writing devitalised American. In his *Autobiography* he attributes the quality of his style to his early exercise of reproducing *Spectator* essays in his own words, versifying the result, then re-expressing it in prose. 'I sometimes had the pleasure of fancying,' he records, 'that, in certain particulars of small import, I had been lucky enough to improve the method or the language.' Elsewhere in the *Autobiography* Franklin sets out some of his ideas on language. He requires clarity, simplicity, conciseness, euphony: 'It should proceed regularly from things known to things unknown', and 'the whole should be so placed as to be agreeable to the ear in reading'. He enters a plea, too, for a democratic spirit in style, which we may see as an American longing to extend the range of communication with an audience relatively uneducated and widely bound to physical labour or commerce. 'The words used,' he insists, 'should be the most expressive that the language affords, *provided that they are the most generally understood.*' While the Augustans would have considered most of this unexceptionable, altogether it has an experimental cast and a popular inspiration which are not strictly Augustan. His own style reflects these prescriptions. It is not the Puritan, it is not Addison's style, but it contains something of each. The following passage from the *Autobiography* exemplifies it well:

'At his house I lay that night, and the next morning reached

Burlington, but had the mortification to find that the regular boats were gone a little before and no other expected to go before Tuesday, this being Saturday. Wherefore, I returned, to an old woman in the town of whom I had bought some gingerbread to eat on the water and asked her advice; she invited me to lodge at her house till a passage by water should offer; and being tired with my foot travelling, I accepted the invitation. Understanding I was a printer, she would have had me remain in that town and follow my business, being ignorant of the stock necessary to begin with. She was very hospitable, gave me a dinner of ox cheek with a great goodwill, accepting only a pot of ale in return. And I thought myself fixed till Tuesday should come. However, walking in the evening by the side of the river, a boat came by, which I found was going towards Philadelphia with several people in her. They took me in, and as there was no wind, we rowed all the way; and about midnight, not having yet seen the city, some of the company were confident we must have passed it and would row no further; the others knew not where we were, so we put towards the shore, got into a creek, landed near an old fence, with the rails of which we made a fire, the night being cold in October, and we remained till daylight.'

Franklin's style is not quite the tremendous novelty patriotism would have it. If we are to institute comparisons, then we must remark on its likeness to the pace and texture of Defoe's prose. As the extract shows, it is a style very appropriate to narrative, elegant, with its sprinkling of multi-syllables, without being at all precious. Franklin's eye looks perceptively outward to record the concrete detail—the gingerbread, the ox tail, the old fence burning in the cold night. The passage moves briskly along with the run of active verbs and the informal grammar. With no straining for effect, no affectation of ornate mannerisms, Franklin brings his modest scenes to life. Irving's early writing is more ambitious, but in basically the same matter-of-fact way, to which he added what Franklin notably lacked, a terse, disrespectful and at times ribald humour. In his *History of New York* (Murray 1820) he describes the attempt of William the Testy to hold back the invading Yankees by proclamation: 'The proclamation was perfect in all its parts, well constructed, well written, well sealed, and well published—all that was wanting to ensure its effect was that the Yankees should stand in awe of it; but, provoking to relate, they treated it with the most absolute contempt, applied it to an unseemly purpose, and thus did the first warlike proclamation come to a shameful end' (p. 230). This is the same William the Testy, Irving tells us, who before his martial career had 'passed with great credit through a celebrated academy at the Hague, noted for producing finished scholars with a dispatch unequalled, except by certain of our American colleges'.

Irving, however, was not taken with this, as it seemed to him, uncouth manner and went on to cultivate the superficially Augustan artifices and refinements. It must be said that his later writings are not uniformly desiccated. Parts of *A Tour of the Prairies* are fresh and individual still. His account of the journey through the forests of the Cross Timber has none of the inappropriate elegances he usually cherished, and its worth quoting for its own sake:

'The Herbage was parched; and the foliage of the scrubby forests was withered; the whole woodland prospect, as far as the eye could reach, had a brown and arid hue. The fires made in the prairies by the Indian hunters had frequently penetrated these forests, sweeping in light transient flame along the dry grass, scorching and charring the lower twigs and branches of the trees, and leaving them black and hard, so as to tear the flesh of man and horse that had to scramble through them . . . It was like struggling through forests of cast iron.'

But this is not the kind of writing on which Irving most prided himself, nor is it typical of most of this book. In general his tendency is to relegate the scene to a secondary position, its character to be defined by (and its beauty approved so far as it approaches) the quality of European landscape. We are for ever being asked to admire 'stately groves' of trees, looking 'as if planted for ornament and shade in the midst of rich meadows' and with 'the air of noble parks'. Meadows are 'finely deversified by groves and clumps of trees, so happily disposed, that they seemed as if set out by the hand of art . . . The whole had the appearance of a broad beautiful tract of pasture land, on the highly ornamented estate of some gentleman farmer . . .' Another part of the prairie resembles 'a beautiful champaign country of flowery plains and sleeping uplands, diversified by groves and clumps of trees, and long screens of woodland; the whole wearing the aspect of complete and even ornamental cultivation'. In the forest he reminds himself 'of the effect of sunshine among the stained windows and clustering columns of a Gothic cathedral. Indeed, there is a grandeur and solemnity in some of our spacious forests of the West, that awakens in me the same feeling that I have experienced in those vast and venerable piles'. Irving's memories of Europe got between him and the scenes he wanted to describe, very much as the Augustan mannerisms he imitated crippled his natural style.

The conflicting emphases we glimpse in Franklin and Irving occupied the magazine editors in the years after the Revolution. All were anxious that literary should follow political independence. The disagreement was upon the procedures that would most effectively stimulate a national character in the country's literature and at the same time raise it to more than parochial stature. 'Our national associations are necessarily few,' *The Atlantic Monthly* argued in 1824, 'so that some reliance on European literature will be necessary for a very long time.' From F. L. Mott's account of the controversy it is apparent that even those who called most loudly for independence prided themselves on the airs and graces of their summons. The *Portico*, in 1816, wrote, 'Dependence is a state of degradation, fraught with disgrace; and to be dependent on a foreign mind for what we can ourselves produce, is to add to the crime of indolence, the weakness of stupidity'. The theme is developed in the same elegant periods: 'The fancy of the Patriot catches the spark of enthusiasm, and flames with a desire of excellence . . . He is animated by the nobler feelings of a laudable fame, that whisper a recompense of renown, to him who shall advance the national character, and place the genius of the country on a permanent basis.' Above all they wanted, these patrons of conscious Americanism, grandeur, romance, solemnity, 'to make,' according to the Philadelphia *Literary Gazette* in 1821, 'our poetry national and peculiar, to hang its flowers around our history, to interweave it with our local attachments, to dye it deeply in the grain of our prejudices and passions'. To their disquiet, America gave easier audience to hayseed humour. In 1849 the *Literary World* spoke ruefully of the number and popularity of the humorous magazines: 'The American face is best daguerrotyped with a broad grin upon it . . . Too late to quarrel, were we disposed to it, with the patronage that crowds the Drama's temples whenever Momus presides, and leaves empty boxes to catch the tears of Melpomena.'

The showy circumlocutions at the end of this passage distinguish it sharply from the style of the humorists it reproves. Their prose, though often enough tedious, and in a way as stereotyped as the 'fine' writing of its critics, did work on the resources of the vernacular. A burlesque country newspaper, the *Bunkum Flagstaff*, printed as part of the *Knickerbocker Magazine* (in 1846) typifies both the language and a broad and bawdy humour of the kind we have seen in the early Irving. One of the advertisements extols the virtues of *Grandfather's Life Pills*, bequeathed from his death-bed to 'the bowels of posterity'. It will 'cure the jaundice, extirpate worms, and is good for fits . . . his grandfather has been heard to say they would open a garden gate . . . In Poor-Houses they will be found an excellent specific to relieve the town from porpuses, and the county from tax. In several of these institutions they have been known to make those die easy that would 'a died at any rate, and squenched their sufferings some months previous to the ordinary time. Come and let us reason, fellow citizens, on the philosophy of the pill. Why is it?—— What is the source of health, strength, happiness, nay, life itself? Common reason will tell you that it is the BLOOD; its circulation discovered by HARVEY some years ago, and has continued ever since . . .'

The greatest representative of this tradition is Mark Twain and the greatest work written wholly in the idiom, *Huckleberry Finn*. Yet while Huck's language is authentic, no one in real life would use it with the consistent imagination, the energy and the complex artifice Twain bestows on it. Nor is this novel Twain's only manner. His more formal prose is, like Franklin's, a blend of native and European elements, capable, as in *The Mysterious Stranger*, of a piercing simplicity quite different from the 'simplicity' of Huck's heightened dialect. Twain does with his linguistic raw material what English writers—we think of the Elizabethan and Jacobean dramatists—do with theirs—organise and manipulate it by conscious art through the whole range of variation on the colloquial base. For the subtle processes which accomplish the transformation, the American writer will draw upon European precedents, whether he goes directly to the European sources or takes them from the increasing body of his own literature, which has grown from them. American prose never entirely cuts its ties with the parent language—which is not, of course, to be equated with the kind of imperfect imitations practised by Irving and his fashionable contemporaries. While it is not the purpose of this study to examine in detail the ways in which American diverges from English prose, it may be said in general that the native and the European attachments are complementary parts of it, both indispensable. Valuable though it is, the untutored vernacular must be confined to the narrow range of a ballad literature. Franklin arrived at a just balance, and though Irving did not, his writing did serve to keep in being the necessary sense of union with the source of America's linguistic heritage.

Oddly, it was the critics pleading most vehemently for national inspiration who failed to appreciate the really significant developments. Scornful of the humorists, they despised the vernacular—a not uncommon pattern in literature; insistent on conventional ideas of humour, romance and dignity, they regretted the prosy character of the subject matter offered by American life. In 1799, Brown's *Monthly Magazine* gave as one of the reasons for the lack of an American literature, 'occupation with business and industry'. Six years later, the *Monthly Anthology* ascribed it to 'the mutual clamours of contending parties'. Ironically, it was to just these occupations that writers had to turn, and to which, like Cooper, they in fact did turn, for the material which would, on inquiry, yield the indigenous themes they sought.

Appendix B

THERE is little point in reiterating here the cautions about the philosophical imprecision of the term 'realism'. Its literary application is long enough established to be unambiguous. In American literature it covers the work of writers as various as W. D. Howells, for whom realism meant treating of the familiar and commonplace, and Theodore Dreiser, a doctrinaire determinist, of all major American novelists perhaps the most wedded to the subject of low life. In Dreiser, realism has become full-bodied naturalism, accepting a range of subject matter which Howells, although he saw the logic of the extension, excluded from his own work.

Naturalism was based on philosophical as well as aesthetic postulates. Aesthetically, it demanded scientific accuracy in the fictional use of social backgrounds and the admission into the novel of all aspects of experience, particularly the sordid and the socially unjust. Philosophically, it depicted man as largely the product of his environment and his heredity: thus from people reared in the violence, dishonesty and squalor of slum life we can expect only violence, dishonesty and dirt. Clearly there is a leaning towards Marxist socialism and the evolutionary theories of the formative effects of environment on species. For the outright naturalist, man was the helpless plaything of impersonal economic forces, and life a struggle for existence which only the strongest survive. This did not, however, prevent his believing that humanity might somehow rise against these forces and direct them to more beneficent ends. The anomaly appears in the disorderly philosophisings of Jack London, who, as Henry Steele Commager points out, 'subscribed to a philosophy which dictated the inexorable triumph of the strong over the weak and advocated a revolution by the weak against the strong'. (*The American Mind*, p. 111). In the late nineteenth and early twentieth centuries, many American novelists turned to naturalism as the system of thought which seemed capable of giving shape to the mass of unfamiliar data their society was thrusting upon them. In the abstract, its intellectual shortcomings are obvious, but it is to be judged finally, in this context, by whatever success the novelists who practised it achieved.

Most of their considerable output is now of historical interest only. To see it in little we may turn to a novelist who, assenting to the assumptions of naturalism, sought an additional dimension in the flatly materialistic settings it recorded. In outline, Stephen Crane's fiction seems often purely naturalistic in subject and theme. In *George's Mother* a young man, spoilt by his mother, consorts with evil companions, turns to drink, and fails to reach his mother's death bed. *Maggie, A Girl of the Streets* narrates the history of a girl seduced by a slum gallant, driven to prostitution and, finally, suicide. These stories barely escape the simplicities of the Victorian 'moral tale', the Awful Warning of the temperance tract. The similarity is reinforced by Crane's awkward attempts to spell out the slum accents of New York, by his somehow stagey dialogue, the slang he never quite makes convincing because it is never, as in Twain it always is, the essence of the vulgar tongue. For the confident Victorian call to self-discipline, repentance, salvation through the Gospels, Crane substitutes, of course—on the whole no less confidently—the lesson that the environment in which they abound makes these squalid tragedies inevitable. But at another level he is much less concerned with slamming home his moral than with the primary imaginative act of recreating the life which he observed.

To this end Crane describes, in the naturalist manner, the life of city bars, theatres, streets and slums. He aims to assault our senses with the physical characteristics, the sights, sounds, and smells of this degraded and degrading world, still, then, excitingly unfamiliar material for the novelist and his public:

'Eventually they entered a dark region where, from a careening building, a dozen gruesome doorways gave up loads of babies to the street and the gutter, A wind of early autumn raised yellow dust from cobbles and swirled it against a hundred windows. Long streamers of garments fluttered from fire-escapes. In all unhandy places there were buckets, brooms, rags and bottles. In the street infants played or fought with other infants or sat stupidly in the way of vehicles. Formidable women, with uncombed hair and disordered dress, gossiped leaning on railings, or screamed in frantic quarrels. Withered persons in curious postures of submission to something, sat smoking pipes in obscure corners. A thousand odours of cooking food came forth to the street. The building quivered and creaked from the weight of humanity stamping about in its bowels.'

Such is the quarter in which, through rapidly changing episodes, we see Maggie falling in love with her brother's friend, the spuriously glamorous Pete, his easy conquest of her, the sleazy entertainment he offers her in the local saloons and theatres, his growing (though uneasy) contempt for her—the appetite satisfied —and her brother's pathetically confused indignation when he discovers that she has become Pete's mistress. He is vaguely conscious of the similarity to his own dealings with women, and in consequence vaguely ashamed of himself, but he cannot bring himself to forgive Maggie. There are effective echoes here of the irony Twain finds in Huck's efforts to allow the conventions in which he is trained to submerge the decent impulses he instinctively feels.

The final sequence, occupying only a few pages, compresses Maggie's years of degradation into what seems to be a single night, culminating in her drowning herself (as we are left to suppose), after a walk, vainly soliciting, through successively drearier quarters of the city:

'The girl went into the gloomy districts near the river, where the tall black factories shut in the street and only occasional beams of light fell across the sidewalks from saloons. In front of one of these places, whence came the sound of a violin vigorously scraped, the patter of feet on boards, and the ring of loud laughter, there stood a man with blotched features.

'Farther on in the darkness she met a ragged being with shifting, bloodshot eyes and grimy hands.

'She went into the blackness of the final block. The shutters of the tall buildings were closed like grim lips. . . .

'At the feet of the tall buildings appeared the deathly black hue of the river. Some hidden factory sent up a yellow glare, that lit for a moment the waters lapping oilily against timbers. The varied sounds of life, made joyous by distance and seeming unapproachableness, came faintly and died away to a silence.'

This particularly striking dislocation of time is an intensification of the episodic method by which the action advances, moving, as we afterwards realise, towards the insanely accelerated final declension by way of rapid shifts of time and place. Despite such descriptive passages as the one quoted first above, with its mainly documentary intention, scenes are often designed to equivocate rather than to present realistically either the locale or the 'real' duration of an episode. Crane is interested in getting beyond the surfaces, in making appearances, as symbols, carry their own ulterior meanings. Smoke-filled interiors, desperate revellers, city throngs, swirl in manic sequence. The garish, flickering settings convey not just the evil facts of urban poverty but a condition of the soul, a desolate rush to annihilation, reckless and involuntary. Thus the theatres, where the harsh lights beat on automatic pleasures joylessly experienced, become 'places of forgetfulness'. Thus a 'concert hall gave to the street faint sounds of swift, machine-like music, as if a group of phantom musicians were hastening'.

It is in this kind of procedure that we see Crane trying to break from the limitations of pure naturalism, first because he is not content to assemble facts which will 'speak for themselves', second because he is suggesting, not spelling out, the meaning. Neither, that is, does he accept the facts as an ultimate reality, nor explicit commentary on them as aesthetically satisfying.

But the naturalist preference for straight talk affects Crane's use of symbol. Too often the symbols are blatantly moralising, read into, not growing from, the reality to which they refer. Instead of the cinema's slow dissolve we have the clumsy magic-lantern operator superimposing one slide upon another. All too clearly the city streets are paths of temptation where murky saloons are 'open mouths' which call 'seductively to passengers to enter and annihilate sorrow or create rage'. In this novel certainly Crane was too committed to naturalism and was dealing with too basically naturalistic a subject to be able to escape its influence where this interfered with what he wanted to do. Our final impression is of styles confused, Zola and Kafka in uneasy collusion.

In *The Red Badge of Courage* Crane again attempts, and with more success, to extend the limits of naturalism. Writing of the Civil War, Crane, who had no direct experience of it, was forced back on his imaginative capacities, and so, perhaps because relieved of the obligation to apply the naturalist formulae, he elevates his episode of war to the universality where most of his other tales—*The Open Boat* excepted—establish only a shaky tenure. Before the battle the brigade halts 'in the cathedral light of a forest. . . . Through the aisles of the wood' they see the distant skirmishers. From the imagery he uses to describe the setting Crane draws the references by which the spiritual significance of the battle is to be interpreted. It is a proving ground for its hero, Henry Fleming, and Crane is as much interested in what goes on inside Fleming as—the naturalist emphasis—in presenting a realistic, deglamourised picture of modern warfare. All the hero's spiritual crises are referred to the churchlike setting of the forest, in a manner not unlike that in which Cooper, though the two authors' intentions are so different, used the Fort William Henry episode. After Fleming has fled from the first brush with the enemy he wanders in the forest until 'at length he reached a place where the high, arching boughs made a chapel. . . . There was a religious half light'. Here he comes upon the sickening dead body, sacrificed in some earlier encounter, bringing to his mind the fate from which his cowardice has perhaps saved him and thoughts as well of his unworthiness. He runs off, and behind him, 'the trees about the portals of the chapel moved soughingly in a soft wind. A sad silence was upon the little guarding edifice', and the trees 'began softly to sing a hymn of twilight'. Fleming is so scared by what he has seen that when the noise of firing shatters the peace he begins to run towards the firing line, this time seeing the action through.

These are the merest notes on Crane, their purpose only to show how naturalism failed to satisfy the needs of its most gifted adherent. Crane's instincts did not betray him. He groped towards an individual use of the two great American symbols of the city and the forest, hampered by an aesthetic which had little place for interpretation of this kind. The naturalist movement was an enlivening experiment which opened new areas of experience to the artist, but most modes of interpretation ran counter to the main American traditions.

Index

Index